EMINENT ELIZABETHANS

Piers Brendon is the author of more than a dozen books, including biographies of Churchill and Eisenhower, the bestselling *Eminent Edwardians* and *The Dark Valley*, and, most recently, the highly acclaimed *The Decline and Fall of the British Empire*. He also writes for television and contributes frequently to the national press. Formerly Keeper of the Churchill Archives Centre, he is a Fellow of Churchill College, Cambridge. He is also a Fellow of the Royal Society of Literature.

ALSO BY PIERS BRENDON

Hurrell Froude and the Oxford Movement
Hawker of Morwenstow
Head of Guinness
Eminent Edwardians
The Life and Death of the Press Barons
Winston Churchill: A Brief Life
Our Own Dear Queen
Ike: The Life and Times of Dwight D. Eisenhower
Thomas Cook: 150 Years of Popular Tourism
The Windsors (with Phillip Whitehead)
The Motoring Century
The Dark Valley: A Panorama of the 1930s
The Decline and Fall of the British Empire

PIERS BRENDON

Eminent
Elizabethans

VINTAGE BOOKS
London

Published by Vintage 2013

2 4 6 8 10 9 7 5 3 1

First published in Great Britain in 2012 by
Jonathan Cape

Vintage
Random House, 20 Vauxhall Bridge Road,
London SW1V 2SA

www.vintage-books.co.uk

Addresses for companies within The Random House Group Limited can
be found at: www.randomhouse.co.uk/offices.htm

The Random House Group Limited Reg. No. 954009

A CIP catalogue record for this book
is available from the British Library

ISBN 9780099532637

The Random House Group Limited supports the Forest Stewardship
Council® (FSC®), the leading international forest-certification
organisation. Our books carrying the FSC label are printed on FSC®-
certified paper. FSC is the only forest-certification scheme supported by
the leading environmental organisations, including Greenpeace. Our
paper procurement policy can be found at
www.randomhouse.co.uk/environment

Typeset by Palimpsest Book Production Ltd, Falkirk, Stirlingshire

Printed and bound by Clays Ltd, St Ives plc

To my beloved grandchildren,
Beau, Sonny, Lucas, Anya and Eliza

Contents

Acknowledgements

I would like to express warm thanks to all who helped me with this book, some of whom wish to remain anonymous. Lord Broers shared his memories of Geelong Grammar School with me. Professor Marcial Echenique discussed Prince Charles's views on architecture for my benefit and lent me his incisive paper on the subject. Andrew Riley, the Thatcher archivist at the Churchill Archives Centre, put his unrivalled knowledge of sources about the Iron Lady at my disposal and went far beyond the call of duty in giving me assistance in other ways. Ian Whitcomb and Graeme Davies afforded me valuable insights into the world of Mick Jagger. So did Tom Findlay, one half of Groove Armada, who subjected my essay to expert scrutiny. Rex Bloomstein and Anthony Heath were also well-informed critics. Tom Rosenthal, formerly my publisher and long my literary guru, read the entire text, improving it in countless ways and giving me inestimable encouragement. My present publisher, Dan Franklin, edited the book with his usual brilliance and precision. I am particularly indebted to him for commissioning it in the first place and for backing it with such enthusiasm. He also provided me with additional aid from Jane Selley, who copy-edited the book, Alison Tullett, who proofread it, and Steven Messer, who took it through the press. Above all and as always, I am grateful to my wife Vyvyen for her love and support. Needless to say, I alone bear the responsibility for the opinions expressed in these pages and for any errors they may contain.

Introduction

Lorem

The reign of Queen Elizabeth II, a monarch whose prime purpose was to provide continuity, has seen change on an almost inconceivable scale. Perhaps the most astonishing change is the revolution in information technology brought about primarily by the computer – a word not mentioned in H. G. Wells's otherwise prescient interwar volume, *The Shape of Things to Come*. Today there are some eight million books in print but over 550 billion documents on the internet. If Gutenberg made a pond, Google has spawned an ocean; and web surfers, however powerful their search engines, can easily drown in its depths. All too often the glut of knowledge obscures truth and darkens understanding. That monument to incontinence, Wikipedia, provides a comprehensive barrier to the comprehension of events and individuals. The most famous figures of the new Elizabethan age (a term here signifying a measure of modern time not a reprise of Gloriana) are well-nigh submerged under the weight of words devoted to them.

Indeed, the situation is far worse now than it was when Lytton Strachey complained about the tombstone 'Lives and Letters' that threatened to obliterate eminent Victorians, prompting him to create his brilliant cameos. Take Margaret Thatcher, for example. Not only has she been the subject of media excess and biographical overkill; she is electronically enshrined in a CD-ROM that contains every one of the 7,500 extant public statements she made between

1945 and 1990. If Mrs Thatcher's voice resembled a dentist's drill, as one of her ministers remarked, what exquisite pain might her collected utterances inflict? It is the premise of this book that only a distillation of the flood of data can capture the essence of a personality, only a snapshot can seize the moment in the flux of time. Simply because of the plethora of evidence, the second Elizabethan era is best represented in miniature.

Here I pen four vignettes, which together form a sequel to my *Eminent Edwardians*, itself published over thirty years ago and in print ever since. Inspired by Lytton Strachey, that book aspired to unlock the Edwardian age by means of a few key figures: Lord Northcliffe, Arthur Balfour, Emmeline Pankhurst and General Baden-Powell. Those dramatis personae, all of whom acted out their roles on a global stage, made an indelible impression on the period in which they lived. Northcliffe, born Alfred Harmsworth, created the popular press; Balfour was prime minister and gave his name to the declaration establishing a national home for the Jews in Palestine; Mrs Pankhurst led the militant campaign for women's votes; and Robert Baden-Powell, hero of the siege of Mafeking, founded the largest youth movement in history. The present volume brings together a fresh quartet of brief lives that have loomed large in the annals of their own time – all but one still alive as I write but here treated as historic figures. My subjects are Rupert Murdoch, the international media mogul; Prince Charles, heir to the throne; Margaret Thatcher, the first female prime minister of Great Britain; and Mick Jagger, lead singer of the Rolling Stones. Each member of the current foursome played out a major theme – economic, social, political or cultural – in the new Elizabethan medley. Each transcended national boundaries, attracting attention in the furthest corners of the earth. Each aroused intense controversy, stirring passions as much by personality as by performance. And each was ambivalent towards the great contemporary process of change, promoting it and opposing it, flirting with radicalism yet embracing conservatism.

Each tilted against the old order to maintain the status quo. Thus Rupert Murdoch always presented himself as the populist foe of a snooty, complacent and degenerate elite. He gloried in being a reformer, a republican and a muckraker. It is clear, though, that Murdoch was reactionary at heart. Avid for power and pelf, he became a fervent neocon who served his own purposes by espousing capitalism red in tooth and claw. The Prince of Wales also paraded as a dissident. He proclaimed his hatred of privilege, his penchant for innovation, his unorthodox ideas about alternative medicine, organic farming, communion with nature and so on. In practice, however, Charles was indissolubly wedded to tradition, whether in the shape of fox-hunting, neo-Georgian architecture, the hereditary peerage or other such causes. He only favoured novelty when it embodied spiritual or holistic qualities calculated to sustain venerable institutions like the monarchy. Margaret Thatcher claimed to be the rebel leader of a Conservative administration. She abandoned 'one-nation' Toryism for the so-called enterprise culture, attacking entrenched interests in the civil service, the professions, the trade unions and elsewhere. But she regarded revolution as a means of redemption. Her crusade, which was convulsive rather than comprehensive, aimed to make Britain great again. Its purpose was to restore dignity, wealth and moral fibre to a nation that had won the war but lost its dominant position in the world. Mick Jagger seemed to be the embodiment of a counter-culture that celebrated sex and drugs and rock 'n' roll. He dramatised his revolt against the bourgeois society of the post-war world through subversive antics, regicide threats ('I'll kill the king'), invocations to Satan and stage performances that provoked riots. But these were impudent attempts to identify himself with the latest fashion, displays of radical cheek as much as radical chic. As evidenced by his anachronistic ambition to become a gentleman and his eventual acceptance of a knighthood, the essential Jagger was a grasping social climber, eager to join the Establishment, not to beat it.

In their different ways, then, each of these four new Elizabethans sheds light on times that were, as Bob Dylan croaked, a-changin'. Every age, to be sure, is an age of transition. But from at least the 1960s, the wind of change became a gale. The British Empire was reduced to a few islands and – for all the post-imperial drum-beating of Rupert Murdoch and Margaret Thatcher during the Falklands War – the Queen presided over a Commonwealth that was its ghost. The growth of affluence coincided with a decline in deference, which eroded the hitherto sacrosanct status of royalty – a transformation furthered by Prince Charles's foibles, which gave the Murdoch press ample scope for lese-majesty. The satire boom and the explosion of popular culture also helped to sap reverence for tradition; and no one expressed the new mood of iconoclasm more vociferously than Mick Jagger, who sang raunchy African-American blues when *The Black and White Minstrel Show* could still attract television audiences of twenty million people, among them Queen Elizabeth II. Jagger, too, was an emblem of the sexual revolution of the sixties, a revolution that fell far short of women's liberation. Indeed, the permissive currents of what Mrs Thatcher regarded as that modern devil's decade did less to sweep out the old and sweep in the new than the market forces she unleashed during the 1980s. As communism collapsed, rampant capitalism carried nearly all before it – though during the banking crisis of 2008, New Labour reaped the whirlwind. Long before that, there was widespread concern about the moral, social and ecological damage wrought by unregulated private enterprise, which encouraged the Prince of Wales to promote his alternative nostrums. Hence, for example, his bid to become, in an increasingly secular and multicultural community, the defender of faith. It was an earnest of his desire, shared to a greater or lesser extent by each protagonist in the following essays, to ensure that *plus ça change, plus c'est la même chose.*

In this they were representative of their compatriots, who aspired to progress while cherishing a nostalgia for the past. Britons endorsed a white-hot technological revolution but embraced quasi-archaic pageantry. They entered the European Union but remained Little Englanders with far-flung special relationships. They favoured an egalitarian society but countenanced nothing that met the hopes or expectations of sea-green sixties radicals – an elected head of state, a democratic second legislative chamber, open government, a disestablished Church of England, the withering away of the public schools and the collapse of the class system. Benefiting from a huge expansion in foreign travel and higher education,[1] Queen Elizabeth's subjects recognised that their country was no longer a great power; yet they were not averse to jingoism, and the monarch's reign was topped and tailed by two disreputable military adventures, the invasions of Suez and Iraq, reminiscent of Victorian gunboat diplomacy. However, my four eminent Elizabethans, although in many ways typifying the ambiguities of the age, are anatomised in their own right. They are treated not just as symptoms of their time but as idiosyncratic creatures of flesh and blood. They are depicted for the intrinsic interest of their characters as much as for the significance of their achievements. In the Stracheyesque manner, moreover, these portraits are executed by acid etching rather than pastel shading. Undue reverence is death to biography, which demands the incisive analysis of temperament and the steely dissection of personality. Equally deadening to the genre is solemn detachment, for individuals are revealed most vitally in a critical and even a satirical light, through pungent anecdote, piquant quotation and sharp, ironic commentary. In the following pages it is my aim to illuminate, to inform and to entertain.

Piers Brendon
Cambridge
May 2012

Rupert Murdoch

When Rupert Murdoch bought the *New York Post* in 1976, its staff expected to meet 'a three-headed monster with an Australian accent'.[1] And certainly the new proprietor of America's largest evening newspaper arrived with a fearsome reputation. Only son of the leading editor in the Antipodes, Rupert had served an apprenticeship on the London *Daily Express*, which he described happily as Lord Beaverbrook's brothel. On his father's death in 1952, he inherited (aged twenty-one) the Adelaide *News* and plunged into a competitive arena that was too brutal even for the potent Canadian press magnate Lord Thomson – Australians carried guns, he said, and their main occupation was rape. Murdoch employed, as he later acknowledged, hooligan methods to expand his business. He hired thugs to repel rivals. He intimidated politicians. He fired employees at will, breaking men as readily as he broke stories. And he practised the most jaundiced kind of yellow journalism, summed up in the memorable headline of an early acquisition, the Perth *Sunday Times*: LEPER RAPES VIRGIN, GIVES BIRTH TO MONSTER BABY.[2] Equally prone to sleaze and sensationalism were his first British newspapers, the *News of the World* and the *Sun*, which he purchased in the late 1960s. They titillated readers with photographs of bare-breasted girls – all the nudes that's fit to print, as one editor put it, since Murdoch banned pubic hair, remarking sagely that 'Cunt is not our line.'[3] Terror was his line, and he

I

scared senior managers into states ranging from panic and para-
noia to paralysis. The editor of the *Sun*, Larry Lamb, doctored
his paper's horoscope in an effort to improve the disposition of his
superstitious boss, who was born under the sign of Pisces. He
might as well have tried to tame a shark. Murdoch invited
witnesses to watch him chew up Lamb. The descent of Rupert
Murdoch upon New York was famously likened to the coming
of King Kong.

The *Post* soon stoked fears that he was a horrific throwback:
when an electricity failure blacked out Manhattan in July 1977,
its headline screamed HOURS OF TERROR and a pull-out supple-
ment told tales of a Stygian metropolis ravaged by arson, looting
and murder. This was a gross exaggeration, but it set the tone for
still more hysterical coverage of the so-called 'Son of Sam' serial
killings. Murdoch, whose favourite son Sam was said to be,
demanded a fresh revelation every day. And he got fake stories
set in red type bold enough to herald the last trump. Subsequent
headlines were equally gruesome: MENTAL PATIENT MURDERS WIFE
ON STREET, WARPED GENIUS TORTURES HIS MOM, MASS BABY KILLER
STALKS HOSPITAL.[4] Murdoch told reporters to 'juice up' news
items.[5] His broadsheets also endured this sort of pressure, so
much so that when he looked set to take over the London
Observer, its television critic, Clive James, likened it to handing
over your beautiful daughter to a gorilla.[6] But tabloids, Murdoch
urged, should always be 'violent and blood and guts'.[7] Like his
predecessors, he knew that gore was good for the circulation. And
journalists spotted further similarities to press barons of the past,
to those gaudy beasts of the newspaper jungle who were notoriously
mad, bad and dangerous to know. As an American commentator
wrote, Murdoch was 'a late nineteenth century Hearstian figure
who has seemingly materialised in the New York City of the late
1970s through some curious time warp'.[8]

It seemed obvious that he had much in common with William
Randolph Hearst himself, immortalised in Orson Welles's film as
the megalomaniac Citizen Kane. Awed by Murdoch's power and
terrified by his sudden, ghostly appearances, one *News of the*

World editor exclaimed: 'He truly is Citizen Kane.'[9] Even Murdoch's crony Woodrow Wyatt, subjected to a tirade about how his media empire made him more powerful than the British government, 'wondered whether he hasn't gone absolutely Citizen Kane'.[10] But there were other analogies. Like Albert Pulitzer, Murdoch sold sex in words of one syllable. He professed prudery but peddled prurience, like Joseph Pulitzer, who (according to the younger James Gordon Bennett) stuck his nose into every putrescent dunghill to rut out filth for the consumption of the dregs of society. Like Bennett himself, who once sacked everyone on the right-hand side of his newsroom, Murdoch was a man of mercury with a whim of iron. Like Northcliffe, who conjured marvels out of nothing, he initiated campaigns, competitions and stunts. Like Colonel Robert R. McCormick, who was said to possess 'the finest mind of the thirteenth century'[11] and created the Chicago *Tribune* in his own image, he was a born-again reactionary. Like Lord Beaverbrook, whose hirelings felt that they were working for a Benzedrine factory, he used the telephone as a deadly weapon. Like Lord Thomson, with his 'deep affection for banks',[12] he lived in a vicious financial circle, buying newspapers to make money to buy more newspapers to make more money. But like Cecil King, who tried to mount a coup against Harold Wilson's government, Rupert Murdoch aspired to be much more than the autocrat of the breakfast table.

Certainly he was keen to sway the mass mind. He boasted that his newspapers mobilised voters and filled ballot boxes. He prided himself on making and breaking politicians. 'I elected them,' he said of Gough Whitlam's government in Australia. 'And, incidentally, I'm not too happy with them. I may remove them.'[13] Of course, the pretensions of press despots had often run along similar lines, and they had been vilified as Murdoch was – one member of the Australian parliament called him 'a lying, perjuring pimp'.[14] Northcliffe had claimed dictatorial authority over public opinion – 'we can cause the whole country to think with us overnight whenever we say the word'[15] – which prompted Lloyd George to denounce his diseased vanity, tapping his finger suggestively on his head. Beaverbrook had said that the press was 'a flaming sword which will cut through any political armour', provoking Stanley Baldwin's classic riposte that he aimed at 'power without responsibility – the prerogative of the harlot throughout the ages'.[16] What distinguished Murdoch, however, was that his ambitions were not confined by national boundaries. As his media empire grew, he aimed to create an international communications conglomerate, a network spanning the planet. Did he envisage leading democracy by the nose, even holding hands with tyranny? Competitors had no doubt that he aspired to be the information overlord of the global village.

This scheme was satirised in the plot to achieve world domination hatched by crazed media tycoon Elliot Carver in the James Bond film *Tomorrow Never Dies*, but it was no mere fantasy where Murdoch was concerned. It developed from a strategy of 'synergy', whereby the diverse media he acquired – newspapers, books, magazines, films, TV channels, radio stations and so on – sustained and promoted one another at home and abroad. The *New York Post*, for example, became a serial advertisement for the movie *Titanic*, produced by Murdoch's film company 20th Century Fox. Similarly, as an ex-editor recalled, Murdoch used the *Post* to club Time Warner, Fox News's foe in a battle over cable television rights in New York, 'for his own monetary gain'.[17] Such commercial cross-fertilisation gave Murdoch's News Corporation immense vigour. This was augmented through creative accounting and tax avoidance on a cosmopolitan scale, achieved by offsetting profits in one place against losses in another. Moreover, Murdoch was reluctant to dilute his control by issuing shares. Instead he financed expansion by borrowing. 'OPM', Other People's Money, enabled him to take over companies that dwarfed his own. This inspired a writer for the *New York Times* to dub Murdoch the 'Tasmanian Devil', a creature that one encyclopedia defined thus: 'Extremely voracious marsupial. Its expression appears evil and it has a fierce snarl. It is very strong for its size and preys on animals larger than itself.'[18]

Other commentators regarded Murdoch as the Devil *tout court*.

They detected something Mephistophelian in his presence, a whiff of brimstone or a glimpse of Hades. They called him 'Satanic' and 'Lucifer-like'.[19] And his fiendish aura was enhanced by the Faustian pact into which he supposedly inveigled politicians. Did they sell their souls for power? Undoubtedly Murdoch won favours in return for the slanted news and partisan views he disseminated, to say nothing of the generous book contracts and article fees he offered, let alone more sinister inducements. The odd maverick dug his toes in: Sir Robert Menzies apparently said that he wouldn't give Murdoch the steam off his piss. But most were eager to collaborate. John Gorton circumvented Australia's exchange control rules to allow Murdoch to buy the *News of the World*. Margaret Thatcher passed laws that made it possible for him to defeat the British print unions. Ronald Reagan eased regulations on media concentration to permit him to own newspapers and television stations in the same cities. Tony Blair repealed the ban on alien ownership of commercial television companies for his benefit. David Cameron endeavoured to facilitate his acquisition of the entire satellite broadcasting company BSkyB. When Ed Koch abandoned long-held liberal principles, the *New York Post* virtually turned itself into his mayoral election broadsheet. Even hardened hacks protested, but Murdoch angrily said that he would decide what went into his own newspaper. Critics denounced the *Post* as 'a force for evil'.[20]

In truth Murdoch was no more demonic than the other wild newspapermen of his native land. John Norton, for example, the owner of *Truth* until his death in 1916, was said to have earned 'a seat in the Council of Beelzebub, to represent the constituency of Sodom and Gomorrah'.[21] Norton's exploits were, indeed, so diabolical that his son Ezra tried to use *Truth* to suppress the truth, getting the New South Wales government to make it a criminal offence to defame the dead.[22] Sir Frank Packer and his son Kerry, the most ferocious media moguls of their day, employed their organs as blunt instruments and were more inclined to ravish than to seduce politicians. Beside such tigers, Rupert Murdoch seemed a pussycat. Furthermore, he was a less baleful figure, despite superficial resemblances, than others of their ilk – less fascist than Hearst, less fickle than Bennett, less demented than Northcliffe, less depraved than Beaverbrook. However, when the old press barons prostituted their newspapers for personal gain, it had scarcely mattered. As in the fable of the bees, their individual iniquities even worked for the common good. By their sulphurous intransigence they preserved a vital diversity of news and opinion, ensuring that truth would out. This justified their independence from political control. As Thomas Jefferson said in 1813, although popular taste was being debauched by the malignity, vulgarity and mendacity of the press, this was 'an evil for which there is no remedy; our liberty depends on the freedom of the press, and this cannot be limited without being lost'.[23]

Murdoch's exploitation of his media for private advantage was a more serious threat to the public interest because in middle age he realised his expansionist ambitions – by 2007 his conglomerate, worth over fifty billion dollars, included 175 newspapers and a broadcasting network that encompassed the globe and dominated the heavens. With such an unparalleled accumulation of power he appeared capable not only of monopolising the channels of communication but of poisoning the wells of knowledge, and thus frustrating the purposes of democracy. But power bred hubris, which in turn spawned corruption, manifested in the great phone-hacking scandal that brought Murdoch's career to such a humiliating climax in 2011. He was forced to close the *News of the World* and there were calls for his overweening stake in the media to be further reduced. To date, though, News Corporation survives intact. The sun never sets on Rupert Murdoch's empire. Perhaps, to paraphrase his oft-repeated joke about the British Empire, God doesn't trust him in the dark.

Yet Murdoch always professed to be on the side of the angels. He was a child of the manse – his paternal grandfather, Patrick Murdoch, had been a minister in the Free Church of Scotland. His father, respected head of the largest press group in Australia, instilled in him a belief in 'the high, moral *purpose* of news-papers'.[24] Rupert, a committed Christian, would often declare that membership of the Fourth Estate was an important public trust.[25] And in 1964 he launched the *Australian*, the country's first real national daily, expressing the hope that it was something his father would have been proud of – as he would have been of his son's other respectable papers, such as *The Times* and *The Wall Street Journal*. Contrasting himself with Robert Maxwell, his rival in the struggle to acquire the *News of the World*, Rupert Murdoch said: 'I'm not an evil man.'[26] Once in charge of this scandal sheet, he claimed to be acting in the fine tradition of the muckrakers, exposing vice in order to promote virtue. Far from peddling pornography, as opponents charged, he was putting on a weekly morality play. In it the wicked wrought their own destruction for the delectation of the good. His papers were instruments of justice as well as agencies of improvement. As Woodrow Wyatt tried to tell Mrs Thatcher, who was offended by their salacious content, 'Rupert is a Puritan.' Murdoch shared, indeed, her radical idealism, her resentful sense of being an outsider and her antipathy to a smug, privileged, hypocritical Establishment. He even shared her nonconformist disapproval of a national lottery, saying that it 'offends my Presbyterian instincts'.[27]

Admittedly he himself was a compulsive gambler, one with extravagant faith in his star. From his youth up Rupert had been addicted to games of chance, trying everything from pitch-and-toss to billion-dollar hazard. He often lost, though he had more than his fair share of luck. He raised the money for his first divorce settlement on the racecourse, making £100,000 at the Melbourne Cup. Later he risked his entire business on the success of Sky Television, a punt that hit the jackpot. Murdoch scorned to play safe, reckoning that fortune favoured the bold. Like Hitler, he always aimed to break the bank. Whatever the stakes, he loved to back winners – commercial or political, equine or divine. Betting on God was a sure thing, as Pascal's wager demonstrated, and Murdoch invariably sought to associate himself with the deity. He went to church. He hobnobbed with Billy Graham. He announced that Pope John Paul II was becoming a columnist in his newspapers, though it turned out that they had merely acquired the rights to print the Holy Father's English-language writings – which did not stop Murdoch from gaining a papal knighthood after donating $10 million to build a new Roman Catholic cathedral in Los Angeles. Murdoch also bought into Beliefnet, the largest 'faith and spirituality information site'[28] on the World Wide Web, thus generating advertising revenue on earth while laying up treasure in heaven. Maybe getting God online makes prayer passé, but Murdoch's own minions communed with him from afar. At a London staff party a high priest in News Corporation spoke of its chief as if he were the Almighty: 'He is thinking of you. He has sent you a message. He wishes he could be here but he is in Hong Kong, or China, or Hollywood, I am not quite sure where – he hovers over the world and us.'[29]

Despite the awe that Murdoch engendered, he was courteous and modest in person. When he took over the London *Times*, he surprised its editor, who had expected an Outback yahoo, by speaking softly and drinking tea from a bone-china service. Murdoch travelled without an entourage, preferring hotel rooms to suites and taking taxis (occasionally even buses) rather than limousines. He was, indeed, frugal to the point of miserliness: refusing to buy footwear at Mayfair prices, he once had lunch at the Savoy Grill with the sole of his shoe attached to the upper by an elastic band. True, he acquired luxury yachts, executive jets and millionaire mansions. But until late in life his tastes remained simple. He wore Wal-Mart shirts. He had no pretensions to culture, read little and associated aesthetic interests with epicene inclinations. He liked swimming, sailing, skiing, riding and playing tennis – he would challenge every line call, even when the ball was clearly out, giving a sheepish grin when he did so. With his furrowed brows, blubber lips, dark jowls and hunched shoulders, he cut an unimpressive figure. Shy with women, nervous with the great, diffident when appearing in public, Murdoch often fizzed with good cheer in private. He swapped gossip. He made mischief. He exercised his well-known lethal charm. He treated underlings with breezy bonhomie and sometimes worked beside them in his shirtsleeves. At one party he even allowed them to throw him fully clothed into a swimming pool. He had a crude sense of humour and could sometimes laugh at himself. When, just after his second marriage, Frank Packer outmanoeuvred him in a share transaction, Murdoch remarked: 'While I was honeymooning in London I was raped in Sydney.'[30]

So Murdoch was a quicksilver compound of high spirits and base conduct. He professed piety and practised profanity. He smiled like a seraph and struck like a serpent. Was his religious credo mere humbug? Was it a fig leaf to cover monstrous indecency? Was it even a cloak to hide the cloven hoof? Murdoch's claim to be a magnanimous muckraker clearly smacked of cant, as *Private Eye* intimated when it nicknamed him the 'Dirty Digger'. Like earlier press moguls, he wanted to sell newspapers and his real interest in muck was to turn it into brass. Equally spurious was his assertion that critics of his tabloids were elitist snobs, as though only they could recognise moral squalor. Murdoch always justified himself by saying that he gave the public what it wanted, but this too was specious pleading: the argument might have been used by any drug-dealer or, as one writer remarked, by Nero throwing Christians to the lions. If Murdoch was two-faced, however, he was also in two minds. Oscillating between elevated principles and ruthless pragmatism, he tried to serve both God and Mammon. He produced some of the best newspapers in the world and some of the worst, evidently setting more store by the latter. He refused to sell out to the Establishment yet he was eager to consort with the powerful. He advocated republicanism, as if the spirit of young Red Rupert lingered on, yet he thrilled to the attentions of royalty like the diehard conservative he had become. He trumpeted democratic capitalism in America yet toadied to communist dictatorship in China. Were these paradoxes or contradictions? How can they be explained or resolved? What made Rupert run? These are puzzling questions but they are not beyond all conjecture.

Rupert Murdoch's divided self stemmed in part from his divided family. His two grandfathers could hardly have been more antithetical: one a stern presbyter in an evangelical sect that had asserted its spiritual independence by breaking away from Scotland's established church; the other a scapegrace Irishman who wasted his substance on riotous living – drinking, woman-ising, gambling and hell-raising. He was Rupert Greene, a Melbourne wool merchant who was often fleeced at the gaming tables or on the turf; he incurred such debts that he sometimes had to rent out his house and move his wife and children into lodgings. Rows ensued and he once told his daughter Elisabeth, 'I'm going to cut your mother up and put her in a little black box under the gardenia.'[31] Rupert Murdoch said his own father had nightmares that he (Rupert) would turn out like his Greene grandfather, 'which I probably did . . . a bit'.[32] Unquestionably young Rupert showed signs of becoming a prodigal son. But this was not so much because he was attracted by Greene hedonism as because he was alienated by tartan spartanism. His father Keith, born in Melbourne in 1885, was brought up in the Calvinist discipline of the kirk and he remained a harsh taskmaster all his life. He was as severe with himself as with his children and employees, grimly resolved to cultivate the 'tremendous strength of mind', as he put it, 'needed to force one's way along'. Although the Revd Patrick Murdoch would have liked his boy to follow him into the ministry, Keith rejected the call of Jesus for the calling of journalism. It too was a vocation, he argued, in which he could accomplish great work. It offered him enormous opportunities to do good and the chance to become 'a power in Australia'.

In this ambition he was handicapped by a crippling stammer, which he fought to overcome for many years. Moreover, having served an apprenticeship on the Melbourne *Argus* and saved £500 to take him to London in 1908, he seems to have suffered a nervous breakdown. Frustrated by his failure to get a job, ashamed of his intellectual callowness (which he tried to correct by attending lectures at the London School of Economics) and worried that he lacked strength of character, Keith confessed to being 'in an almost haunted and tortured frame of mind'. He had 'fits of beastly depression', doubtless exacerbated by the dinginess of his flea-ridden billet in the Caledonian Christian Association hostel. He was offended by the 'beastly humbug' of the quasi-religious ceremonial he witnessed at the royal opening of parliament, saying that though the monarch was a useful public servant, Australians would admit no claims of sovereignty or divine right. And he was shocked by the parade of immorality in the imperial capital, not just ambulant members of the oldest profession but prostitutes of the press, Fleet Street-walkers. The English were brutes and savages, he thought, and most of their newspapers were dirty and dishonourable.

As Keith slipped into the slough of despond, he experienced an acute crisis of faith. For days, he told his father, he was in 'an agony of chaotic ideas'. In a country where the churches had very little hold, he longed to 'get back to Christianity'. To judge from his letters, what shook him was the prevalent notion that science had discredited religion, that human destiny was governed by a mindless process of evolution rather than by the hand of God. Having had a vested interest in the saving blood of Christ, he now felt spiritually destitute. He was fogged by doubt. He was beset by temptations in a hard, hostile metropolis that 'shatters the knees of a stranger when he knocks against it'. However it was a short step, psychologically, for a man raised in the conviction that he was one of the Lord's elect to believe that he was the finished product of natural selection. Keith evidently took that step, thus recovering his equilibrium. He distilled Protestantism into the spirit of capitalism and fervently embraced the tenets of social Darwinism. Like those who tried to show by works that they were redeemed by grace, he was determined to prove himself in the struggle for existence. 'The survival of the fittest principle is good,' he wrote, 'because the fittest become very fit indeed.'[33]

So, despite paternal concerns that the press would bear evil fruit, Keith returned to labour in his chosen field. First he resumed work as a reporter on the *Age*, where fluent shorthand made up for stuttering speech. Then he directed the cable service of the Melbourne *Sun* and *Herald*, simultaneously cultivating present and future prime ministers, Andrew Fisher and Billy Hughes. In

1915, Murdoch was sent to England to supervise the transmission of war news and en route he got a scoop that transformed his life, winning him the success and power he devoutly craved as well as laying the foundation for his son's career. Fisher had asked him to examine the flawed postal arrangements for Australian forces in the Middle East. Informing the commander of the expeditionary force to the Dardanelles, General Sir Ian Hamilton, that duty called him to wield the pen rather than the rifle, Murdoch wheedled permission to visit Anzac troops on the 'sacred shores of Gallipoli'. He spent a short time with them, sending home a story about the invincible spirit of men who 'died charging with the light of battle in their eyes'.[34] But he talked at length to the British correspondent Ellis Ashmead-Bartlett, a flamboyant figure with champagne tastes and his own French chef, who was an outspoken critic of the top brass. The Anzacs were lions led by donkeys, Ashmead-Bartlett thought, and Gallipoli was the bloodiest military fiasco since Bannockburn. Ashmead-Bartlett enshrined this verdict in a cogent report to the London government, which he entrusted to Murdoch in order to evade the censor. However, Hamilton got wind of it and an army officer confiscated the report in Marseilles. Murdoch then wrote a more lurid letter of his own, plagiarising Ashmead-Bartlett without acknowledgement. It was an exercise in sensationalism that prompted the cabinet secretary, Maurice Hankey, to call Murdoch 'a horrible scab'.[35]

The letter, which was addressed to Andrew Fisher, performed the remarkable feat of exaggerating the 'continuous and ghastly bungling' at Gallipoli of the 'chocolate general staff officers'.[36] It was full of mistakes, among them the assertion that an order had been given to shoot without mercy laggards at Suvla Bay. Murdoch presented rumour as fact and gossip as first-hand experience. 'From what I saw of the Turk . . .' he wrote, when he had seen no Turks.[37] He frequently contradicted himself, saying that the troops were dispirited but morale was good. 'Sedition is talked round every tin of bully beef on the peninsula, and it is only loyalty that holds the forces together.' Murdoch's tone throughout was egotistical and hysterical, indicating that here, masquerading as a military dispatch, was a tabloid exposé. Yet like many such exposés it contained a germ of truth, namely that Hamilton had led his men into a disastrous 'series of cul-de-sacs'.[38] Moreover, at a time when almost everyone was seeking an exit, Murdoch let it be seen in Fleet Street and Westminster. Lord Northcliffe seized on the letter, Lloyd George endorsed its message and H. H. Asquith, the prime minister, published it as a state paper. Within a month Hamilton was recalled and at the end of 1915 Gallipoli was evacuated. Many years later Rupert Murdoch, who financed Peter Weir's film about the campaign, claimed that although his father had made errors, he 'changed history'.[39] This was a myth. Keith Murdoch merely helped to substantiate the cabinet's conclusion that the entire operation had been a gigantic blunder. Northcliffe liked to discover government policy in advance so that he could take credit for it and Murdoch, who became his protégé, did little more than anticipate the inevitable.

Nevertheless, Murdoch had gained entry into the inner circles of the British Empire. He was soon hobnobbing with the likes of Lord Milner, Lloyd George and Bonar Law. He devilled for the dynamic Billy Hughes, who said that Asquith 'looked upon action as a kind of disease'.[40] Murdoch treated with General Haig and vainly tried to induce Australian soldiers in France to support Hughes's doomed plebiscites in favour of conscription. Crucially he also obtained the patronage of the Napoleon of Fleet Street. Northcliffe was erratic as well as autocratic, inspiring such awe that one journalist bowed and raised his hat while talking to him on the telephone. But the creator of the *Daily Mail* took a fancy to the burly, bustling, wavy-haired Australian. He taught him the meretricious tricks of the inky trade and invited him to his country house, Sutton Place, for what Murdoch called 'lovely girls, golf and one week more of your [company]'. The young man confided in Northcliffe about his romantic entanglements: 'I recently met an Adorable Person in the shape of a Slade School art student.' He also flattered him shamelessly, lauding his virtuoso control of a vast organisation and hailing the 'Chief' as the greatest force in his life. After the war Northcliffe offered Murdoch a job with golden prospects but he was loath to serve such a manic puppet-master. Still, he did report the Prince of Wales's Antipodean tour for Northcliffe's *Times*. And in 1921, single-mindedly set on emulating Northcliffe down under, he followed his patron's advice and accepted the editorship of the Melbourne *Herald*. Soon Keith Murdoch was nicknamed 'Lord Southcliffe'.

He earned the title, importing the techniques of the *Daily Mail* to galvanise the *Herald*. He introduced stunts, serials, campaigns, competitions and insurance schemes. He peptonised the news, sharpened the editorials and started a women's page. He improved the pictures and layout. He focused on local issues and highlighted human interest, liking nothing better than a good murder. Northcliffe sent him sagacious counsel – 'you don't have enough stockings in the paper' – and Murdoch replied slavishly, 'Your notes are my bible.'[41] Thus inspired, he promoted one of the first beauty contests in Australia. Within a year the *Herald*'s circulation had risen from 95,000 to 140,000. It was not plain sailing. Murdoch had to resist interference from above, asserting that it would be disastrous if the proprietor 'overrides the editor'[42] – hardly a sentiment shared by his son. Moreover the competition from Hugh Denison's *Sun* was cut-throat. Murdoch's building was set on fire, his newsvendors were assaulted by hoodlums wielding bicycle chains and he sometimes had to distribute his paper through tobacconists, fruiterers and barbers' shops. He retaliated in kind, turning his workforce into a private army, building a grey fortress on Flinders Street and employing a pistol-packing bodyguard. For Murdoch, as for his son in after years, journalism was a form of warfare.

Keith also sought safety in size. He founded radio stations, launched periodicals, created a newsprint industry, bought provincial papers and eventually built the *Herald* group into one of Australia's media giants. As it grew, Murdoch attempted to make it respectable. He hired genteel reporters, insisting that they should dress smartly and shave properly – like Northcliffe, he suspected that men with beards had something to hide. Murdoch moralised about the Fourth Estate. He denounced dishonest journalism as worse than perfidy: it was folly, 'for the Australian public soon finds out'. Yet in pursuit of profit, like the most vicious of his breed, he used the press as a cosh. Murdoch revelled in the political fight, the intrigue, the inside information, the clash of personalities. He wooed adherents, vilified opponents and probably 'felt that he was a king-maker'.[43] During the Depression, he attacked the Labor leader James Scullin, who had imposed a duty on newsprint, and backed Joseph Lyons, the Ramsay MacDonald of Australia, who advanced his interests. 'Lord Southcliffe' was accused of manipulating ministers like marionettes and trying to usurp the powers of parliament. Lyons ingratiated himself with Murdoch, calling at his office and getting him a knighthood. But the prime minister had no illusions about the press magnate. He acknowledged the truth of a warning by the chairman of the Australian Broadcasting Commission, who said that Murdoch's favour was always ephemeral and never disinterested – Lyons himself had been transformed into a 'dreadful person' when he 'stood between Sir Keith and his ambitions'.[44] True to form, Murdoch soon damned Lyons as a conciliator. He had put him into office, Murdoch said, and he would put him out.

In this boast, of course, as in so much else, Sir Keith anticipated Rupert. Indeed, through nurture as well as nature the father exercised a seminal influence over the son's destiny. Keith Rupert Murdoch (always called Rupert) was born on 11 March 1931, the second child of Elisabeth, née Greene, whom Keith had married three years earlier. Rupert and his older sister Helen at once became the subject of a family tussle. They were much spoilt by their Greene grandfather, who gave them lavish toys and treats. This angered Sir Keith, who applied to domestic matters all the finesse he had acquired in the journalistic bear-garden. He insisted that Rupert needed stiff discipline to meet the deadlines and make the headlines in life. When the boy was only six, Sir Keith interrogated him at formal Sunday lunch about the Revd Patrick Murdoch's sermon. Later, as if to imbue his son with the true grit of the noble bushman, he made Rupert sleep in an outdoor hut at Cruden Farm, his country estate thirty miles south of Melbourne.

Here Sir Keith lived like a lord with his attractive young wife, herself a mixture of saccharine and steel. He drank French wines and smoked Havana cigars in a colonnaded mansion filled with Georgian porticos and open fireplaces, antique furniture and Chinese porcelain, surrounded by rockeries, sunken gardens and tennis courts, and approached along an avenue of eucalyptus. However he remained tight-fisted in spirit and imposed thrift on Rupert, who earned cash both by selling bags of horse manure from the stables and by catching rats, paying Helen a penny to skin them and selling the fur for sixpence – enterprises curiously akin to journalism. His father, increasingly dour and brusque, was not impressed. Rupert tried hard to please. He even invented achievements, in tabloid fashion, to elicit paternal praise. But Sir Keith issued public rebukes and punishments instead, sowing the seeds of adolescent rebellion.

Rupert reacted against everything his father represented. Sir Keith loathed communism, nursed dark prejudices against Roman Catholics and endorsed a white Australia policy. He shared the predilections of what was the most conservative, class-conscious and Anglophile city in Australia. He favoured Melbourne's militant patriotism, its cult of masculinity and its addiction to sport (though not its devotion to gambling). He accepted its stunted night life and its stifling sabbatarianism – as in Toronto, visitors joked that they could spend a week in Melbourne on a Sunday. He approved of the metropolitan ban on drinking after six o'clock and the restrictions on mixed bathing – Sir Keith was so prim that when a female editor urged the omission of 'social *piddle*'[45] from the women's page he waved a bunch of gum leaves in front of his nose to purify the atmosphere. Rupert proved more robust when snatched from his governess and sent to Geelong Grammar School, the Eton of the South. Its charismatic headmaster James Darling had a progressive reputation but he was a bully who employed the traditional methods of the English public school to suppress 'the poisonous passions of puberty'. Muscular Christianity, cadet drill, cold showers, prefect canings and organised games were the order of the day. Rupert detested the regime and (perhaps inspired

by his radical history teacher Manning Clark) became ostentatiously 'bolshie'. He advocated pacifism and socialism. He
defended trade unions and proposed the nationalisation of banks.
He denounced private education and racial discrimination. Rupert
was lonely and unpopular, partly because of his father's dictatorial
pretensions, partly because of his own 'obnoxious personality'.
He did badly at his studies and often sneaked away to bet on the
horses. Darling regarded him as a nuisance at the time and later
as a canker in the heart of Australian life.

Meanwhile Sir Keith, knowing that Rupert had always enjoyed
the fruits of affluence, reckoned that his egalitarian views were
insincere. Like other worldly Presbyterians, Sir Keith was a
connoisseur of hypocrisy, and he was not far wide of the mark.
Throughout his career Rupert combined the satisfactions of posing
as an outsider with the rewards of having an inside track. He
attacked privilege while benefiting from it. The Digger aped the
Leveller. He needed to kick against the pricks and found them in
the Establishment of which he himself became a virile member.
At Oxford, where he gained entry in 1950 thanks to his father's
influence and occupied the grandest room in Worcester College,
Rupert discovered an enemy within, a ready-made elite to challenge. He regarded his gilded contemporaries as effete snobs and
tagged them with epithets like 'putrid little shit'.[46] Fellow undergraduates patronised him as a poor little rich boy with an
outlandish accent, uncouth habits and a chip on each shoulder.
At worst, indeed, Rupert seemed to have the manners of a convict
and the morals of a commissar. He gambled recklessly and indulged
in drunken horseplay. He broke the rules by canvassing for
office in the University Labour Club, which banned him after a
hearing in what he called, without irony, a kangaroo court. At a
time when Stalin was still spilling buckets of Soviet blood, 'Red'
Rupert famously kept on his mantelpiece a bust of Lenin, paying
homage to the great teacher of communist revolution. In middle
age Rupert confessed to having been a papier-mâché radical; but
the pulp fiction alarmed Sir Keith during his final years. He died
in October 1952. In his will he expressed the desire that Rupert

should fulfil his father's ideals by devoting his life to useful and altruistic work in the field of newspapers and broadcasting. It would prove a memorable injunction.

Rupert was shocked to discover that his father had left him relatively little apart from good wishes. Sir Keith had been director but not proprietor of the *Herald* group and he owned only a couple of provincial newspapers, one of which was sold by the trustees of his estate – to his son's lasting chagrin. Thus Rupert's inheritance consisted of not much more than the small Adelaide *News*, described as a nothing paper in a nothing city,[47] and a radio station in remote Broken Hill, a cockleshell that scarcely prefigured the armada he would build to rule the airwaves. He determined thereafter to secure a controlling interest in all his enterprises. Meanwhile, after much coaching, he got a third-class degree in PPE: politics (which fascinated him), philosophy (which he despised) and economics (which bored him). He learned less from Oxford than from raffish continental tours and a subeditorial stint on the *Daily Express*, where he earned £10 a week and lived at the Savoy Hotel. In 1953 he flew home to claim his birthright. Under the tutelage of the red-haired and once redtainted Rohan Rivett, Sir Keith's surprising choice as editor of the *News*, Rupert published a paper that was both populist and progressive. It was replete with headlines such as QUEEN EATS A RAT.[48] And it opposed the right-wing policies of its larger rival, the *Advertiser*, whose monopolistic ambitions it lambasted. Rupert interfered in all departments of the *News*, getting his fingers inky and running his staff ragged. He was as rumbustious as the Great Dane that accompanied him on forays to the racetrack, the boxing ring, the poker saloon and the pub. Rupert could also be ferocious, a crouching attack dog with narrowed eyes and bared teeth.[49]

Inevitably he clashed with Rivett, who had spent three years in a Japanese prisoner-of-war camp and himself possessed a savage temper. Rivett wanted the *News* to make waves, whereas Rupert wanted it to make money. Rivett gave to stories space that

Rupert required for advertisements. Rivett acted as the keeper of Rupert's radical conscience, which proved about as durable as snow on the Flinders Ranges. Yet for the time being the proprietor let the editor have his head. Rupert (who did find time to address the local branch of the Fabian Society) was preoccupied. Although he remained gauche with women, especially with the 'big-hipped, stately Amazons'[50] of Melbourne, he pursued them eagerly, and in 1956 he married an airline stewardess named Patricia Booker. Their union, which produced a daughter, Prudence, was doomed. Like most Australians then, Rupert thought that a wife's place was in the home and that a husband should mix it in a man's world. Emulating his father, he embarked on a relentless course of expansion. He bought the Perth *Sunday Times*, taking six-hour flights across the continent most weekends to inject energy, inflate headlines and invent melodrama – he not only printed all the news that didn't matter but some news that didn't exist, such as 'How to Keep UFOs Out of Your Garden'. Then he broke into television, acquiring a station in Adelaide and starting a successful imitation of America's *TV Guide*. Meanwhile Rivett became embroiled in a bitter cause célèbre. It concerned an Aborigine called Max Stuart, who had been sentenced to death for the murder of a nine-year-old white girl. There was evidence that racist police had framed Stuart, and it seemed that his conviction was upheld thanks only to a local ruling clique so Neanderthal that it banned Tom Lehrer's songs and J. D. Salinger's *Catcher in the Rye*. The *News*'s raucous campaign saved Stuart from the gallows and Rivett was hailed as the 'Zola of South Australia'.[51] But his attack on the judges, in which Rupert himself played a virulent part, goaded the authorities to prosecute him for seditious libel. Shortly after a jury acquitted Rivett, in 1960, Rupert fired him by post.

The episode marked an epoch in Rupert Murdoch's life. It inclined him to avoid crusades that might offend the masses or antagonise the powers that be. His newspapers should aim at entertainment before activism, titillation before investigation. And they should be created in his own image, its liberal gilt now tarnished by a leprous pragmatism. Thus Murdoch, who disparaged 'Abos' and privately doubted Stuart's innocence, at once reversed Rivett's opposition to the government's white Australia policy. He appeased the Adelaide conservatives and veered towards a prime minister, Robert Menzies, who was anti-socialist to his bootstraps. No one demonstrated the advantages of backing Menzies better than the Sydney media tycoon Sir Frank Packer, whose knighthood was the least of his rewards. Murdoch, who had failed in takeover bids elsewhere, set out to challenge Packer in his own domain. It was a rash move, since Sir Frank was the most brutal tyrant ever to run an Australian newspaper. Profane, drunken and licentious, he had a fist to 'fell an ox' and a boot to 'kick a mule'.[52] He scourged his offspring, disinheriting his elder son. He blasted his underlings, screaming at reporters and forcing one leader writer to stand in the corner. He printed diatribes about the Red Menace and the Yellow Peril, and urged Americans to kill 500 black civil rights protesters at a time to discourage the others. Sir Frank was the Cullinan of rough diamonds. He confused Parkinson's law with Parkinson's disease, and proposed to call one of his magazines *Women's Monthly*, conflating a period and a periodical. But he made a fortune, flagrantly using his organs to promote his other enterprises, to blackmail politicians and to secure secrecy for his own misdeeds, such as tax evasion. By comparison Murdoch was a cultured pearl. But he learned a lot from his struggle with Packer, whom he described as the biggest, cleverest crook in Australian newspapers.

Murdoch did not tackle Packer head-on. He entered Sydney though the back door, buying a chain of suburban publications called the Cumberland Press. Sir Frank retaliated, determined to send Murdoch 'back to Adelaide with his fookin' tail between his fookin' legs'.[53] Both sought extra printing capacity, and on 7 June 1960, Packer's plug-uglies occupied a plant claimed by each side, the Anglican Press. Murdoch quickly recruited another bunch of toughs, led by his boon companion Frank Browne, journalist, jailbird and neo-Nazi. Having dispensed wads of ten-pound notes, Murdoch retired to a safe distance while Browne's bruisers evicted the opposition, beating young Kerry Packer severely – he hid his black eyes behind dark glasses. Murdoch gleefully recorded the discomfiture of this 'knight's son' in the *Daily Mirror*, which (with its bilious Sunday sister) he had just bought from the city's other major press gang, the Fairfax family. The Fairfaxes hoped that this loss-making paper would sink 'the boy publisher'. Instead, after some false starts, he transformed it into a voyeuristic scandal sheet full of rapes and murders, soaring headlines and plunging necklines. As one old hack said, 'The *Mirror* had to out-lie the liars, out-distort the distorters, out-shock the shockers. And it did. It raised the standards of Australian journalism to a new low.'[54] One story, concerning a SCHOOLGIRL'S ORGY DIARY, which turned out to be a virgin's sexual fantasy, caused a boy to hang himself. In the spirit of Thomas Jefferson, mature citizens who saw anything in the *Mirror* that they knew to be true immediately began to doubt it. A report concocted by the editor about a small war in Dutch New Guinea, replete with cannibals and shrunken heads, elicited this telegram from the *Mirror*'s correspondent on the spot: 'Nearest shrunken heads to Dutch New Guinea are in Sydney.'[55]

Cannibalism in Sydney was the peculiar prerogative of the media barons. Dog ate dog, or at least, as Randolph Churchill once remarked, son of a bitch ate son of a bitch.[56] And Murdoch stimulated rival appetites by snapping up a television station in Wollongong (south of the city) plus American programmes to go with it. To limit damaging competition, though, he eventually reached an accord with Packer and Fairfax. They carved up the available territory like so many mafia bosses. Such pacts are temporary: Murdoch's *Mirror* soon breached its agreement with Fairfax's *Sun* to use the word OUTRAGE in headlines instead of RAPE. But Packer made a permanent impression on Murdoch, who in some ways modelled himself on Sydney's dark knight. It is true that Murdoch modernised the *Mirror*, whereas Packer's hacks had to scramble for desks and typewriters, and to hand in used ballpoint pens before they could get new ones. And 'Rupert the Chick', as the fledgling press magnate was sometimes called, never became an unbridled primitive to match Sir Frank. But as Murdoch's marriage disintegrated, he, like Packer, did everything to excess: 'Drinking, smoking, gambling, whoring, you name it.'[57] After one binge an editor vomited over him in a taxi and Murdoch afterwards apologised, assuming that he himself had been sick. He was more indulgent than Packer towards his employees, many of whom liked working for such a live wire. But he also had a short fuse and exploded in the face of opposition. Moreover, he shared some of Sir Frank's obscurantist views, an aversion to short-haired women in trouser suits and long-haired men in suede shoes, which probably meant that they were homosexual. And he recognised that Packer's alliance with Menzies brought him incomparable commercial benefits. Denied them, Murdoch poured the vials of wrath on the prime minister's head. It was partly to gain political leverage that in 1964 he launched the country's first proper national daily, *The Australian*. He acted, too, in response to his mother's plea that he must rescue the family name, which his horrid newspapers had sullied, by publishing something decent for a change.

The quest for respectability was arduous. Murdoch's broadsheet was initially based in the federal capital, where he aimed to establish a monopoly by running the *Canberra Times* out of business – as he kindly informed its proprietor, who sold out to the Fairfax group, which then beat *The Australian* on its home ground. Moreover Murdoch, who had got rich by peddling trash to the masses, hardly knew how to cater for the top end of the market. Indeed, in his organisation, said one of its senior managers, John Menadue, 'talk of quality is snobbery'.[58] Murdoch hoped that his gifted first editor, Maxwell Newton, would attract a large and classy readership. But Newton was as volatile as gelignite, intermittently manic and alcoholic yet committed to sober intellectual journalism. Murdoch himself craved heavy type and light entertainment. He wanted pin-ups, sport and stories about drug rings, call girls and decapitated corpses. He also insisted on a column called 'For Those Who Trust the Stars', seeing nothing astrologically untoward about reprinting, under the Southern Cross, the charts of a London paper showing the northern sky. As sales fell and losses mounted, Murdoch's interventions grew more frenetic. 'Here comes that big hairy bastard again,'[59] Newton would mutter, dismissing the proprietor's contributions as 'rubbish'[60] and sometimes pretending to fall asleep in his presence. After angry words and banged doors Murdoch sacked Newton, who proceeded on a remarkable career as publicist, pornographer and brothel-keeper – useful preliminaries no doubt for his final incarnation, after a rapprochement with Rupert, as a business columnist on the *New York Post*.

At the 'mausoleum on Mort Street' in Canberra, Murdoch hired and fired vigorously. He excited and intimidated his staff, who christened him 'Puff the Magic Founder'. He struggled with the distribution system, urging his pilots to take off in fog that he described as light mist. Then, in 1967, he moved *The Australian* to Sydney. Although still a financial drain, it now paid handsome political dividends. Money was vital to Murdoch, but what really drove him, wrote Menadue, was the desire to influence or control people in power.[61] And no one had a more tenacious hold on power than the formidable protectionist Minister of Trade and Industry 'Black Jack' McEwen. Murdoch cultivated him assiduously, going beyond the bounds of Australian cronyism or 'mateship' and treating McEwen almost as a surrogate father. Their relationship was sustained by a valuable exchange of favours. Thus in 1968 Murdoch assisted Black Jack in his campaign to prevent Billy McMahon, a scheming free-trader rumoured to fancy trim sailors in tight bell-bottoms, from becoming prime minister. Using secret service information supplied by Black Jack, *The Australian* alleged that McMahon's leading journalistic champion was a 'foreign agent'.[62] This was none other than the paper's ex-editor Maxwell Newton, who now derided Murdoch as a 'whipper-snapper from Adelaide'.[63] Whatever the truth of that, the charge against Newton was entirely false: he was merely acting as consultant to a Japanese trade organisation. Nevertheless some mud stuck to McMahon, who lost the premiership to the scarred war hero John Gorton. He helped Black Jack to repay his debt to Murdoch a thousandfold, by authorising the release of the foreign currency he needed to invade Fleet Street.

Murdoch was grateful to Gorton, a hard-drinking nationalist who presided over a 'cocktail cabinet'. So *The Australian* duly changed tack (for a while) to support the government's hawkish policy over the Vietnam war. Murdoch also entertained Gorton at Cavan, the spacious new estate north of Canberra that he shared with his beautiful new wife Anna (née Torv), a cub reporter with whom he had become involved well before his divorce from Patricia. Needless to say, newspapers generally maintain a decent reticence about the love affairs of press magnates, even when they are competitors – a convention Murdoch endorsed. But all too soon *The Australian* signalled the breakdown of Murdoch's liaison with Gorton, who did not improve his position by appointing as his principal private secretary a twenty-two-year-old pocket Venus called Ainsley Gotto, better known as 'Miss Wiggle'. Like a Machiavellian prince in some tale of Renaissance treachery, Murdoch even administered the poisoned chalice. This was a lucrative commission, which Gorton found irresistible, to write a series of articles for the short-lived *Sunday Australian* entitled 'I Did it My Way'. In them, as Murdoch expected, Gorton criticised colleagues and fatally discredited himself. McMahon succeeded him in 1971. The following year Packer reluctantly disposed of his unprofitable *Telegraph* newspapers to Murdoch, selling the estate with the serfs – many of whom were quickly evicted. McMahon rang Sir Frank, who was having a drink with the new owner, to protest about the loss of press support. Packer handed the telephone to Murdoch, who promised to be as fair to the prime minister as he deserved. In the background Sir Frank growled, 'If you do that you will murder the silly little bugger.'[64]

He was a true prophet, and Murdoch later confessed that his newspapers had conducted a dreadful campaign against McMahon. Full of distorted news and biased views, it was his first serious effort to decide the outcome of a general election. Murdoch was convinced that twenty-three years of conservative rule were coming to an end and he championed the pugnacious Labor leader Gough

Whitlam. Apart from an unapologetic Australianism, however, the two men had little in common. Murdoch confessed to being 'a bit dull and humourless',[65] whereas Whitlam was flamboyant and witty – asked by a tailor whether he dressed to the left or the right, he replied, 'Both sides, Comrade, both sides!' Murdoch talked in vehement platitudes where Whitlam effervesced with insolent aphorisms – describing himself as a Christian fellow-traveller, he promised that when he met God, 'I shall treat him as an equal.'[66] Murdoch was a man of action where Whitlam was a man of ideas – he found none at Cavan, spending there one of the most 'excruciatingly boring' evenings of his life. Still, Murdoch associated himself with Whitlam's brand of radicalism and took credit for Labor's victory, asking afterwards: 'How many seats do you think we won?'[67] Probably he reflected rather than directed the opinions of his readers. But future Australian ministers were awed by his supposed ability to brainwash the public. They caved in to him because, as one delicately put it, there was no way 'we can fuck Rupert Murdoch without fucking ourselves'.[68]

Whitlam was not intimidated, saying simply: 'Fuck Rupert!' He refused to 'duchess' the media magnate, withholding favours and declining his request, evidently made in all seriousness, to become Australian High Commissioner in London.[69] Murdoch, whose global empire now included some eighty newspapers, eleven magazines, and television and radio stations as well as printing, paper, transport and mining concerns, was personally miffed and politically affronted. Having become an admirer of Richard Nixon and a critic of the kind of investigative journalism that exposed the Watergate scandal and led to the president's downfall, he now campaigned unrelentingly against Whitlam. His administration, which exuded what one senator called 'an air of magnificent chaos',[70] offered scope for valid criticism as well as vile calumny. And in 1975 Murdoch played a role in precipitating its demise. He urged the governor-general, Sir John Kerr, to take the reckless step of dismissing the Labor government when the opposition majority in the Senate denied it supply. In general Murdoch's media responded to his direction like an orchestra under the baton of a conductor. But journalists found his control odious, according to Whitlam,[71] and some now deliberately struck wrong notes. Others protested about the barrage of anti-Labor propaganda, holding strikes and demonstrations. As a fig leaf of decency *The Australian* had withered, and copies were burned in the streets. Murdoch was unmoved, nursing his own grievances about long-haired tree-huggers on the paper who wanted to proselytise for bleeding-heart causes and to see 'the country turned over to the blacks'.[72] However by this time he was, as one editor wrote, 'an absentee landlord visiting Australia for short periods, three or four times a year'.[73] While there he made snap decisions; but since 1968 his attention had been focused on Britain, an old world to conquer.

The opening offensive was laughably simple, and Murdoch described his first acquisition in Fleet Street as the 'biggest steal since the Great Train Robbery'. This was the *News of the World*, the largest and most venerable scandal sheet in the country, full of stories about gay vicars, bent coppers, kinky peers, stoned pop stars, suburban sex fiends, celebrity love triangles, spanking television 'personalities' and randy judges in frolics with vice girls. Ironically the paper's chairman and chief shareholder, Sir William Carr, was a pillar of Conservative rectitude. But he had allowed the circulation of the so-called *News of the Screws* to become sadly detumescent. His control of the company was threatened by a contumacious cousin, Derek Jackson, who wanted to sell his twenty-five per cent of the shares. And he was confronted by a takeover bid from the publisher Robert Maxwell, a Jewish Czech who, as a fellow British MP observed, liked to play God on five telephones.[74] Or, as the tabloid journalist Joe Haines said, before he became Maxwell's authorised hagiographer, the man was a crook, a monster, a creature 'fundamentally corrupt'.[75] Indeed, Maxwell looked like the prototypical rapist or serial killer so dear to the heart of the *News of the World*: his body was bearish and his face was 'not so much lived-in as taken over by squatters'.[76] In comparison Murdoch's knotted visage seemed cherubic. He stemmed from sound stock. His manner was unassuming. Beside Maxwell, whom he would defeat in several battles, Murdoch was a white knight in shining armour. To all appearances riding to the rescue, he was wryly amused by Carr's greeting: 'Thank God, you've come!'[77]

Of course Murdoch had not travelled halfway round the world, as he put it, just to toss Maxwell a concrete lifebelt. He had come to dispossess Carr, who represented everything the Australian despised about the decadent British Establishment. Murdoch sneered at Carr's antique furniture. He scorned his champagne-swigging corporate entertainments at Ascot, remarking that he himself was sober after lunch, which in some parts of Fleet Street 'makes you a genius'.[78] He was impatient with Sir William's old-fashioned business methods, warning that dither would hand the *News of the World* to a really undesirable alien. Murdoch himself might be a coarse colonial who appalled Lady Carr by lighting a cigar before lunch and eventually insisted on becoming the paper's sole managing director. But he promised that Sir William would remain chairman and that he (Rupert) would restrict his own stake in the company to forty per cent. So, during the tortuous manoeuvres whereby Murdoch completed the take-over, padding out an inferior offer with charm and artistry, Carr threw his considerable weight against Maxwell. The 'bouncing Czech', as he was inevitably called, warned Sir William that he would be out before his feet touched the ground, describing Murdoch as 'a moth-eaten, empty-pouched kangaroo'.[79] Carr insisted that Rupert was a gentleman. He was quickly disillusioned. Once in charge, Murdoch bought Jackson's shares, thus acquiring forty-nine per cent of the total, and forced Carr to resign as chairman. The excuse he gave for breaking his word was that the *News of the World* was in an even more parlous state than he had realised. His expressions of displeasure were not inhibited by good taste. When told that Jack Miller, the paper's media correspondent, had dropped dead, Murdoch rasped: 'Well, it wasn't from overwork.'[80]

He was equally abrasive towards the trade unions, opening

one meeting with the words: 'I'm now going to fucking tell you . . .'[81] But when the print workers' leader responded robustly, advising him to wash his mouth out, they soon struck a deal. Murdoch stopped at nothing to galvanise the *News of the World*, which was still bought by over six million people each Sunday. Doubtless recognising this as a commentary on the British educational system, he lowered the paper's tone in a bid to broaden its appeal. It seemed impossible to insert more sex but, as one observer noted, Murdoch 'made it with several orgies to spare'.[82] In September 1969, he published a warmed-up version of the memoirs of Christine Keeler, the call girl at the centre of the scandal that had destroyed the career of Harold Macmillan's war minister, John Profumo. As the Press Council immediately judged, to rehearse the salacious details of this affair was to exploit sex for gain. While living off immoral earnings was hardly a novelty in Fleet Street, Murdoch had hurt a man who merited privacy – for the past six years Profumo had been doing social work in London's East End. The owner of the *News of the World* might boast about the hundreds of thousands of extra copies he sold and refuse even to meet the Press Council. Ironically, though, Murdoch was not just arraigned before the bar of public opinion but cross-examined by an unelected tribune of the people and hoist with his own petard of publicity. Every inch the cocky colonial, he allowed David Frost to interview him on television in front of a studio audience. It proved to be one of the worst humiliations of his career.

The programme, a pioneering live colour broadcast, revealed Murdoch as a kind of cinematic villain, blue-jowled, shifty and inarticulate. Under Frost's inquisition he sweated, fidgeted and contradicted himself. He claimed that there were important new facts in the story but then had to admit that it was a twice-told tale. He had personally deleted indecent passages, yet he could not deny including elements of sexual titillation. Worse still for Murdoch, Frost showed a film clip of Cardinal Heenan anathematising the *News of the World* for cynically raking up the sordid past of a sinner who had repented. To call his paper dirty, Murdoch expostulated, was a downright libel. But the audience (apart from Murdoch's public relations man, whose lonely applause for his boss Frost sarcastically commended) found him guilty as charged. No one appreciated better than Murdoch the unfairness of trial by media, though his own victims could not respond as he did. As Murdoch left London Weekend Television, he swore to buy the 'blankety-blank company'.[83] It was a vow he would keep. Meanwhile he was reviled as a smut merchant and treated as a social pariah, which especially upset his wife, Anna. Murdoch blamed the Establishment for whipping up the row, though Frost ridiculed this as a conspiracy theory based on the anachronistic assumption that Britain was still governed by an old-boy network. But there was no more convenient enemy than 'the Establishment', that 'harlot of a phrase'[84] as the journalist Henry Fairlie called it. So Murdoch continued to maintain that he was the target of powerful forces scheming to resist change. All his foes were implicated in the plot. Murdoch even claimed that *Private Eye*, whose 'Dirty Digger' alias he hated, was 'almost a sort of Establishment'.[85] Of course the magazine specialised in subversion and Murdoch deemed it not funny but negative, detritus from the sixties satire boom.

He was still less amused after he acquired the *Sun* in 1969 and began to flesh out the news with generous views of 'Page Three girls', for *Private Eye* memorably christened him 'Rupert "Thanks for the Mammaries" Murdoch'. His Catholic wife was as much appalled as his Protestant mother, who doubtless recollected that the strait-laced Sir Keith had secured the rejection of a Renoir nude from Canberra's National Gallery. But Rupert was determined to beat Hugh Cudlipp, boss of the London *Daily Mirror*, who had sold him the *Sun* in the hope that its losses would cripple him. Murdoch got the paper for a song, describing it as 'the steal of the century'.[86] He concluded that Cudlipp no longer deserved his reputation as the doyen of tabloid journalism. This was true, though Cudlipp's radical edge had never been sharp. The *Mirror* had long claimed to be irreverent and outspoken, the scourge of the Establishment and the champion of the common man. It did, indeed, cock a snook or two, opposing the invasion of Suez, for example. But it was essentially populist, dressing transient content in garish style and nailing its colours to the weathercock of public opinion. This had been the standard practice of the popular press since the days of Grub Street. It was at once adopted by Murdoch's *Sun*, whose first editor, Larry Lamb, copied many of the *Mirror*'s best features. Like his chief, he knew that plagiarism is the soul of journalism.

However, Murdoch galvanised the *Sun*, which was housed in a rat-infested slum in Bouverie Street, charging it with his own energy and audacity. In a perpetual purge he cleansed the paper of 'intellectual bullshit'. In a seismic break with twentieth-century tradition, he treated royalties as celebrities instead of divinities. He set out the *Sun*'s principles in an impudent oxymoron. Among other things it passionately endorsed the ideals of truth, beauty and justice, while asserting that everyone from the Archbishop of Canterbury to Mick Jagger should be free to evolve his own moral code. The tabloid dealt in fantasy as much as fact, especially when conjuring up melodramas about the lives of the stars of television soap operas. But Murdoch made the *Sun* snappy, pithy, sexy. He got what he wanted, 'a tear-away paper with a lot of tit'.[87] Reeling from the competition, the *Mirror* too printed nipples, withdrawing them after protests and then promising that they would only appear 'where relevant'.[88] The *Sun* could always eclipse it in lubricity, here reporting Rolling Stones' debauches, there indicating 'The Way into a Woman's Bed', elsewhere offering its readers an 'Antipodean erotica kit'.[89] In 1970 the National Union of Journalists censured Murdoch for debasing the standards of their profession. The *Sun* also sinks, critics said, from gutter to sewer. According to one rival, indeed, it was less like a sun than a paraffin lamp in a brothel.

Murdoch loved the *Sun*, which tripled its circulation (to three million) within four years and in 1978 overtook the *Mirror*. The 'Currant Bun', to use its relished sobriquet, was the most profitable unit in his empire, enabling him to expand its boundaries across the Atlantic. It also gave him unprecedented political leverage, as epitomised in the famous boast about the Conservative general election victory of 1992: IT'S THE SUN WOT WON IT. Above all, Murdoch found the *Sun* fun, an arena of absurdity as well as a theatre of cruelty. He enjoyed the humour: the paper's cheekily advertised 'pussy week' turned out to be all about cats. He liked the drama of last-minute decisions, brightening headlines, subbing copy, moving photographs, working on the stone, getting his hands dirty. He revelled in the romance, the outrageous escapades, scurrilous exposés, pitiless vendettas and incandescent language of a world glamorised for the ages by Ben Hecht and Charlie MacArthur in *The Front Page*. His favourite editor, the foul-mouthed Kelvin MacKenzie, was Murdoch's id. Technically adept, freakishly hyperactive and scabrously funny, MacKenzie appealed to the basest instincts of his readers. Indeed, his description of the typical *Sun* reader might almost have fitted its proprietor: 'a right old fascist, wants to send the wogs back . . . he's afraid of the unions, afraid of the Russians, hates the weirdos and queers and drug dealers'.

Thus MacKenzie abused 'darkies' and 'poofters', 'Krauts' and 'Frogs'. He had one word for students, squatters, demonstrators, 'Gypsies' and others: 'scum'. He called Margaret Thatcher 'Maggie' and nicknamed the militant mineworkers' leader, Arthur Scargill, 'Mine Führer'. He subjected the toilers on his treadmill to wild and obscene harangues, coining words like 'fan-fucking-tastic' and 'soci-fucking-ology'.[90] He transformed news into vaudeville, favouring zany proclamations such as the notorious FREDDIE STARR ATE MY HAMSTER. Avid for sensation and consumed by bigotry, he made awful mistakes. MacKenzie blamed drunken Liverpool fans for the fatal crush at Hillsborough football stadium, and alleged that Elton John had sex with underage rent boys – a libel that cost the paper a million pounds, John ignoring Mick Jagger's advice that it was 'not worth fighting because they'll try to rake up so much muck'.[91] Slavering over reports about a 'blind rapist' or a pop star's 'lust for bondage', MacKenzie delighted in salacity and mendacity. He was much amused by a journalist's mock epitaph: 'Here lies Kelvin MacKenzie, and lies, and lies, and lies . . .' Murdoch called him 'my little Hitler' and encouraged some of his worst excesses, such as the brutally illiterate headline that announced, during the Falklands War, the sinking of the Argentine warship *General Belgrano*: GOTCHA. This conflict gave MacKenzie scope for uninhibited xenophobia as he turned the paper from 'bingo to jingo'.[92] When *Private Eye* satirised his antics with a competition to KILL AN ARGIE AND WIN A METRO, he was furious that he had not thought of the idea himself. Under Murdoch's auspices, in short, MacKenzie's *Sun* became a bizarre combination of circus, penitentiary, bordello and madhouse.

Despite its best efforts, though, the paper hardly plumbed new depths of degradation and its owner devised few fresh techniques of intimidation. Like earlier press barons, he harried subordinates mercilessly, driving some to resignation or nervous breakdown. To enforce his will he employed hatchet men described as 'terrorists in suits'.[93] He imposed rigorous economies, charging a deposit of fifty pence for cutlery in the Bouverie Street canteen and earning his company the nickname 'Shoestring International'.[94] He responded with thunderous brow and crashing fist to the remark that an advertising campaign for the *Sun* would only cost peanuts: 'Yeah, but they're my fucking peanuts!'[95] Murdoch would sweep clutter off reporters' desks and then say that the newsroom was a pigsty.[96] He would tear the paper to bits ('that story is a crock of shit')[97] and spurn editors' attempts to defend it ('Don't give me any of that crap'),[98] reducing Lamb to mincemeat and MacKenzie to jelly. He would appoint two men to do the same job and watch them struggle for dominance. Like his father, Rupert believed that journalism was a matter of survival of the fittest. There was little room for human sympathy in a world where the best catalyst was sudden carnage. As an employee said, 'One minute he's swimming along with a smile, then snap! There's blood in the water. Your head's gone.'[99] Murdoch was liberal only when it came to dismissals, keeping everyone in his organisation on tenterhooks. His prime instrument of torture was the telephone. He issued 'bollockings' at all hours and repeatedly told the editor of the *Sun* that he was a 'fucking idiot'.[100] MacKenzie griped, 'The Boss has been at the gorilla biscuits again.' Nothing was more frightening than Murdoch's angry silences: 'You're losing your touch, Kelvin. [Pause] Your paper is pathetic. [Pause] You're losing your touch, Kelvin.'[101] And the line would go dead.

Murdoch's moods were made worse by jet lag, treated with pills and purges, which became chronic after his move to the United States in 1973. Although seeking fame and fortune across the Atlantic, he was also disenchanted with Britain. He and Anna were shocked by an attempt to kidnap her that went wrong and resulted in the murder of Muriel McKay, the wife of the deputy chairman of the *News of the World*. And they were alienated by the persistent hostility of those Rupert called 'the chattering classes'[102] or 'bloody pinko Islington liberals'.[103] Murdoch's popular papers also increased his unpopularity among the top people who were said to read *The Times*. Boasting about his refusal to join the system, he complained of being barred from everything because 'we'd catch Lord Lambton in bed or something'.[104] But although Murdoch felt more at home in the less stuffy atmosphere of New York, he continued to exploit opportunities in London. He bought a substantial stake in London Weekend Television, for example, getting it after giving his word that he would not interfere in the content of programmes. Needless to say, he could not resist doing so; and when reminded of his promise he replied: 'Yes, but that was before I came.'[105] After a bitter dispute, in which he claimed to be the victim of character assassination, Murdoch had to obey regulations that prevented a newspaper owner from controlling television output, and he eventually sold his shares. However he was not hampered by guarantees of editorial freedom he gave in order to acquire *The Times* and *The Sunday Times* in 1981. In theory these guarantees were validated by independent directors and they could not be torn up, Murdoch said, without creating a destructive 'public stink'. In practice he tossed them aside like confetti, telling a *Times* journalist, 'They're not worth the paper they're written on.'[106]

Murdoch felt that he had every reason to crack the whip at his two new papers. He was able to buy them (with help from Margaret Thatcher, who ensured that his bid escaped the scrutiny of the Monopolies Commission) for a mere £12 million because their owner, the Thomson organisation, would no longer bear *The Times*'s huge losses, caused largely by atrocious labour relations. But he was confronted by 'a barnacle-covered whale'[107] that had scarcely changed since Lord Northcliffe tried to drag it into the twentieth century. At *The Times*'s office in Gray's Inn Road, internal telephone numbers were unlisted, manual typewriters were chained to desks and reporters still seemed to believe that news, like wine, improves by keeping. Critics mocked *The* (behind the) *Times*. Murdoch called the place a 'graveyard'[108] and sent in tanned Australians wearing short-sleeved white shirts and carrying clipboards who looked, said Bill Bryson, as if 'they were measuring people for coffins'.[109] The workforce was slashed, some abruptly sacked, others made voluntarily redundant. Murdoch stalked about like a caged lion, one witness noted. He had much to be angry about and he made no attempt to conceal his feelings, crouching low in his chair and tapping his gritted teeth with his folded spectacles. His flushed face was said to resemble a bruised knuckle. His eyes, under bushy eyebrows, glittered with feral intensity. His voice, normally a nasal mumble and often so quiet that underlings had to strain to hear him, became hard and menacing. His mordant discourse was punctuated by brittle laughter and he seemed insensitive to the pain he inflicted. The backs of his hands, observed *The Times*'s new editor, Harry Evans, were covered with thick black hair.

Murdoch had persuaded Evans, formerly a courageous and successful campaigning editor of the *Sunday Times*, to try to revive its sister paper. And Evans had succumbed to Murdoch's beguiling charm, the obverse of his chilling hostility. Under this spell, he could not believe that the proprietor would renege on his pledges about editorial independence. However, he underestimated Murdoch's will to power – the term 'control freak' might have been invented for him – and his compulsion to intervene while *The Times* continued to haemorrhage cash, his cash. Furthermore, Evans failed to appreciate his boss's essential contempt for high-minded broadsheet newspapers and for the highbrow journalists who worked on them. Murdoch's instinct was to shorten leaders, strengthen headlines, highlight sport, introduce Tombola ('up-market Bingo') and exploit royalty – the republican prompted a full-colour front page for the wedding of Prince Charles and Diana, herself soon adored in Fleet Street as the 'Princess of Sales'. To purge the staff he appointed as managing director Gerald Long, gastronome, logophile, martinet and, as Evans said, 'very much the Governor of a Victorian colony'.[110] Murdoch himself poured streams of profanity over top people who wrote for *The Times*. They were 'pissing liberals', limp-wristed left-wing layabouts and stuck-up, self-important, expense-padding Trotskyites. Altogether he seemed bent on killing the old Thunderer and resurrecting it as a de luxe edition of the *Sun*. On his fiftieth birthday, 11 March 1981, which was celebrated at Cavan with fireworks, skydivers and general razzmatazz, Anna gave him a cake iced to look like the front page of *The Times*. Excitedly, he plunged a knife into it.

Evans made life difficult for himself by introducing his own team and by applying the goad too liberally, for he shared Murdoch's reforming zeal and conducted what one senior man called 'journalism by orgasm'.[111] But his troubles were as nothing to those of Frank Giles, urbane editor of the *Sunday Times*. Murdoch regarded him as a wimp and from his window overlooking Giles's office he would fire mock pistol shots into the editor's back. He told Evans with a sidelong grin: 'I'm just going over to terrorise Frank.'[112] The terror became acute on Saturday nights. Murdoch would jab his finger at the paper and say, 'What do you want to print rubbish like that for?' or 'That man's a Commie.'[113] He was especially vituperative about the treatment of Margaret Thatcher and Ronald Reagan, interpreting impartial reports as covert criticism – in the words of Hugo Young, the deputy editor, Murdoch 'didn't believe in neutrality'.[114] The editor remained silent in the face of the proprietor's 'disagreeable and intemperate' language, though his colleagues engaged in undignified 'slanging matches'.[115] Someone less phlegmatic than himself, Giles thought, would have gone to hospital with acute ulcers. But

Murdoch had worse in store for him. Under threat of dismissal, he made the editor tell the national directors that staff changes that Murdoch himself had demanded, including the demotion of Young, were his own idea. Giles's humiliation was complete in 1983 when Murdoch, rejoicing that he had 'just pulled off the biggest coup in the history of journalism',[116] implicated him in one of the great newspaper debacles of all time – the *Sunday Times*'s publication of the forged Hitler diaries. Having originally declared that they were 'the real McCoy',[117] the historian Lord Dacre (Hugh Trevor-Roper) changed his mind at the last minute. Unperturbed, Murdoch uttered the immortal words: 'Fuck Dacre. Publish.'[118]

Almost equally celebrated was his comment when the truth about the confidence trick emerged: 'After all, we are in the entertainment business.'[119] This hardly squared with the *Sunday Times*'s attempt to justify its gullibility and irresponsibility by arguing that serious journalism is a high-risk enterprise. As far as his newspapers were concerned, of course, Murdoch wanted it both ways. Rupert the publisher favoured printed histrionics; Rupert the Puritan aspired to produce the first rough draft of history. Whatever his ambitions, they were not to be thwarted by his editors. Murdoch soon replaced Evans with a true-blue Conservative, the main protest coming from Anthony Holden, who said that the proprietor wanted a poodle as editor and that he was not going to work for a poodle. Giles was kicked upstairs, where his scheme to write foreign features was wrecked by Murdoch, who told his right-wing successor, Andrew Neil: 'Let him do it then don't use the stuff.'[120]

The independent directors were supine. But one of them, Dacre, denounced Murdoch as 'a megalomaniac twister'[121] when he arbitrarily transferred the titles of *The Times* and the *Sunday Times* to his British subsidiary, News International. Murdoch had to reverse the move, which was made to back up his threat to close the papers unless he got more staff cuts. These he achieved, but the workforce continued to sap profits by engaging in restrictive practices known as 'old Spanish customs'. Originally designed to protect jobs in an industry with execrable management, terrible conditions and a perishable product, these ranged from overmanning and wildcat strikes to systematic fraud, extortion and sabotage. One technique was to hold up production of the *Sunday Times* on Saturday nights by complaining of a bad smell in the foundry, which could only be wafted away with five-pound notes. Union 'chapels', run by quasi-independent shop stewards known as fathers, ensured that their members got the 'most pay for the least work', Murdoch said, of anyone else in Britain.[122] He vowed to retaliate, visiting the sins of the chapel fathers on their children for all generations.

He first built a new plant at Wapping in London's docklands, replacing a fine group of Georgian warehouses with a construction likened variously to a giant incinerator, a global air-conditioning unit, a high-security prison and George Orwell's Ministry of Truth. Equipped with few windows and much concrete, it was guarded by searchlights, CCTV cameras, electronic gates, a twelve-foot-high steel fence and spools of German razor wire. Goss rotary presses were installed, operated by members of the maverick electricians' union, with whom Murdoch had done a secret deal, and journalists could type in their copy directly from desktop computers. Under the pretence of launching a new evening paper from Wapping, Murdoch lured the print unions into what he called his 'bear trap'. Having spun out negotiations with them, he made a set of unacceptable demands, which they denounced as a 'serfs' charter'. He was thus able to provoke a strike, which began in January 1986, and to sack 5,500 employees without compensation, saving £40 million in redundancy payments. After some soul-searching most journalists agreed to move to Wapping. Rejecting bribes and threats, one of the 'refuseniks', Claire Tomalin, condemned 'a ruthless and bullying management which regards all employees as cattle'.[123] Others recalled Patrick Brogan's assertion that no honest journalist could work for Murdoch, and his warning to *Times* colleagues that 'he will cut all your balls off, if you have any'.[124]

Certainly Wapping, which was besieged by pickets in one of

the longest and most ferocious strikes in British history, aggravated Murdoch's militant tendencies. Dressed in a cardigan, an open-necked shirt, casual trousers and trainers, he rampaged around his bunker, shouting instructions, uttering curses and creating an aura of fear. Stabbing one manager repeatedly in the chest with his finger, he raged: 'You fuckwit! You bastard! Get this fucking newspaper out.'[125] 'Rambo Rupert' even tongue-lashed Charlie 'Gorbals' Wilson, the new editor of *The Times*, himself said to be an 'arse-kicking machine'[126] and (in the columnist Bernard Levin's phrase) 'the man who knows how to put the razor blade in the snowball'.[127] Evidently trade union anarchy had given way to managerial tyranny. The inmates of 'Stalag Wapping', who were not only treated like helots but attacked as scabs, made sporadic protests. Murdoch told Neil, who acted like a deputy dictator, to 'be a bit more two-faced . . . soft-soap them a little bit'.[128] Thus Neil averted trouble with the promise (not kept) of a swimming pool and a health centre. Murdoch himself tried to buy off the print unions, offering them the Gray's Inn Road premises so that they could start their own newspaper – with a sardonic smile he also offered to advise them on manning levels. But they rejected this and other inducements. He therefore relied on Margaret Thatcher's measures outlawing secondary pickets and making trade unions liable for damages. She supported him to the hilt, protecting his delivery trucks with posses of police, who met violence with violence and sometimes got their aggression in first. They became known as 'Murdoch's paperboys'.[129] While the strikers proclaimed, 'Murdoch is bad news',[130] the Prime Minister declared: 'Rupert is marvellous.'[131]

He clearly played a major role in her campaign to unbridle capitalism, for the printers' strike collapsed after fifty-four weeks and other press magnates embraced the new technology, moving to Docklands and consigning inky Fleet Street to the dustbin of history. Although more of a pragmatist than a pioneer, Murdoch alone had possessed the resources and ruthlessness – or as admirers said, 'the guts and tenacity'[132] – to spearhead a revolution of inestimable benefit to the newspaper industry, though not to its workforce. Moreover, he shared the prime minister's sense of being a dissident bent on smashing archaic vested interests and viscerally hostile to the liberal mandarinate. The two radicals were not altogether in harmony: Murdoch disliked being shouted down by a mere woman, and Mrs Thatcher, who did not mention him in her memoirs, thought the *News of the World* 'such a filthy paper'.[133] He was the more fanatical anti-communist, reviling Gorbachev, supporting the American invasion of Grenada and urging her to tell China that if the Red Army occupied Hong Kong, 'we'll nuke Beijing'.[134] Nevertheless, for ideological as well as commercial reasons, Murdoch's papers became more stridently Thatcherite after the move to Wapping. News reports reflected editorial opinions. Facts became subservient to dialectics. When a Labour MP, Ken Livingstone, said on television that his party's defeat in the 1987 general election had been caused by media lies and smears, Murdoch cried out delightedly: 'That's me!'[135]

Murdoch treated his readers as consumers rather than citizens and he often directed them towards his own products, such as Sky Television, while competitors like the BBC were disparaged. *The Times* became not so much a newspaper of record as a newspaper of accord with Murdoch's views. It lost distinguished reporters such as Robert Fisk, who deplored its strong pro-Israeli bias and refused to work for a newspaper he could not respect. And it opened the way to a new broadsheet rival, the aptly named *Independent*, which used computerised technology. The *Sunday Times* became, as Hugo Young said, 'a hard-line paper of the Right'.[136] For example, during the controversy over *Death on the Rock*, Thames Television's critical documentary about the shooting of three IRA members by the security services at Gibraltar in 1988, the paper was an echo of the government information service. It is true that Neil was a bulldog editor and that Murdoch kept him on a long leash. Thus the *Sunday Times* serialised Peter Wright's book *Spycatcher*, which Mrs Thatcher had tried to suppress. It also backed Michael Heseltine, whom Murdoch disliked, as her successor in 1991. Often, indeed, Murdoch was glad of an excuse to disclaim responsibility for the content of his newspapers – while in the next breath dictating their editorials over the telephone. But editors inattentive to his prejudices were liable to be fired sooner than yes-men and yes-women – he preferred to exclude females from the boardroom, saying that they talked too much, but advanced them on his newspapers, favouring stiletto-heeled battleaxes.

Murdoch had no friends, only interests. He walked by himself . . . and simply walked away from people who bored him. He seldom expressed affection or gratitude, sacking his Geelong schoolmate and long-time legal counsel Richard Searby by fax. Sometimes even his wife Anna found him cold, remote and impatient. She complained that he was in perpetual motion. She nagged him to attend to his parental duties, insisting that he teach his adolescent boys the facts of life – convinced that they knew already, he told them while going down in a lift. As a form of therapy Anna took to writing novels, which he failed to appreciate. Murdoch did show warmth to newly promoted functionaries, encouraging them to think that they had a special relationship with the boss. But his favourites were as perishable as peaches. One manager said, 'He has built his empire by using people, then discarding them when they have passed their sell-by date.'[137] So Charlie Wilson was abruptly removed from his editorial chair at *The Times*, taking his dismissal, Murdoch said, like 'a gentleman who has just been hit in the stomach'.[138] And Neil, whose coverage of a corruption scandal in Malaysia threatened News Corporation's expansion there, was eventually sidelined – even though he had made Murdoch a small fortune. Wapping made him a large one, reducing his workforce by three-quarters (with further cuts to come as machines drove out humans) and increasing the profits of his British papers from £38 million in 1985 to £150 million in 1987. He desperately needed the cash. Indeed, he had fled from Fleet Street mainly to escape ruin. Thanks to his colossal purchases in the United States, the entire edifice of News Corporation was in danger of being crushed under a mountain of debt.

* * *

Murdoch bought his first American newspapers, the *San Antonio Express* and *News*, because they were there. He had considered other acquisitions, but in 1973 these Texas rags were available and, at less than twenty million dollars, affordable. Obtaining them was not part of a long-term commercial strategy so much as a characteristic piece of opportunism. It is true that Murdoch saw a bright future for himself and his family in the New World, where money talked and class seldom answered back. He was excited by the 'mind-boggling'[139] size of the transatlantic market. Furthermore, heading westwards coincided with moving to the right. Murdoch found a ready audience in God's own country for his view that 'the energy and prosperity of industrious white America was being drained by the tremendous black problem' and that criminals should be killed before they could kill others, electrocution being 'a waste of good electricity'.[140] However San Antonio gave him the chance to exploit his tabloid techniques in a challenging new environment, and he jumped at it.

The *News* soon eclipsed its yellow Hearstian rival, the *Light*. Headlines blazed: VAMPIRE KILLER STALKS CITY, ALIENS FOUGHT OVER URINE IN DESERT BATTLE and, most famously, KILLER BEES MOVE NORTH.[141] News items were equally febrile:

> A divorced epileptic, who told police she was buried alive in a bathtub full of wet cement and later hanged upside down in the nude, left San Antonio for good this week-end. The tiny, half-blind woman, suffering from diabetes, recounted for the *News* a bizarre horror story filled with rape, torture and starvation.[142]

In the end, though, Murdoch only succeeded by moderating his tone and merging his papers, for it turned out that you could go broke by underestimating the intelligence of the American public. This was because sensationalism might increase circulation without attracting advertisements, thus raising costs. The problem recurred in acute form when, late in 1976, Murdoch bought the *New York Post*. It was summed up in a story, often repeated but apparently apocryphal, that Bloomingdale's chief executive refused his request for advertising on the grounds that 'Your readers are our shoplifters.'[143]

Having promised the *Post*'s previous owner, Dorothy Schiff, that he would maintain its time-honoured liberal policies, Murdoch transformed it into a flaming paper of the right. Although he liked to do business in restaurants, he enjoyed his new eminence on the sixth floor of the *Post*'s office, saying that it felt real, and he relished his augmented influence with politicians. He got a kick out of campaigning and, as Hazlitt had said of the archetypal Tory, he was ever strong upon the stronger side. Asked why he backed Ed Koch against Mario Cuomo in the 1977 mayoral election, Murdoch did not mention the Democratic candidate's opportune conversion to conservatism. Instead he replied: 'It's very simple. There are two and a half million Jews in New York and one million Italians.'[144] Murdoch's stated aim was to sell the *Post* to as many millions as possible. 'We're not here to pass ourselves off as intellectuals,' he said superfluously, but to appeal to a popular audience.[145] There was nothing vulgar in this: 'Shakespeare wrote for the masses.'[146] The *Post* would attract them by 'telling it like it is – directly, simply, entertainingly and, most important of all, accurately'.[147] Here was an audacious inversion of the truth, comparable to Murdoch's subsequent Fox News slogan, 'Fair and Balanced', a slogan he would repeat with every sign of sincerity.

In fact the *Post* followed the lurid, slanted trajectory of the *Sun*. It became a printed expression of its proprietor's personality and was prized by him accordingly. As one witness recorded, the look, mood and feel of the paper was in 'a continual state of frantic flux, depending on Murdoch's restless and changing sense of what will attract readers'.[148] News had to be spangled with stardust and inflated with ballyhoo. To quote the *Post* reporter Bill Hoffmann: 'We would hype things up here and there to get people interested. We basically took one or two facts and created a whole scenario around them . . . it sort of becomes larger than life.' It became Grand Guignol during the Son of Sam murders, and even Murdoch laughed at the *Post*'s bizarre conceit that the Mafia had joined in the hunt for the killer. Fortunately journalists are seldom troubled by scruples, but those who did demur Murdoch crushed like cockroaches. He said, 'Anyone who thinks I don't have integrity should resign.' Some obliged. Others were fired – Murdoch called them 'dead wood'. Editors were replaced as swiftly as typefaces. Murdoch despised American journalists, whom he thought smug, lazy, pretentious and incompetent. He imported larrikins from Australia who would spin yarns about anything from VD to voodoo. They also imbued the *Post* with their carnal fixations. Murdoch did not seem to mind. His bosom pal was the former nightclub bouncer Steve Dunleavy, whose exploits were legendary. An exponent of truly creative journalism, he specialised in stories about flying saucers, priapic pop singers, miracle cancer cures and AIDS being spread by kisses. He also claimed credit for the *Post*'s most famous headline: HEADLESS BODY IN TOPLESS BAR.[149] After a snowplough ran over Dunleavy's foot while he was having sex in a New York alley, a colleague remarked, 'I hope it was his writing foot.'[150]

Murdoch needed muscle, since the *Post* was grappling with the *Daily News* in what he called 'a dance of death'.[151] Indeed, at a time when most American cities could support only a single newspaper, he also aspired to beat the *New York Times*, which he disdained as the house organ of liberal elitists, or 'liberal totalitarians'. To combat the printers, who went on strike in 1978 to prevent staff cuts, Murdoch did act in concert with his rivals. Fearing their treachery, however, he betrayed them. He reached a separate agreement with the unions, which enabled him to bring out the *Post* while his competitors were still embroiled in the dispute. Murdoch had no qualms about exploiting this temporary advantage. 'Monopoly is a terrible thing,' he remarked, 'till you have it.'[152] His enemies had long maintained that he was debasing the currency of American journalism, bad newspapers driving out good in compliance with a version of Gresham's law. Now they bombarded him with abuse: he was an amoralist who lied easily and vended acres of printed falsehood; he was a dark, evil, contaminating presence slinking out of the night. The publisher of the *Times* deemed him 'charmingly repulsive';[153] the general manager of the *News* called him a 'dirty street fighter'.[154] Murdoch concluded that they were out to get him. He had, after all, sharpened their antagonism by predatory raids in Manhattan, the hostile takeover of *New York* magazine (at the expense of its editor, Clay Felker, who had befriended him) and the surprise capture of the *Village Voice*. To dominate the metropolis, moreover, Murdoch was clearly determined to keep the *Post* despite losses of nearly $15 million a year. For him to sell the paper, one journalist memorably remarked, 'would be like Dracula selling his coffin'.[155]

Actually in 1988 Murdoch was forced to sell the *Post*, only to buy it back later, on resuming the acquisitive blitz he had carried out during Reagan's presidency. The *Post*'s temporary alienation resulted from a law that stopped anyone owning both a newspaper and a TV station in the same city at a time when Murdoch was turning News Corporation into a multimedia conglomerate with a major presence on global screens. 'The electronic revolution is part of our lives and if one wants to stay in communications, you can't turn your back on it,'[156] said Murdoch with a characteristic clash of pronouns – he often used the royal we, like Margaret Thatcher, to disguise the absolutist nature of his regime. The speed and cost and scope of Murdoch's advance during the Reagan years were breathtaking. In 1979 he gained control of television channels in Sydney and Melbourne, the latter by dint of buying half its parent company, Ansett Airlines. After engorging *The Times* and the *Sunday Times*, he made two (short-lived) American purchases, the Boston *Herald American* in 1982 and the Chicago *Sun-Times* the following year. In 1985 he bought the Hollywood film studio 20th Century Fox, a clutch of magazines and Metromedia, owner of half a dozen metropolitan TV stations, which formed the basis of his newborn Fox television network. In December 1986 he acquired the *South China Morning Post*. Two months later Murdoch won back his father's old fiefdom, the *Herald and Weekly Times* group. This was the largest newspaper takeover in the English-speaking world, he boasted, a sweet revenge that gave him control of some two-thirds of the Australian press. In the same year he augmented his publishing interests, subsequently merging them to form HarperCollins. In 1988 he announced the launch of Sky TV in Britain. And he paid Walter Annenberg $3 billion for Triangle Publications, which included *Racing Form, TV Guide* and *Seventeen*, a young women's magazine of such virginal wholesomeness that it banned the word 'pimple' from headlines, which did not stop jokers calling it 'The Acne and the Ecstasy'. Thus ended what Murdoch called his 'expansionary lunge'.[157]

This outline hardly conveys the bewildering complexity of his manoeuvres. He resembled a *condottiere* fighting on many fronts, with no clear strategy but much tactical guile. He relied on improvisation and energy. He specialised in feints, ambushes and subterfuges. He formed and dissolved alliances, employing diplomacy as much as propaganda. Above all, Murdoch indulged his addiction to risk. In doing deals he suffered many reverses. But he had a vulpine capacity to twist, turn, wriggle and dodge. Failed takeover bids gave him the chance to make money by greenmail. A false start in satellite broadcasting during the early 1980s merely whetted his appetite. When he was being bled dry by Sky TV, which was said to differ from the Loch Ness Monster in that fewer people had seen it, Murdoch arranged a successful merger with its rival, BSB. The more stringent the government regulations, the more adept he became at circumventing them. When his 1979 television purchases in Sydney and Melbourne were challenged because he lived abroad, Murdoch argued that he was 'a good Australian'.[158] But in 1985 he took American citizenship in order to buy television stations in the United States, jeopardising his bid for the *Herald and Weekly Times* group because of an Australian ban on foreign ownership. This he overcame by promulgating the transparent fiction that he no longer controlled his subsidiary down under, News Ltd. By a similar feat of legerdemain he managed to possess but not to own the Adelaide *News* and the Brisbane *Sun*. Murdoch also benefited from a craven relaxation of rules preventing such a concentration of the media in his hands, which (as he himself had once piously acknowledged) was 'against the public interest'.[159] No one was more obliging than the prime minister, Bob Hawke, who told Labor colleagues that Murdoch and his minions were 'the only mates we've got'.[160]

In truth Murdoch was a citizen of the world, relishing the ambiguity of ubiquity and exploiting his international position for all it was worth. Although qualified to fly the Jolly Roger, he sailed under shifting flags of convenience. He sheltered in offshore tax havens such as Bermuda and the Cayman Islands. He set profits in one country against losses in another, paying in tax as little as three per cent of News Corporation's income. He shuffled cash between his family trusts and private and public companies on five continents. His finances were a monstrous spider's web, stretching across frontiers and defying disentanglement. In America Murdoch employed curious Australian accounting practices that enabled him to revalue his assets and to represent stock issues (in effect debts) as equity. All this, plus a deluge of lucre from the sale of junk bonds, increased his capacity to borrow from the banks, which geared their loans to his supposed means. They largely funded the spending spree that made him a commercial titan with a personal fortune of three billion dollars. He lost over a billion during the stock-market crash in 1987, when the Commonwealth Bank of Australia was worried enough to take a lien on his New York penthouse. However he could not resist appropriating Annenberg's Triangle, which turned out to have only one side, a down side. Murdoch tried to recoup through piecemeal disposals. But by 1990, when Sky TV was losing £2 million a week, News Corporation's debts amounted to $7.6 billion. For several months it seemed about to go bust and Murdoch's hair turned completely grey. He was too vain or too mean to have it dyed professionally, doing the job himself and achieving hues that ranged from orange to aubergine.

Murdoch liked to dramatise his financial crisis by telling how a Pittsburgh bank almost liquidated his empire when it demanded the immediate repayment of a paltry ten million dollars. But this anecdote concealed the fact that his troubles were deep-seated and long-lasting. Essentially he had paid more for his acquisitions than they were worth and far more than he could afford. The situation was made worse by Murdoch's managerial weakness. He never exercised calm supervision. He alternated between excessive delegation and rabid totalitarianism. He was variously said to descend on his subordinates like a lion among wildebeest, like a cult leader among acolytes and like a thunderbolt from hell. As he thrashed about trying to fend off insolvency, therefore, staff demoralisation increased, business suffered and earnings shrank. Eventually Murdoch ran out of other people's money. By a familiar paradox, what saved him was that he had borrowed so *much* – from a total of 146 banks. The largest of these, his greatest creditors, could not afford to let him fail, and they put pressure on the smaller ones to join in a grand scheme to reschedule the debt. He cut costs, reduced salaries, sacked employees and sold assets, often at a loss. To help him in the immense task of retrenchment, the big banks even supplied a bridging loan. No doubt they were impressed by Murdoch's mystique, by his Houdini-like ability to escape disaster. But he had to accept stiff terms and to provide security. It took the form of the mastheads of the *Sun* and the *News of the World*, together with the 'Page Three trademark'.[161] Thus topless models reduced the banks' exposure and the world was treated to the spectacle of capitalism in action, naked and unashamed.

To give him his due, Murdoch could be embarrassed by nudity. In 1992, a bright young man at Fox Television, Stephen Chao, illustrated a lecture (about censorship) at News Corporation's annual Colorado conference with a male stripper who disrobed immediately in front of Murdoch and his guests of honour, Mr and Mrs Dick Cheney. There was a stunned silence. It was broken by Patsy Chapman, editor of the *News of the World*, who said: 'Can I get that guy's telephone number?' Visibly perturbed, Murdoch did not join in the titters. He at once fired Chao, who had devised lucrative programmes such as *America's Most Wanted* and *Cops*, only to re-employ him later. Thus Murdoch pandered to the proprieties while attending to the practicalities. It was the same in the realm of finance, where he satisfied the bankers while hatching new speculative ventures. The recovery of his fortunes, assisted by lower interest rates, proved surprisingly swift. By 1992 he had made early repayments and could negotiate better terms on the rest of his borrowings. He also bought out his sisters and his aged mother from the family holding company, a dynastic coup that caused them some anguish. The following year, as Fox and BSkyB television networks began to thrive, News Corporation returned to profit. Murdoch discerned 'a window of opportunity to take a quantum step forward'.[162] The scrambled clichés reflect the fact that he had been discomposed by his brush with bankruptcy. Thereafter his progress, though still impressive, became more erratic. He worried especially about which of his children was worthy to succeed him, gnawing the index finger of his right hand. To adorn the lobby of a new 20th Century Fox building in Los Angeles, Anna would commission a thirty-six-foot-high mural modelled on the print of this finger. Its significance was obscure. The artist said that it could represent a leader pointing the way but, although positively identifying Murdoch, it gave no sense of direction. Perhaps it was a version of Michelangelo's finger of God, enhanced for the digital age.

As Murdoch embarked on further expenditure, he certainly seemed set to create the first globally integrated media enterprise. In 1993 he bought a majority interest in Star TV, which covered the whole of Asia. He also began satellite operations in Mexico, South America and Japan. In 1994 he purchased a stake in New World Communications, which transferred the affiliation of its twelve local television stations to the Fox network in America. In 1995 he entered into a joint pay-TV undertaking with Australia's state-owned telecommunications giant Telstra, which hugely benefited his own company Foxtel at the taxpayer's expense – the deal, pressed through by prime minister Paul Keating, was said to be 'straight out of a banana republic'.[163] Murdoch made progress in Europe, caught his audience young with Fox Kids Worldwide and combined with organisations such as John

Malone's Liberty Media to distribute sports programmes to an international audience. In short, through shifting alliances and adroit manoeuvres he advanced on all fronts. By 1996, when he launched the Fox News Channel, he had transformed key stretches of the information superhighway into a toll road. Murdoch understood that to dominate the mass media in the modern world he had to control dissemination as well as supply content. What mattered first was command of electronic impulses and airwaves. This was why he invested so heavily in computer software, lithographic technology, encryption systems, television stations, cable networks, satellite channels, interactive services and broadcasting frequencies. No more ambitious attempt had ever been made to distil power from the ether.

At the beginning of President Clinton's second term, *Time* magazine ranked Murdoch as the fourth most powerful person in the United States, a position he owed not just to his media but to his message. After a shaky start, Fox and Sky began to transmit programmes that attracted viewers. Having hired some of the best writers in Hollywood, Murdoch put out hit shows such as *Married ... With Children* and *The Simpsons*, both comedies about dysfunctional families. He used his papers to promote his television offerings – a particularly shameless puff in *The Times* provoked the resignation of its arts editor Tim de Lisle. Murdoch stole a march on competitors (as well as revolutionising the economics of international sport) by paying vast sums for the TV rights of events such as the American Football League and Britain's Premier League. Moreover, he provided spicier fare on the small screen than was usual, especially in pap-fed America, admitting that some of his early-evening material was unsuitable for children. Critics denounced Murdoch's slick melange of crime, race, sex, religion and populist politics as tabloid television. Aimed at rednecks in blue collars, it proved that 'shit sells'.[164] The apotheosis of this type of broadcasting was Fox News, which set out to challenge its mighty rival CNN, dubbed the Clinton News Network. The struggle prompted CNN's founder Ted Turner to compare Murdoch's global ambitions to those of Hitler. The *New*

York Post responded with characteristic delicacy: IS TED NUTS? YOU DECIDE.[165]

By 2002, Fox was on top. It was a triumph of glitz over probity. The news channel, controlled by President Nixon's former TV adviser Roger Ailes, featured electronic fanfares, flashy graphics highlighting the American flag and shouting heads with neoconservative sound bites. It shunned laborious and costly investigative journalism. Instead it delivered tawdry 'infotainment' and arrant demagogy – with the result, for example, that two-thirds of Fox viewers believed that America had discovered links between al-Qaeda and Iraq after the 9/11 terrorist attack on New York's Twin Towers. The political commentator Bill O'Reilly became especially notorious for conducting interrogations in the style of Senator McCarthy and expressing opinions worthy of Father Coughlin, the quasi-fascist radio priest of the New Deal era. Murdoch allegedly despised O'Reilly as a loud-mouthed bully. And in private he distanced himself from the neocon fundamentalism of Ailes, telling a colleague: 'You know Roger is crazy. He really believes that stuff.'[166] But he did not publicly repudiate Ailes who, Goebbels-like, systematically subordinated news to propaganda, making nonsense of the slogan 'We Report, You Decide'.[167] By now, in fact, Murdoch had fully fledged right-wing views on a gamut of issues ranging from abortion to law and order. As Margaret Thatcher's successor he favoured Norman Tebbit, a political skinhead in whose mouth, it was said, the word 'permissive' sounded like a sexually transmitted disease. As Ronald Reagan's successor, Murdoch plumped for Pat Robertson, a homophobic 'televangelist' who spoke in tongues and had prophesied that the world would end in 1982. Fox employed hacks to echo its master's voice. Their reports were carefully monitored and they themselves lived in 'an environment of fear', subjected to what one called a 'Stalinist system'.[168] This term, however overblown, reflected the omnipresence of Rupert Murdoch. According to an Australian academic, Murdoch's media responded in unison to his wishes as though to some 'divine wind'.[169] In liberal nostrils it was a toxic eructation tainting the atmosphere of the entire planet.

Yet Murdoch's achievement in transcending national boundaries, which made him uniquely powerful, also made him uniquely vulnerable. This became all too apparent when, still shaken by his financial ordeal, he tried to extend his television network to China. He was thrilled by the prospect that Star TV would now reach an Asian marketplace containing three billion people. But Murdoch forgot that while he could condemn government regulation of his media expansion in America, he must kowtow to it in China. In September 1993 he made a speech in which he posed as the champion of liberty, declaring that George Orwell had been wrong about modern telecommunications, which were not a support but 'an unambiguous threat to totalitarian regimes everywhere'. Fax machines, direct-dial telephones and satellite broadcasting, he said, undermined state control of information. The Chinese leaders had been mortified by television coverage of the bloodshed in Tiananmen Square – observing it in June 1989, Murdoch had wanted Britain to shun China and to keep Hong Kong. Now they were incensed by what looked like a deliberate assault on red absolutism by the autocrat of the yellow press. Premier Li Peng, 'the Butcher of Beijing', at once banned the sale and use of satellite dishes anywhere in the People's Republic, effectively excluding Star TV. Murdoch's speech was not his own work – he acquired ideas just as he acquired words, off the peg. But he at once saw that it had been a ruinous miscalculation. His response was revealing. The champion of capitalism embarked on a degrading campaign to appease the communist colossus.

Thus in October 1993 Murdoch sold his Hong Kong newspaper, the *South China Morning Post*, to a pro-Beijing Chinese businessman. The following year he dropped the BBC, which the Chinese rulers hated for its studiously objective coverage, from his Star satellite service. At first Murdoch presented this as a purely commercial decision, but he later confessed that his purpose was to obtain entry for his own channels. Chris Patten, the last British governor of Hong Kong, called it the seediest of betrayals. When HarperCollins bought Patten's vivid account of his endeavours to establish democracy in the colony, Murdoch ordered its chairman to 'kill the fuckin' book'.[170] The publishers, who then claimed that it was too boring to sell, were forced to apologise and pay damages, whereupon Murdoch blamed them for having 'screwed it up'.[171] By contrast HarperCollins shelled out nearly a million dollars for the English rights to a dull biography of Deng Xiaoping written by his daughter. Such gestures did not allay suspicions about a man apparently intent on beaming advertisements into every household in the country. An official at China's Foreign Ministry said: 'It is like having Genghis Khan at the Palace Gates – he may tell you he is your friend, but then he might also rise up and strike at once [in a] thousand places.'

Murdoch took endless trouble to ingratiate himself with the Chinese leaders. He gave them presents. He helped to set up an online edition of the *People's Daily*, a propaganda sheet in which nothing could be trusted but the date. He opened a Sky News bureau in Beijing and promised 'fair and balanced' reporting of Chinese matters in all his organs. One result was that the London *Times* spiked many articles by the respected China-watcher Jonathan Mirsky, who soon resigned. Murdoch argued that to try to impose 'Western notions of decency and openness' on China was cultural imperialism.[172] He suggested that the Dalai Lama was 'a very political old monk shuffling around in Gucci shoes'. And he did not dissent when his son James defended Beijing's vicious crackdown on the Falun Gong cult. Eventually Murdoch became impatient, hectoring officials, replacing employees and infiltrating by stealth. In 2005, therefore, to protect their air space from 'spiritual pollution',[173] the Chinese authorities definitively banned foreign participation in domestic broadcasting. By the new millennium Star TV had thirty channels in seven languages reaching 300 million people in over fifty Asian countries. But the vast majority of China's 1.3 billion were denied it. Orwell was right after all: totalitarian states can control mass communications. It's small compensation that their leaders, unlike democratic politicians, are largely immune to the corrupting influence of alien media moguls.

Although deputy premier Zhu Rongji disconcerted Murdoch

by joking that he might take Chinese citizenship to pursue his media interests in the People's Republic, there is no reason to suppose that the Australian American married a Chinese citizen for this purpose. Admittedly business dominated his family life. His devotion to it undermined his relationship with Anna. Their offspring, Elisabeth, Lachlan and James, called him 'the Boss'. They had had a disturbed upbringing, with long periods of inattention interrupted by expressions of paternal solicitude, and they now competed for promotion as well as affection – Murdoch once referred to 'my three children',[174] forgetting his first-born Prudence to her fury and then saying that he meant the three working at News Corporation. Furthermore Rupert's abrupt rejection of Anna in 1998 smacked of a sacking, just as their divorce settlement, in which the wife sacrificed her own interests in an attempt to safeguard those of her children, had the hallmarks of a demerger. His clandestine courtship of Wendi Deng, an intern at Star TV, also had commercial dimensions. It was apparently consummated between deals in Shanghai, where the twenty-nine-year-old Wendi made the sexagenarian Rupert glow with pleasure and excitement by taking him to a barber who cut his hair for less than a dollar. It seems, though, that he really was in love. Wendi, who had a business degree from Yale, was tall and attractive. Shamelessly flirtatious, she was fond of exclaiming: 'Oh, Lupert!'[175] She was an old man's fancy – or folly, according to his mother, who could hardly bring herself to 'look at the girl'.[176] Indeed, Wendi was the calculating one. She was especially circumspect about her previous liaisons, including a brief marriage to a middle-aged American engineer. When Rupert read an account of all this in the *Wall Street Journal* a couple of years after their wedding, which took place aboard his garlanded yacht the *Morning Glory* in New York in June 1999, he was said to be 'ashen-faced'.[177]

Wendi appeared to give Rupert another lease of life. Senior employees noticed a new gleam in his eye and a fresh spring in his step – some followed his lead and left their own wives for younger women. One paper reported that Murdoch was full of vim, vigour and Viagra – Wendi was quoted as saying that he took the drug but did not need it. In 2000 Rupert even survived prostate cancer, boasting that he did not miss a day's work during the treatment and that after it he was convinced of his own immortality. Egged on by his wife, he exercised with a personal trainer and later took up yoga. He wore younger and smarter clothes, jeans and sneakers as well as Prada suits. He sired two daughters, Grace in 2001 and Chloe in 2003 – the former eventually acquired a godfather in the person of Tony Blair. Rupert scowled less and mixed more in high society. After a spell living in Greenwich Village, he spent $44 million in 2004 on a twenty-roomed penthouse overlooking the Central Park Zoo, the highest price ever paid for a Manhattan residence. Having sold his adored yacht *Morning Glory* to the Italian prime minister and media magnate Silvio Berlusconi, in a bid to seduce him, Rupert purchased, with Wendi's encouragement, the still more sumptuous *Rosehearty*. She also seems to have induced him to break the divorce settlement with Anna by persuading his older children to share their inheritance with the two younger ones. This further aggravated family relations. Anna herself, who had long proclaimed her husband a man of principle, was bitter. In the wake of Rupert's betrayal, she especially resented his assertion that he only took up with Wendi after separating from her, stating that this was a lie.

Although personal problems compounded commercial difficulties, Murdoch continued to exert inordinate influence over susceptible politicians. None was more susceptible than the ambitious young leader of Britain's 'New' Labour party, Tony Blair. In 1995 he flew halfway round the world to address a News Corporation gathering at the luxury resort of Hayman Island on the Great Barrier Reef. There he met Paul Keating, who told him that Murdoch was 'a big bad bastard'.[178] As such, he only respected strength. Blair shrewdly interpreted this to mean that Murdoch only respected weakness, at least as far as he himself was concerned. So Blair, presenting himself as a radical moderniser in the spirit of Margaret Thatcher, promised to free media enterprises from state regulation. Murdoch was impressed, though he warned that they would have to consummate their flirtation like porcupines – very carefully. Old Labour supporters were appalled. Blair had made the most humiliating odyssey, it was said, since Henry IV abased himself before the Pope at Canossa. The party's former leader, Neil Kinnock, privately denounced his successor for selling out to an evil man, and he correctly forecast that more concessions would follow. In the short run, of course, Blair benefited, since the *Sun* deserted the Conservatives and backed Labour in the 1997 election. But he paid a heavy price for support that he did not need – like Dr Johnson's patron, Murdoch looked with unconcern on sinking politicians but encumbered rising ones with help. The new prime minister was beholden to the media magnate in ways that even his loyal press secretary Alastair Campbell found 'faintly obscene'.[179]

According to Campbell's deputy, Murdoch 'seemed like the 24th member of the Cabinet'.[180] He was in and out of 10 Downing Street, often by the back door. He was assured that there would be no change of policy on Europe without reference to him, and in fact the government took no big decisions of any kind without considering his reaction. His papers were given scoops, even at the cost of infuriating Labour's old ally the *Mirror*. Its editor complained that 'Murdoch's cronies have been courted so hard everyone's forgotten who their real media friend was'. This protest wrung a muted confession from Peter Mandelson, Labour's so-called Prince of Spin, that No. 10's 'relationship with the *Sun* is a fairly grim thing'.[181] Yet Blair buttered up Murdoch's tabloid editor Rebekah Wade, a flame-haired virago whose witch-hunt against child abusers resulted in vigilantes mistaking paediatricians for paedophiles. At Murdoch's behest, the prime minister even asked Romano Prodi if the Italian government would prohibit a foreigner from gaining control of Berlusconi's television network. When revealed, this piece of lobbying embarrassed Blair as much as it delighted Murdoch. He bragged about his access and clearly relished the prime minister's willingness to consummate their relationship despite the pricks. Blair also stifled a legislative proposal to ban predatory pricing, whereby Murdoch was attempting to crush weak competitors such as the *Independent*. The Communications Bill (2002) relaxed rules preventing large newspaper groups and American companies from owning television stations in Britain. Official denials merely convinced critics that this did not so much create 'a level playing field as a landing strip for Rupert Murdoch'.[182]

It is impossible to say how far Murdoch's gung-ho organs influenced Blair's fatal decision to back the American invasion of Iraq in 2003; but the war and its disastrous aftermath discredited not only the prime minister but the media mogul. Indeed, here was one indication among many that the septuagenarian Murdoch was losing his grip. Unable to send an email and barely proficient at operating his mobile phone, he was slow to appreciate the significance of broadband – the signal transmitting high-speed data via digital television and the World Wide Web, which makes available a vast new range of goods and services. Thus he was late in buying internet businesses, with the fortuitous result that his losses were only measured in hundreds of millions when the dot-com bubble burst. On the other hand, he missed golden opportunities to exploit the information revolution. He even made an unusual confession of failure. As news sources proliferated, he said, young people did not want 'a god-like figure from above to tell them what's important'.[183] Successful internet enterprises were both expensive and elusive: having paid $580 million for the online social networking site MySpace, Murdoch could only get $35 million when he sold it six years later. For all his hopes of synergy, moreover, his acquisitions became more piecemeal. In 2003, for example, he spent $6.6 billion to gain control of America's biggest satellite network DirecTV, billed as the key piece in his integrated media organisation. Yet three years later he sold DirecTV to John Malone in exchange for his eighteen per cent shareholding in News Corporation – a menacing stake that Murdoch had dozily allowed him to accumulate. Murdoch himself was now free to concentrate on another glittering prize.

This was the *Wall Street Journal*, a national institution that would give him copper-bottomed respectability in America just as *The Times* did in Britain. To achieve the takeover Murdoch employed tactics that were by now almost comically familiar. He courted and divided its main owners (the Bancroft family), offering them a huge premium on their shares, promising editorial freedom and establishing an independent committee to guarantee it. Within months of buying the paper in July 2007, though, Murdoch made crucial changes of policy and staff, which prompted accusations that he had broken the spirit and the letter of the agreement. This was predictable. But soon afterwards, as the economy dipped, even Murdoch must have realised that the *Wall Street Journal* was worth far less than the $5 billion he had paid for it. When the recession slid into the world-shattering financial crisis of 2008, income from advertising shrank and pillars of the American press such as the *Chicago Tribune* and the *Los Angeles Times* collapsed. During that year News Corporation's shares lost two-thirds of their value (making it worth a mere $20 billion), and in the last quarter Murdoch's business suffered a record loss, $6.4 billion. He took stern measures to reduce costs, sacking employees, cutting salaries and generally drawing in his horns. Murdoch rode out the storm. But his acquisition of the *Wall Street Journal* did not make much financial sense. Nor did the launch of its metropolitan section in 2010, whereby he aimed 'to cripple, really cripple the *New York Times*'.[184] Murdoch's atavistic commitment to print media, which provided only fourteen per cent of News Corporation's revenue, had become a serious drag on its progress. He presided over a paradox, a modern telecommunications company that was technologically retarded. For he himself was more at home with Gutenberg than Google.

Murdoch had always run his organisation by the seat of his pants, relying on instinct and betting on hunches. But his daemon faltered in old age. 'Mr Grumpy', as some subordinates called him, was cut off by deafness. He muttered more, lost his train of thought and subsided into worrying silences. His wife and children spoke up and sometimes stood up to him. His son James, tattooed, pierced and earringed as a Harvard dropout but now an

Armani-suited thruster, once told his father in front of Tony Blair
that he was 'talking fucking nonsense' about Israel, and that the
Palestinians had been 'kicked out of their fucking homes and had
nowhere to fucking live'.[185] In the line of succession James became
the anointed one. The anti-monarchical Rupert embraced the
hereditary principle where his own family was concerned, systematically excluding pretenders who lacked Murdoch blood – though
the phone-hacking imbroglio, which eventually forced the heir
presumptive to resign as chairman of News International and
BSkyB, may well have wrecked his chances. But Rupert did not
want to share power, let alone to abdicate. Indeed, his ukases
were as arbitrary as ever and there was no one to overturn them.
For example, after being the subject of several hostile books, he
instructed his reluctant brood to cooperate with his new biographer, Michael Wolff. Some years earlier Murdoch had had a
facelift, and he evidently expected to receive its literary equivalent.
But even in professional hands such treatments are liable to go
wrong. To be sure, Wolff portrayed Murdoch as a networking
genius, a master illusionist, a possessor of 'dark, magical powers
. . . that border on mind control'. Amid the sycophancy, though,
unpleasing features still obtruded. Wolff recorded, for instance, a
revealing exchange with Gary Ginsberg, Executive Vice President
for Corporate Affairs, the public relations watchdog who attended
most of his interviews with Murdoch. To his boss's assertion that
Muslims were so prone to birth defects because they often married
their cousins, Ginsberg replied: 'Ahhh . . . really? Wow. Hmmm.
. . . That does explain a lot.'[186] He might just as well have said,
'Up to a point, Lord Copper.'

Like Beaverbrook, Murdoch exercised power without responsibility. Nothing illustrated this better than the most recent crisis
to overtake News Corporation – the telephone interception and
police bribery scandal. In 2007, the *News of the World*'s royal
correspondent Clive Goodman, and a private investigator working
for the paper, Glenn Mulcaire, were sent to prison for hacking
into the voicemail messages of members of the royal household.

The *News of the World* held an internal inquiry, which implausibly concluded that this law-breaking was restricted to a single rogue reporter acting without the knowledge or approval of his superiors. The Metropolitan Police, some of whom had received large sums of money from the paper as payment for information and other favours, connived at the cover-up. So did politicians. Furthermore, David Cameron, who employed a former editor of the *News of the World*, Andy Coulson, as his press secretary (until he had to resign), supported Murdoch's attempt to increase his concentration of media power by acquiring the sixty-one per cent of the satellite broadcaster BSkyB that he did not own. The prime minister endorsed the press magnate despite widespread fears that, notwithstanding Murdoch's familiar undertaking to maintain the company's independence, he would turn it into a British version of Fox News.

Moreover, the government's Pavlovian response to Murdoch persisted well into 2011, when it emerged that the *News of the World*'s electronic eavesdropping had been conducted for many years on a large scale. Murdoch maintained that illegal tapping was 'not part of our culture, anywhere in the world, least of all in Britain'.[187] And he subsequently denied knowledge of earlier out-of-court settlements, amounting to more than a million pounds, paid to well-known British victims of telephone interception in what looked like an endeavour to buy their silence. Yet Murdoch could hardly have been unaware that his organisation did have a record of electronic espionage, since News Corporation had recently disbursed a staggering $655 million to resolve lawsuits filed against its subsidiary, News America Marketing, for unfair trade practices, among them breaking into a competitor's computer system to obtain 'proprietary information'.[188] Still, even as the police were compelled to renew their investigation into wrongdoing at the *News of the World*, which led to the arrest of senior figures from the paper, Murdoch conducted a prolonged rearguard action. Again and again he stressed the uprightness of his organisation, which was governed by 'very, very strict rules'.[189] But his assertions seemed mainly designed to establish that he was a fit and proper person to own the whole of BSkyB. Particularly sardonic about his motives, *Private Eye* showed him answering critics with the words: 'I overhear what you're saying.'[190]

The scandal reached boiling point in July 2011, when reports circulated that, far from being confined to politicians and celebrities, the phone-hacking had extended to the families of murder victims, of civilians blown up by terrorists and of British soldiers slain in Iraq and Afghanistan. The most horrifying revelation concerned a schoolgirl called Milly Dowler, kidnapped and killed in 2002, whose mobile phone messages were intercepted, some being deleted, so as to give her distraught parents hope that she was still alive.[191] Public opinion was so outraged that the government had to announce a public inquiry on top of the police investigation. Murdoch himself professed shock and indignation, later confessing to panic. As advertisers and readers boycotted the *News of the World*, he approved the drastic course of sacking its 200 staff and closing down the 168-year-old paper – its final edition appeared on 10 July. This sacrifice, rightly suspected of making way for a Sunday edition of the *Sun* (launched in February 2012), was actually a prelude to further woes. More denizens of Wapping were arrested, among them Andy Coulson. Scotland Yard admitted that some of its officers had taken 'inappropriate payments'[192] from the *News of the World*, and shortly thereafter the Metropolitan Police Commissioner and his deputy resigned, both of them alleged to have been too close to News International. As politicians sensed that it was safe at last to call for a healthy diversity in media ownership, Murdoch had no option but to withdraw his bid for BSkyB. News Corporation's share price plunged and, amid threats of further costly lawsuits, some perhaps in America, the whole organisation tottered on its foundations.

Murdoch was caught between two alternatives, both of which had the potential to bring down his grey hairs with sorrow to the grave. If he knew about the telephone surveillance, he was party to a criminal conspiracy. If he did not, he was unfit to run a business that owed its success to a lifetime of intense personal supervision. Facing extreme moral and commercial pressure, as well as public obloquy, Murdoch veered between defiance and penitence. He blamed rival papers for stirring up hysteria, avowed that his top executives had handled the crisis well and defended Rebekah Brooks (formerly Wade), who had been editor of the *News of the World* when Milly Dowler's voice mailbox was infiltrated – despite being a famously 'hands-on'[193] editor, she claimed to have known nothing about this ghastly episode. However, on 15 July he apologised in person to the Dowler family and accepted Brooks's resignation – she was arrested two days later. Finally, after first refusing to appear before a select committee of MPs, he was obliged to do so. Their first televised inquisition – a second occurred nine months later at the public enquiry conducted by Lord Justice Leveson – took place in Portcullis House, opposite the House of Commons, on 19 July. Millions of viewers watched the stark epiphany of Rupert Murdoch.

Flanked by his son James, slick in crew cut and rimless glasses, and backed by his wife Wendi, feisty in pink, as well as by a phalanx of granite-faced advisers, he looked tragically old. Like one of Swift's Struldbrugs, humans who aged but could not die, Murdoch seemed constitutionally senescent. He misheard and misunderstood questions. He stumbled over the answers, punctuating them with long pauses and banging the table for emphasis. He was vague about crucial details, admitting that 'I'm not really in touch.' Whether any of this was feigned in order to evade accountability or to garner sympathy, it is impossible to say. Still, Murdoch's performance was more convincing after its fashion than that of James, whose fluent responses were couched in business jargon and voiced in an American accent ringing with insincerity. Rupert did express shame and contrition, however gruffly, ineptly and Heepishly: 'This is the most humble day of my life.' He stated that the *News of the World* only represented one per cent of News Corporation, which had over 50,000 employees. And he brusquely refused to acknowledge personal responsibility for its 'sickening and horrible invasions of privacy'. This was because he had been let down by people he trusted, who had themselves perhaps been let down by people they trusted. As an earnest of his integrity, Murdoch harked back to his father, expressing immense pride at his exposure of the Gallipoli scandal and declaring that Sir Keith had launched him into journalism specifically to give 'me the chance of doing good'.[194] This emotional invocation struck many witnesses as risible, among them no doubt the protester who interrupted the proceedings by shoving a plate of shaving foam in Rupert Murdoch's face with the cry, 'You are a greedy billionaire.'[195] But at what might be regarded as the moral nadir of Rupert's career, it was natural that he should conjure with his father's idealistic injunction.

In an era of soulless conglomerates, Rupert Murdoch was a throwback to the age of the press barons, but he eclipsed them all in terms of money, power and reach. Since his corporation was international he could exert unprecedented pressure on national governments. At their worst his media behaved like the old communist propaganda machine, whose apparatchiks disseminated their message without regard to frontiers or veracity. Over the air waves Fox, Star and Sky took part in synchronised sinning, under the aegis of a kind of global Big Brother. In reality, perhaps, Murdoch was more of a paper tiger. He did not so much change minds as haunt imaginations – the playwright Dennis Potter famously nicknamed the cancerous tumour that killed him 'Rupert'. Instead of riding a juggernaut, Murdoch jumped on bandwagons. He told people what they wanted to hear. Nevertheless, he did have access to leaders from Canberra to Ottawa, from China to Peru. His influence on the White House increased his leverage in Downing Street, where successive prime ministers bent to his will. Murdoch's vendettas against the likes of Edward Kennedy, Neil Kinnock and Barack Obama terrified liberal politicians everywhere, just as his assaults on the BBC and his designs on the *New York Times* horrified all but the most rancorous neoconservatives. Perhaps the phone-hacking scandal, compounded by recent charges that News International paid large sums to a 'network of corrupted officials,'[196] has broken his spell. Perhaps the select committee's majority verdict that he is unfit to run a major international company has smashed his thraldom.

No one can tell, and it is even conceivable that Murdoch might fall like Lucifer. The present crisis is pregnant with future possibilities. But past apprehensions about him were entirely understandable. Murdoch was, as detractors charged, a cynical pragmatist whose business had an ethical hole in its heart.

Yet with another lobe of his brain Murdoch believed what he saw on his own TV channels and read in his own newspapers, sure that their far-right message was the true gospel and that by promoting his other interests they were carrying out the Lord's work. At the Leveson enquiry, in a remarkable assertion of his own bona fides, Murdoch reiterated that he had never used his media for improper purposes. He consistently maintained that, strange as it might sound, he was a God-fearing altruist with a mission to improve the world and a commitment to 'the values of my Calvinistic background'.[197] This was not complete hypocrisy. By birth Rupert was a cross between Irish larrikin and Scottish Puritan, and he invariably justified ruthlessness as a form of righteousness. Like his father (and like Protestant capitalists down the ages), he regarded worldly success as a cosmic stamp of approval. He conducted his own commercial battles so unscrupulously because he always saw himself as a lonely crusader fighting the good fight, challenging iniquitous monopolies and attacking unholy establishments. The least introspective of men, he continued to play the part of David even when he had become Goliath. Those keen to demonise Murdoch assumed that he had deliberately adopted the creed of Satan: evil be thou my good. This was to miss the point. Murdoch was no intellectual and he had only a callow knowledge of good and evil. But thanks to nature and nurture, he possessed a priceless moral confidence. However evil his deeds might seem, Rupert Murdoch was always able to convince himself that he was as good as gold.

Prince Charles

It is all too easy to portray Queen Elizabeth's eldest son in tabloid fashion as the 'Clown Prince'. His upbringing seemed calculated to produce a zany: aged eight, in 1956, he asked, 'Mummy, what *are* schoolboys?' As a schoolboy himself, Prince Charles formed a lifelong admiration for the *Goon Show* and, according to his father, when acting the role of Macbeth at Gordonstoun he sounded just like the Goons. At Cambridge he took part in undergraduate burlesque, cracking laughably unfunny jokes. A gauche young man with big ears, a bobbing Adam's apple and a lopsided grin, Charles admitted that he sometimes regarded himself as 'a bit of a twit'.[1] He certainly lived up to that characterisation in his own social realm, a chinless wonderland of tiaras and trumpets. In such time as he could spare from polo, field sports and playing at soldiers, sailors and airmen, he developed ideas that ranged from the cranky to the crackpot. He ate birdseed muesli and talked to his plants. He promoted the use of carrot juice and coffee-bean enemas in the treatment of cancer. He attended to the quasi-mystical effusions of Sir Laurens van der Post, who urged him to be 'outward-bound the inward way'[2] – which was no doubt preferable to being inward-bound the outward way.

Equally striking were Charles's amorous exploits, chronicled with lascivious glee by Fleet Street. What the Prince lacked in erotic expertise, one lover recalled, he made up for in 'Hanoverian enthusiasm'.[3] But he remained bashful, and there was always the problem of undress address. Throughout their liaison Lady Jane Wellesley never called him anything but 'sir'. During his affair with Camilla Parker-Bowles, they adopted Goonish nicknames, Fred and Gladys. Christabel Barria-Borsage reported that just before sex Charles invited her to call him Arthur – perhaps he was thinking of Excalibur, possibly Lancelot. More seriously, the Prince of Wales botched the only important task he had to perform: finding a suitable wife. After his fairy-tale wedding to Lady Diana Spencer in 1981, the royal soap opera, as Charles himself termed it, descended into tragic farce. *Private Eye* lampooned their stormy relationship in a series entitled 'Heir of Sorrows', which it had to drop when truth became stranger than satire. Nothing was more bizarre than the Prince's famous speculation, during a bugged telephone call to Mrs Parker-Bowles, that he might be reincarnated as a Tampax. Before Diana's death he publicly confessed to adultery, and after it he married his mistress. Popular newspapers, like many of their readers, concluded that Charles was a 'total chump'.[4] He seemed about as fit to be king as Ethelred the Unready.

Yet it would be wrong to dismiss the Prince of Wales as a mere buffoon. Indeed he was more like Hamlet than the Fool: earnest, melancholy, peevish, sensitive, introspective and indecisive. Of course Charles *was* also eccentric, as he himself acknowledged. He sported on his lapel a fox's penis bone mounted on a silver pin presented to him by members of the Belvoir Hunt. He had a silver key, embossed with Prince of Wales feathers, attached to the end of his toothpaste tube, which his valet turned to squeeze just the right amount on to the brush. According to a story heard by the television reporter Jeremy Paxman, the heir to the throne was served seven boiled eggs ranging from hard to soft so that he could select the one that was 'just right'[5] – a story officially denied but partially confirmed from another source. Charles instructed the butler at Highgrove, his Gloucestershire mansion, to tell guests not to put condoms or tampons down the lavatory because they blocked his reed-bed sewage disposal system – an innovative way of giving royal sewage special treatment. If tampons were something of a princely preoccupation, so, apparently, were lavatories: Charles not only enjoyed lavatorial jokes but collected lavatory fittings, becoming, as it were, keeper of the privy seat.

At the same time he pursued an erratic quest for spiritual fulfilment, seeking it variously from the monks of Mount Athos, from crofters in the Outer Hebrides and from the Bushmen of the Kalahari Desert. He dabbled in parapsychology, flirted with Buddhism and contemplated 'bringing back the world of Plato'.[6] He advocated organic farming, holistic medicine, education according to 'timeless principles'[7] and architecture in harmony with our 'inward, invisible patterns'.[8] Eager to impart deep insights, he frequently revealed hidden shallows. His agricultural revolution was little more than a rich man's hobby. His defence of homeopathic treatment was based not on science but on super-stition. Keen to restore the sacred dimension to life, he made a fad of faith. Any faith would do, it seemed, so long as it was, like himself, part of a living tradition, integral to the natural order of things. Whether it was natural to kill animals or to be a vegetarian he was not always sure, much to the irritation of his parents. They attributed his foibles to lack of backbone, regarding him as a prize wimp. The Queen thought him silly to the point of dottiness and the Duke of Edinburgh described him as an 'intellectual pillow',[9] bearing the mark of the last head to make an impression on him – or the last bottom to sit on him. They failed to appreciate his virtues or to recognise that his vices stemmed largely from the fact that he was Prince of Wales – which was not so much a position, to paraphrase Alan Bennett, as a predicament.

Over the past two centuries every Prince of Wales has been a rake or a freak, sometimes both. The Prince Regent, profligate son of the 'mad' King George III (who talked to trees rather than plants), was a caricature of the breed. Sybarite, libertine and popinjay, he spent a king's ransom on follies and trifles, from shoe buckles to chinoiserie, from diamond epaulettes to artificial whiskers. A royal bigamist, he officially married Princess Caroline of Brunswick, whose behaviour was even more indecent than his own, though he was so unpopular that she was hailed as a martyr. 'Prinny' attempted courtesy and refinement. He strove to be the arbiter of fashion, blubbering when told that Beau Brummell did not like the cut of his coat. In fact the Regent aspired to be what flatterers dubbed him, the First Gentleman of Europe. But, a monster of extravagance with a rouged face and a florid costume, he was mocked as the 'Prince of Whales'. He was denounced as a royal scoundrel. His language and manner were said to be 'those of a Bedlamite',[10] an opinion borne out by his claim to have personally defeated Napoleon in 1815.

Edward Prince of Wales, Queen Victoria's eldest son, was another of George III's descendants thought to have inherited his malady. Edward's juvenile rages were described as fits and his worried mother had his head examined by a phrenologist. As an adult, the Prince was pathologically incapable of concentration, almost of cerebration – he tended to echo the opinions of the last person he had met. Signalling his boredom by the impatient drumming of podgy fingers on his knee, Edward needed ceaseless diversion. In lieu of work this took the form of pleasure: dressing and undressing like a man mannequin, presiding over the social round of the beau monde, racing, shooting and yachting, eating twelve-course meals, gambling (illegally) at cards and engaging in multiple adulteries. Some of them caused a scandal. Kipling called the Prince 'a corpulent voluptuary', and Henry James nicknamed him 'Edward the Caresser'. The press said that there was nothing between him and Lily Langtry, 'not even a sheet'. Although cheered as a sportsman, the Prince was booed as a roué. Ministers such as Gladstone and Salisbury tried to shield him; anything but Edward the Silent, he subjected them to a barrage of 'royal twaddle'.[11]

Edward's indiscretions were modest beside those of his grandson, another Edward Prince of Wales, who abdicated in 1936 within twelve months of becoming king. Known as David to the family (and afterwards as the Duke of Windsor), he at least had the excuse of an upbringing that was traumatic even by Hanoverian standards. It was dominated by a martinet and a marionette: his father, King George V, bellowed and bullied like a latter-day Captain Bligh; his mother, Queen Mary, conveyed love with all the warmth of a majestic automaton. In due course the Prince of Wales learned to perform ceremonial functions with grace and charm, winning unparalleled adulation. But the spoilt youth revolted against regal flummery and complained about 'this thankless & rotten job of P. of W.'.[12] It was no job at all, he said, certainly not for a modern man – although wedded to precedence and precedent, the Prince fancied himself a progressive and aspired to be known as 'Edward the Innovator'. Assertive yet easily led, he 'reset his watch by every clock he passed'.[13] He even succumbed to the fashion for fascism, much to the fury of his father, who rebuked him for unconstitutional interference in politics. But the Prince devoted nearly all his energies to amusement: golfing, steeplechasing, playing his ukulele, drinking cocktails in night-clubs, going off on louche holidays and becoming infatuated with a series of married women. The last of these was, of course, Wallis Simpson, who cost him the crown and what little sense it had encompassed.

There are obvious similarities between Prince Charles and his recent predecessors, but compared to them he proved an ornament to his station. He was well educated, the first Prince of Wales to be sent away to school and to gain a university degree. Surrounded by Tories, he was surprisingly liberal-minded. He read books, an unusual accomplishment in a dynasty full of what one Victorian had called 'microcephalous mediocrities'.[14] He took thinking seriously, which was not the same, one of Princess Diana's friends observed, as being a serious thinker; but Charles would hardly have made his great-grandfather's mistake of confusing the word 'highbrow' with eyebrow. Charles had a genuine interest in art, poetry and music – and this in a family whose idea of a cultural evening was (according to Sir Anthony Blunt) 'playing golf with a piece of coal on the Aubusson carpets'.[15] Whereas Edward VII had given less to good causes than he earned in stud fees (for his horses), Charles raised some £100 million annually for philanthropic organisations. He attended over 400 engagements a year to support them, displaying a particular concern for inner cities, minorities and the environment. The Prince's Trust, which he founded in 1976, became the largest youth charity in Britain. Footmen at Buckingham Palace liked to say that the first thing royal children were taught by their nannies was how to ring for service. In contrast to previous Princes of Wales, however, Charles could plausibly claim to live up to the motto of his rarefied caste: *Ich Dien*, I Serve.

Yet membership of that caste corrupts even the best of men. It saps their moral fibre and distorts their character in weird but all too explicable ways. The Prince of Wales is born with a platinum spoon in his mouth and gorged on unearned wealth, privilege and deference. To compensate for this diet his parents invariably impose a harsh regime: like his forebears, Charles was berated, bullied and beaten. Since Victorian times naval training has been used to reinforce domestic discipline, though it did little more than equip princely sailors to become proficient Sea Scouts and enhance their respect for rank. On reaching adulthood, heirs to the throne breathed only the incense of idolatry. Potent enough to turn the strongest head, it encouraged them to behave like little tin gods. As the Victorian author Augustus Hare noted on meeting the future George V, he talked a lot and no one ever contradicts princes, 'however much they disagree; no subjects are aired but those which they choose for themselves, and the merest common-places from royal lips are listened to as though they were oracles'.[16] Democracy did not eradicate sycophancy, as appears from Alan Clark's record of a dinner with Prince Charles in 1988, at which the guests were 'solely interested in scoring goodboy points and ingratiating themselves with the Royal Chair'.[17] In the words of a female friend, Charles lived in 'an isolation ward of flattery'. Hollywood said he was handsome; Peter Sellers laughed at his jokes; women, who thought it an honour to submit to royal desire, hailed him as the greatest lover of their lives. Charles understand-ably concluded that 'he could charm warts off a toad'.[18]

Toadyism compounded the prime difficulty facing every Prince of Wales, namely that his office was a sinecure. Although invested with the glittering panoply of leadership, he remained, until the monarch died, a bit-part player. It was a profoundly frustrating role. The more he was lauded for possessing the wisdom of Solomon and the fortitude of Caesar, the more obvious it became that he had no real function. Some princes responded by confining themselves to ornamental tasks and idle distractions during the long, awkward wait to succeed. Typical of these was Queen Victoria's heir, who once said that he didn't mind praying to an Eternal Father, but he must be 'the only man in the country afflicted with an eternal mother'[19] – a remark that, more than a century later, Charles might well have echoed. Other princes, as if to make up for their lack of proper employment, engaged in hectic bouts of activity. Their prototype was the future Edward VIII, the Prince Charming of the Western world, who did everything to excess: gardening, hunting, fornicating, taking reckless initiatives and, as he put it, performing in the decorated circus. Charles, though more well-meaning than his great-uncle David, followed in his footsteps. His life was punctuated by spasms of animation, many of them induced by lickspittles. The poet Kathleen Raine, for example, urged her 'Dear, dear Prince' not to 'give the riff-raff an inch'. Instead, under divine guidance, he should drive his chariot of fire against the forces of darkness and rescue Albion sunk in deadly sleep.[20] Charles welcomed this sage counsel, despite its unintended implication that he was busy doing nothing.

To his credit, however, no Prince of Wales ever searched more diligently for a significant occupation. It is true that, like his predecessors, Charles was butterfly-minded. He lacked steady purpose, though he was tireless in pursuit of rest and recreation. He drove his staff frantic by the variety of his endeavours, which sometimes duplicated or contradicted one another. Nevertheless, fearful that he would be seen as a playboy, Charles felt a noble obligation to serve the underprivileged and tried 'to help furiously'.[21] He had four hobby-horses – medical, architectural, environmental and spiritual – and he rode them hard. He strove to galvanise British enterprise. He carried out endless public engagements, though he found them so artificial as to be futile. Yearning for responsibilities outside Ruritania, he schemed to become governor-general of Australia. He pestered ministers about rural decay, red tape, political correctness and many other matters – his letters were known as 'Black Spiders', though they often contained melo-dramatic and illiterate addenda scrawled in red ink, with copious underlinings and exclamation marks in the manner of Queen Victoria. These were the emphases of the impotent, for Charles's efforts were often snubbed or mocked. According to his biographer, Jonathan Dimbleby, the Prince 'was frequently consumed by misery and rage as he struggled to prove his worth' and occasionally he came 'close to despair'. This did not prevent him from using Dimbleby to float the notion (in 2008) that the sovereign's role might be redefined to 'allow Charles III to speak out on matters of national and international importance in ways that at the moment would be unthinkable'.[22] It was a rash proposal, redolent of Edward VIII and inimical to the golden mean traditionally symbolised by Britain's crowned head. It also ignored Walter Bagehot's classic warning about the danger of having, 'upon a constitutional throne, an active and meddling fool'.[23]

Charles's project could hardly have increased Queen Elizabeth II's confidence in his judgement. She had always exercised influence in secret and now he seemed to be bidding for overt power. She had always been the centre of patriotic attraction and now he was apparently aiming to fill 'a vacuum of national leadership'.[24] She must have seen his démarche as a slight on her life and an antici-pation of her death. Yet it was the fate of every Prince of Wales to offend the parent whose bittersweet demise would bring about his succession. Charles could not escape it. As holder of the 'rever-sionary interest' in the throne, he presided, like 'Prinny', over a rival court. He became the focus of political intrigue like Queen Victoria's hedonistic son, whom she excluded from affairs of state and instructed that he had '*no* right to meddle'.[25] Like his great-uncle David, Charles personified the future, promising improvement and offering hope. Impatient with pompous formality and archaic formulae (such as the sixteenth-century title Defender of the Faith), Charles campaigned ardently for an alternative vision and a radical approach. He even saw himself as a 'dissident' who was 'working against the prevailing political consensus'.[26] Moreover, he went so far as to attack the Establishment. A Knight of the Garter himself, Charles described the robes of this chivalrous order as 'a crazy outfit'.[27] Born into the purple, he declared: 'I can't bear privilege.'[28] Here was a delusion to match the Prince Regent's fantasies about riding Fleur de Lis to victory at Goodwood races or winning the Battle of Waterloo.

No doubt Charles genuinely regarded himself as a champion of dissent. Like his predecessors, he had to differentiate his coming reign from the ancient regime. He needed to be seen as a man of advanced ideas. Yet a progressive prince, like a modern arquebus, is a contradiction in terms. Although susceptible to New Age panaceas, Charles was wedded to olde worlde usages. He was attached to tradition by silken bonds of sentiment and self-interest. He favoured only such cosmetic adjustments as would perpetuate the status quo – in the manner of his great-uncle David, whose innovations amounted to little more than permitting the gentlemen-at-arms to shave off their spade beards. Charles hated the vulgarity of novelty. He nursed a Bourbon aversion to revolutionaries, clinging to the princely principle that change based on reason was deeply subversive. He did change his clothes – but not their cut or style. He promoted conservation because he was a conservative – in the drive at Highgrove a notice proclaimed, 'You are now entering an old-fashioned place.'[29] He was partial to heritage because he stood to inherit a kingdom. Charles venerated ancestral wisdom on the assumption that monarchy was its embodiment. Poised at its apex, he esteemed hierarchy. Belonging to an elite, he espoused elitism. Being well-bred, he had an innate respect for breeding – like his mother, who refused to allow a mare from her stables to be impregnated by a likely stallion because it belonged to a bookmaker. Indeed, the Prince reminded people of his own pedigree if they seemed inclined to forget it. He extolled the customary appurtenances of his station such as royal trains, planes and yachts. He revered ritual, even the mock-medieval mumbo-jumbo of his investiture as Prince of Wales in 1969. He was especially moved, he later wrote, 'when I put my hands between Mummy's and swore to be her liege man of life and limb and to live and die against all manner of folks'.

In short, Charles was a royal oxymoron. He yearned to be a people's prince, liberated from stuffy palace protocol, yet he expected the genuflections due to his exalted rank. Imprisoned in the gilded cage of convention, he sometimes beat against the bars but more often luxuriated in the privileges of his splendid isolation. He had green instincts but blue-blooded tastes. He aimed to make headway by turning the clock back. He was a dogmatic dilettante, a dynamic scatterbrain, a radical reactionary. But although Charles was confused, he was sincere. Although he associated with the rich, he cared about the poor. No Prince of Wales devoted himself more assiduously to good works. However, Charles hardly proved an exception to Bagehot's rule that no Prince of Wales can resist the temptations of his position. He succumbed to the carnal despite cherishing an acute 'sense of the sacred'.[30] He gave way to fits of arrogance, petulance and giddy extravagance – when incarcerated in Cirencester hospital with a broken arm from playing polo in 1990, he was supplied from home with silver cutlery, engraved crystal glasses and crested bone-china plates. His antics were grist to Rupert Murdoch's republican mill. Like his great-uncle David, Charles shook the throne. Moreover, he suffered from a comparable crisis of identity, precipitated by contradictions in his character and uncertainties about his role. George V had repeatedly told his eldest son, 'You must always remember who you are', which prompted him to wonder: 'Who exactly was I?'[31] Prince Charles himself was asked by a Malaysian boy, 'Who are you?' He replied, 'I wish I knew.'[32]

Doubtless the Prince spoke with more than a touch of whimsy. To be sure, he was perplexed by the personal pronoun, veering wildly from 'I' to 'we' to 'one'. Yet he was also the topmost sprig in a family tree that could be traced root and branch back to the Dark Ages. Genealogists conjure with blood as astrologers read the stars, and no ancestry was endowed with richer qualities: Charles was said to be descended, via Alfred the Great, from the Saxon god Woden. No individual was distinguished by such a plethora of totems and titles: Earl of Chester, Duke of Cornwall, Duke of Rothesay, Earl of Carrick, Baron of Renfrew, Lord of the Isles and, of course, Prince of Wales and King hereafter. Charles's inheritance was a burden to him almost from the start, since it meant that he could never enjoy anything like a normal life. But he was much more weighed down, during the years after his birth on 14 November 1948, by his mother's emotional frigidity and his father's temperamental pugnacity.

Princess Elizabeth, as she was then, had been brought up in strict conformity with the ladylike conventions of her day. Her mother, née Elizabeth Bowes-Lyon, preferred accomplishments to scholarship, and the Princess was taught dancing, drawing, music appreciation, country matters, good manners, perfect deportment and 'all the distinctively feminine graces'.[33] One biographer described such an education as the British equivalent of foot-binding. Certainly Princess Elizabeth, far less pampered than her younger sister Margaret, was told to keep her feelings under tight control in public. Shy by nature, she became more inhibited as the abdication crisis demonstrated the perils of putting passion before duty. When she was only eleven, her stammering father was crowned King George VI, an honour he accepted with weeping and gnashing of teeth. So Princess Elizabeth would succeed to the throne unless her mother produced a son, which seemed unlikely, though not perhaps for the reason adduced by Evelyn Waugh, who maintained that the Queen could only get pregnant if suspended by her legs from a chandelier.

What Queen Elizabeth unquestionably did was to cling to tradition and to stiffen her husband's backbone. Her candyfloss exterior concealed a granite disposition – or, in the metaphor privately coined by her husband's official biographer, 'there was a small drop of arsenic in the centre of that marshmallow'.[34] She ensured that George VI restored the prestige of the monarchy by rigid adherence to the canons of the past, though at ceremonies he sometimes wanted to 'scream and scream and scream'.[35] She also locked up her daughters, keeping them in a patrician purdah tempered by servants – who monogrammed their butter pats with the royal coat of arms. The girls endured a wholly artificial existence in Buckingham Palace, which their governess likened to 'the setting of a luxurious pantomime'.[36] Princess Elizabeth preferred the tartan rustication of Balmoral, which was occasionally enlivened by ghillies' balls. Already skilled at charades and jigsaw puzzles, she became adept at stalking deer and strangling pheasants. But she grew up better able to form relationships with horses and dogs than with people. Despite having a sense of humour, she was too serious and sometimes too imperious to encourage familiarity. Moreover, she was protected from every untoward encounter: the 'new recruits' she joined in the Auxiliary Training Service during the war were really instructors in disguise. It took a handsome prince to break though the forest of briars surrounding the Princess and win her heart.

He was, of course, Prince Philip, a blond Viking with an adventurous past. As the son of Prince Andrew of Greece and Princess Alice of Battenberg, he was descended from Queen Victoria and belonged to the Danish-German ruling house of Schleswig-Holstein-Sonderburg-Glücksburg. But shortly after Philip's birth, which took place on Corfu in 1921, his family was forced into exile. Interwar Europe was haunted by redundant royals scavenging for crowns or half-crowns, and Philip had a knockabout (though well-nannied) childhood. Sometimes he stayed in palaces, sometimes he wore hand-me-down clothes supplied by charitable relations. In 1930 his parents' marriage collapsed, his father retiring to Monte Carlo with a mistress and his mother succumbing to religious mania – she claimed to receive divine messages and to possess healing powers, and she eventually founded an order of nuns. While Philip's four elder sisters married German princelings, most of them pro-Nazi, he boarded at an old-fashioned English preparatory school, Cheam. A hardy, rumbustious boy, he learned to take his lickings like a man. He developed a brash sense of fun. He shone at athletics, though not at study. In fact he was well suited to the kind of education pioneered in Germany by Kurt Hahn, a Jewish headmaster who believed in forging character by spartan means. Philip followed Hahn when he fled from Hitler and set up another academy at Gordonstoun. Here Hahn's 'despotic, overpowering personality' reigned supreme and he became, according to an astute observer, T. C. Worsley, the incarnation of the Führer principle.[37] Philip found him inspiring, enjoyed the brutal regime at Gordonstoun and got to the top.

In 1939 he went on to Dartmouth Naval College, encouraged by his uncle, Lord Louis 'Dickie' Mountbatten, who also harboured dynastic ambitions for him. A prodigy of self-promotion himself, Mountbatten schemed to marry his nephew to Princess Elizabeth and thus make him sire of a new royal house. Despite Philip's later protestations, it is clear that he avidly embraced this prospect – a cousin likened him to a 'huge, hungry dog' without a basket.[38] When the royal family visited Dartmouth, Mountbatten ensured that his nephew was well to the fore. A princely paladin exuding charm and animal magnetism, Philip soon enraptured the adolescent Elizabeth. As early as January 1941, the well-informed socialite 'Chips' Channon stated flatly that Philip 'is to be our Prince Consort'.[39] The sailor corresponded with the Princess during the war, in which he served with courage and distinction – though he was a strict disciplinarian who tended to shout first and ask questions afterwards. He also saw her when possible, though he was not popular with the King, who yearned to keep his family foursome intact. Nor did Philip please the courtiers, who found him loudly Teutonic. Noting his rackety doings and his 'armfuls of girls',[40] they also feared that he would take after his philandering father. One dry old stick-in-waiting summed up the verdict of the 'horrified' royal family and their canny retainers: Philip was 'rough, ill mannered, uneducated and would probably not be faithful'.[41] But the Princess was in love, and, with Mounbatten's help, Philip changed his name and his status. He accomplished a brisk metamorphosis from Glücksburg to Mountbatten and from Greek Orthodox to British Anglican. In November 1947 he married Elizabeth, adding a dash of romance to the drab world of post-war austerity. Normally so undemonstrative, the Princess glowed with happiness. But a journalist who spotted the couple en route to their honeymoon in Mountbatten's country mansion, Broadlands, said that the Duke of Edinburgh (as Philip had become) looked 'grey-faced and already long-suffering'.[42]

Doubtless he saw shades of the palatial prison-house beginning to close upon the thrusting naval officer. Philip had taken pride in his independence and, while enjoying the delicious fruits of his new position, he was humiliated to find himself a kept man. Worse still, the Duke would have to defer to his regal spouse in public for the rest of his life, reversing what he took to be the cosmic order. Sometimes Philip liked to challenge old ways, and he despised crusty court mandarins who regarded horseless carriages as dubious novelties. He had to apologise for calling one Keeper of the Privy Purse 'a silly Whitehall twit'.[43] Accustomed to the gusto of the wardroom, he resented the punctilio of the stateroom. He also objected to the solemnity of what he called 'pomping' – it amused him to wave at spectators clinging to lamp posts in the hope that they would wave back and fall off. He still rarely thought before he spoke and his premature ejaculations seldom erred on the side of delicacy: 'The trouble with you Egyptians is that you breed too much.'[44] Breeding was, as the Duke ruefully appreciated, his own *raison d'être*. This function at least he performed, despite rumours of early infidelities, to general satisfaction. On 14 November 1948, at Buckingham Palace, Elizabeth gave birth to Prince Charles. Arriving to see the new baby after a game of squash, Philip was thrilled to find that he had fathered a boy. As he told his aide Mike Parker, 'It takes a man to have a son!'[45]

With equal sagacity the Duke determined that his son should grow up to be 'a man's man'.[46] Yet Charles was at once consigned to the care of, as Philip disgustedly remarked, 'nannies, nurses and poofs'.[47] He had two Scottish nannies, Helen Lightbody and Mabel Anderson, assisted by nursery maids and footmen. Like Victorians so indolent (it was said) that they would if possible have got servants to masticate their food, royal personages left almost everything to their staff. The nannies did the chores, of course, giving the infant Charles his breakfast and his bath – the two occasions when his mother saw him every day. But they also gave him the hugs and kisses that his parents singularly failed to provide. It is true that Elizabeth was preoccupied with duties to carry out on behalf of her ailing father and that Philip was busy keeping his naval career afloat. When she joined him in Malta, however, Charles stayed at home, and on her return she showed little eagerness to see him, once delaying their reunion for several days while she attended to other matters and went to the races. She was sometimes able to relax with him in private, playing games and even pelting him with rabbit droppings in a mock battle during a picnic on the Isle of Uist. But in public she behaved with chill formality, greeting the small boy with a handshake. In fact Elizabeth's maternal feelings were so cool that (as the Duke of Windsor said of Queen Mary) she might have had iced water in her veins. Philip, on the other hand, blew in and out of his son's life like a cyclone. Charles was timid, shy and gentle, but Philip, who came to prefer his bumptious daughter Anne (born in 1950), thought him soft. He was convinced that the boy was being mollycoddled. So he roared at Charles, who was quiet and apprehensive in his presence. He spanked him for small misdemeanours. Ignoring his screams, Philip threw the three-year-old into the palace pool to teach him to swim. Charles's adored Nanny Lightbody tried to prevent the nursery from becoming an extension of the quarterdeck, for which she was later dismissed.

The Duke of Edinburgh was all the more intent on ruling the domestic roost because he had nothing else to rule. He had to abandon his profession to assist his wife. When King George VI died in 1952, Elizabeth became queen and Philip was snubbed by the likes of her aloof private secretary, Sir Alan Lascelles, who had once described him as 'the matrimonial nigger in the wood-pile'.[48] At the coronation the Duke was little more than an attendant lord, paying homage to the anointed sovereign. When he wanted to remain in newly decorated Clarence House and use Buckingham

Palace as an office, the prime minister, Winston Churchill, insisted that the monarch must live over the shop. Philip's attempts to modernise this mausoleum were largely thwarted, among them his proposal to improve the system of internal communication, substituting the telephone for written messages borne on silver salvers by liveried footmen. His mother-in-law was a trial, taking months to move out of what she regarded as home and maintaining that Charles was, like her late husband, a tender plant to be watered not forced. Moreover, to the Duke's intense chagrin, the Cabinet forbade him (for the time being) to give his children the Mounbatten surname. Philip famously raged, 'I'm just a bloody amoeba'[49] – a curious expression by which he seems to have meant sperm donor. So he asserted himself as head of the family, which he called 'the Firm'. He was often away on business and pleasure, missing six out of Charles's first eight birthdays. But when present, he tried to instil something of his own lustiness into the weak-chested, knock-kneed, flat-footed Prince.

So Charles was detached from the petticoat tails of his fond governess, Catherine Peebles ('Mispy'), and sent to school. In 1956 he became a day boy at Hill House, a smart new establishment in Knightsbridge. For the heir to the throne to be educated outside the royal ivory tower was a break with tradition, and Charles was soon introduced to other novelties. He rode on a bus, entered a shop and handled money, though it was deemed inappropriate for him to visit public baths, tainted as they were by the masses, and Hill House boys used the palace swimming pool. In addition to the usual curriculum, he learned valuable lessons in elementary anatomy from the headmaster's wife, who, according to his first biographer, lay 'on her back on the floor for her young pupil to practise artificial respiration'. Charles was hampered by more than his fair share of juvenile afflictions, including tonsillitis – he once left a bottle containing his tonsils on the altar of the little chapel at Windsor where he liked to preach to imaginary congregations. But he proved a plodder at work and a duffer at games. He was taciturn, diffident, dreamy, vague and vulnerable. Nothing daunted, the Duke pressed him further into the paternal mould. Shortly before his ninth birthday, Charles was dispatched to board at Cheam, his father's old preparatory school. The boy had dreaded the prospect of leaving home, and at the start of the journey from Balmoral, the Queen noticed, he 'shuddered with apprehension'.[50] His worst fears were realised. Charles might have echoed General Sir Ian Hamilton's verdict on his own entry to Cheam the previous century: 'it was, as far as my childhood was concerned, exactly like a dose of poison'.[51]

Homesickness is sometimes worse for children unhappy at home, and Charles suffered acutely, often crying himself to sleep. He was all the more miserable for being lonely in a crowd. His fellows regarded him as a royal peculiar and he was unable to make friends – his closest companion was the only girl in the school, the headmaster's daughter. Occasionally he was victimised. His head was held under a cold tap and he was called 'Fatty' – though he found the food at Cheam too rich after frugal nursery fare. Nothing emphasised his crippling apartness more than the Queen's announcement at the end of the 1958 Commonwealth Games that she was creating him Prince of Wales. Her Majesty had not bothered to inform her son about the impending honour, and as Charles watched her televised address with other boys in the headmaster's study, he was overcome by confusion and embarrassment. In the woodwork class soon afterwards he carved a model entitled 'Gallows and Stocks', a grisly emblem of his stretch at Cheam. Incarcerated, he retreated even further into his shell. During the holidays Philip tried to winkle him out, reading stories, arranging activities, playing games of hide-and-seek and enthusing about the popular new Duke of Edinburgh Award scheme. But he did not conceal his partiality for Princess Anne, a horse-mad tomboy who excelled in the family's mealtime equine quizzes, whereas Charles, to his shame, could not tell a pastern from a martingale. The father indulged the daughter but oppressed the son. His brusque commands, cruel thrusts and abrasive banter often reduced Charles to tears, sometimes in front of shocked guests. The Queen did not interfere, accepting that Philip must be 'boss in his own home'.[52] Once, though, she absent-mindedly said to Charles, 'Goodnight, darling.' He was surprised: 'You called me darling!'[53]

Charles made modest progress with his studies at Cheam, doing well at drama, music and art but badly at mathematics. He also became captain of the football team, though it lost every match and he was criticised for not driving himself 'as hard as his ability and position demanded'.[54] Any such comment was enough to confirm the Duke's belief that his effete offspring must attend a school of even harder knocks. So in the summer of 1962, Charles, aged thirteen, followed in his father's footsteps and entered Gordonstoun. Having done time at a juvenile remand home, he now faced an extended sentence in an adolescent detention centre. Charles himself used prison imagery ('Colditz in kilts') to describe his ordeal, and it was not far-fetched. Like Baden-Powell, Kurt Hahn had been obsessed by the degenerative effects of solitary vice upon the growing boy – he claimed to be able to smell the evil. So Gordonstoun denied its inmates privacy in the spirit of Jeremy Bentham's see-through gaol, the panopticon. Charles slept on a hard wooden bed in a crowded dormitory with uncurtained windows open summer and winter. Equally hugger-mugger were his living quarters, which, with their unpainted walls, bare boards and naked light bulbs, resembled a run-down barracks. Even the lavatories were virtually public. Charles took part in communal exercises: domestic chores, country runs, cold showers, physical jerks and compulsory games. There were also exhausting outward-bound pursuits at sea and in the mountains. These were the moral equivalent of hard labour. They were designed to purge pubertal youth of depraved passions, to produce healthy minds in healthy bodies and to save souls by attuning them to the chaste harmonies of nature. But just in case boys could still find the energy and the opportunity to practise self-abuse, they were put on their honour to confess their faults – an unrivalled method of fostering shame and deceit.

Charles might have braved the borstal rigours of Gordonstoun but for his fellow pupils. However, discipline was erratic under Hahn's successor, Robert Chew, a detached figure with a detachable glass eye. According to the writer William Boyd, there were times when 'capricious thuggery' reigned and the school took on 'certain fascist characteristics'.[55] Moreover, the Prince's housemaster, an irascible boor, did little to curb brutish behaviour among his charges. So they shunned Charles, as at Cheam, but reinforced the ostracism by making foul slurping noises, indicative of bum-sucking, at anyone who fraternised with him. He walked everywhere by himself, a princely pariah to be kept at arm's length in case his condition was catching. There was also positive persecution, starting with barbaric initiation ceremonies. Charles was deliberately roughed up on the rugby field, where well-heeled hooligans relished the chance to kick their future king. In the dormitory he was constantly hit on the head because of his snoring, an experience he found 'absolute hell'.[56] The malevolence unnerved him and perhaps accounted for his most famous schoolboy gaffe. At a Stornoway hotel, which he visited while on a sailing expedition in 1963, Charles ordered a cherry brandy, the only drink he could think of on the spur of the moment. Inevitably the press splashed the news, eliciting the kind of instant denial from Buckingham Palace without which, journalists said, no royal story was credible. Charles was not caned. He was reduced to the rank of new boy again, a crushing humiliation that confirmed his outcast status. His parents hoped that it would teach him a lesson.

They also rejected his pleas to be taken away from 'this horrible place',[57] though Charles was indeed protected from its worst excesses. He had a private detective on the site and was never subjected to naked terror of the kind described by William Boyd. He was allowed frequent visits to Balmoral and Birkhall, where his grandmother, Queen Elizabeth the Queen Mother, gorged him with food and love. Further ailments enabled him to take refuge in the sanatorium. He was helped by one or two sympathetic masters. He found solace in painting, potting, acting and playing the cello. Religion was also a comfort, though Charles disliked worshipping in the chapel at Gordonstoun, a converted barn, because it lacked the mysterious atmosphere of a church. Nor did his father exactly encourage the Prince's spiritual development.

During Charles's confirmation service in 1965, the Duke ostentatiously read a book, moving the pious Archbishop of Canterbury,
Michael Ramsey, to unwonted profanity: it was, he said, 'bloody
rude'.[58] Plainly Philip did not want his son to imbibe the milk
and holy water of Anglicanism, let alone a nauseating draught of
mysticism. Instead he sought further means to grind grit into the
feckless youth, finally hitting on the tried and tested expedient of
sending him to a penal colony in Australia. That, at any rate, was
what Charles anticipated when in 1966 he went to serve a term
at the outback outpost of Geelong Grammar School known
as Timbertop. But although run on the same lines as Gordonstoun,
Timbertop amounted to a deliverance. To be sure, there was a
gruelling programme of activities, ranging from wood chopping,
which rubbed Charles's hands raw, to bush hikes, which blistered
his feet and bloodied his rucksacked back. But most of the boys
were younger than he was, and they directed little in the way of
insult at the legitimate heir to the throne except 'Pommie
bastard'.[59]

Charles was said to have gone to the Antipodes a boy and
returned home a man. He apparently adored Timbertop, learning
to be more independent during his extended time there. Moreover,
he claimed, 'Australia got me over my shyness.'[60] There may be
some truth in all this. Few stood on ceremony down under and
Charles was encouraged to mix by his gregarious new mentor, a
pipe-smoking equerry called Squadron-Leader David Checketts,
who was described as 'one of nature's gym masters'.[61] On holiday
tours the Prince encountered nothing but affection and respect,
which was especially marked in Papua. Here he witnessed
missionary work among befeathered men and grass-skirted
women, who sparked his interest in 'primitive society'. It was a
repository of immemorial tradition, which, he hoped, would not
be adulterated by materialistic European culture. Elsewhere
Charles played polo, which became 'an avid passion'.[62] He enjoyed
teaching Geelong novices to ski. He also sampled normal domestic
life with the squadron-leader's family, though the Queen had not
herself troubled to meet Mrs Checketts. Nevertheless, the Prince

was still tense and withdrawn. Facial tics betrayed his anxieties. Emotionally retarded, he blushed in the presence of girls. Charles liked to say that without his ability to see the funny side of things he would long since have gone mad; yet his sense of humour, often expressed in mimicking the Goons, was callow even by the standards of royalty, for whom the height of comedy was someone getting his fingers shut in a door. The Prince remained ill at ease with his parents, and the first person he telephoned on arriving back in England was his old governess, Mispy.

The Duke hoped that a final year at Gordonstoun would mature his son in body and mind. Charles certainly found life easier there, especially when he duly became head of his house and then captain of the school. His dignity was further enhanced when the Queen made him a member of the Privy Council, an appointment he learned about from the BBC News. At the age of eighteen, Charles passed A levels in History and French, though his grades (B and C respectively) would not have gained anyone of lesser rank a place at Trinity College, Cambridge. Free at last – insofar as he could be free when his ultimate fate was determined by birth and his immediate future had just been decided by a gaggle of Establishment worthies meeting at Buckingham Palace – Charles gave conflicting verdicts on his past captivity. He paid dutiful tribute to his father's wisdom in sending him to places that instilled 'a great deal of self-discipline and experience and responsibility'.[63] He extolled the value of physical challenges and later sought more testing adventure. In lieu of compulsory military service, he even recommended a scheme based on Kurt Hahn's methods for training the nation's youth. As his authorised biography would confirm, however, Charles had found Gordonstoun a purgatory as well as a penitentiary.

If the Prince's accounts of his early education were contradictory, its effects on his character were paradoxical. Charles's schooling wounded a psyche already scarified by parental mistreatment; but it strengthened an overriding sense of uniqueness. It further battered his confidence while teaching him the absolute necessity of self-reliance. It flattened him into worried conformity and he remained cautious, dithering and doubtful about his own capacities. He was still racked by nervous gestures and embarrassed grimaces – stroking his nose, licking his lips, fiddling with his cufflinks, twisting his signet ring. Yet he felt compelled to strive for personal achievement in the spirit of Kurt Hahn, whose training, as one commentator wrote, 'could hardly have been a worse preparation for the life of inert frustration and puppetry to which British heirs to the throne are expected to devote their prime'.[64] Moreover, having survived all the tribulations and got into university despite his poor academic performance, Charles had every reason to put his trust in princeliness. So while he took refuge in self-deprecation, he also grew ever more arrogant, egotistical and opinionated. Superior instinct, he evidently decided, was preferable to vulgar rationalism. A pinch of royal intuition was worth a pound of common sense. Puffed up by sycophancy, a large portion of the air he breathed on entering adulthood, Charles would all too easily succumb to moods of truculence and petulance.

The student Prince's most defiant move was a refusal to move with the times, to tune in to the unruly rhythms of the day and (as the current cliché had it) to swing with the sixties. In an age of flower power, Carnaby Street, alternative theatre, Women's Lib, the Rolling Stones, recreational drugs, university sit-ins over civil rights and protests against the war in Vietnam, Charles was a cultural Canute. There was not a trace of the contemporary scene in his rooms at Trinity, which were redecorated by workmen sent over from Sandringham. His attire, bespoke from Bond Street, was old-fashioned and middle-aged: sober ties, tweed jackets, corduroy or grey-flannel trousers and fogeyish brogues. His haircut was conventional and he groused about mop-topped undergraduates with beards and bare feet. He still assumed that nice girls were virgins at the altar. He revolted against current modes, preferring classical music to pop and stirrup cup to pot. Charles regarded marches and rallies as 'a sort of modern, ghastly phenomenon'. He watched one Cambridge demonstration in disguise and commented judiciously that it was put on 'for the sake of doing something to change things, which, from my point of view, is pointless'.[65]

Charles was more at home in the immutable world of 'the most *primitive* kinds of men'.[66] Against the advice of the Master of the College, the veteran Tory politician R. A. Butler, he therefore insisted on taking a course in archaeology and anthropology, before switching to history in the second part of his degree. At Trinity, where mutual suspicion and reserve made it hard for him to integrate with ordinary students, he acquired only the odd friend. The Prince felt most comfortable with the smart set, which was less interested in studying than in hunting, shooting and fishing for royal invitations – cronies were bidden to Sandringham for avian massacres. He could also relax in thespian company, putting on funny voices and acting in several student revues. These were facetious affairs, which, at a time when mordant television satire was all the rage, harked back to the music hall. In one sketch Charles gave a mock weather forecast: 'By morning promiscuity will be widespread but it will lift, and may give way to some hill snog.' In another he posed as an expert in 'Bong Dynasty Chinese bidets' and, thanks no doubt to his German relations, he was able to put on what *The Times*'s reporter called an 'extremely authentic Teutonic accent, reeking of sauerkraut and pumpernickel'.[67] Audiences were appreciative, but these performances, like royal amateur theatricals down the ages, mainly amused the cast.

Another princely performance at Cambridge attracted no publicity and remains shrouded in obscurity. But it seems that the Master of Trinity arranged for Charles to lose his virginity. In the Prince's delicate (and indelicate) matter Butler appointed himself, so to speak, Pander of the Bedchamber. For his purpose he selected Lucia Santa Cruz, the attractive daughter of the Chilean ambassador, who was acting as his research assistant. She was a happy example, Lady Butler later wrote, of someone on whom Charles 'could safely cut his teeth, if I may put it thus'.[68] As this odd but graphic metaphor suggests, the consummation was sorely achieved.

Charles was eager but innocent and inhibited. He was fearful of exposure. Moreover, despite sharing the royal penchant for dirty jokes, he was prudish about public morality. He took a dim view of the movement towards sexual liberation that occurred between the arrival of the contraceptive pill and the coming of AIDS. America was especially to blame for flouting Victorian standards, as illustrated by the transatlantic slogan: 'Rock and Roll and Dope and Fucking in the Streets'. This sort of thing would frighten the horses. Charles was more discreet, though once he got a taste for the pleasures of the flesh and discovered that he could exercise a kind of *droit de seigneur* over young females, he indulged himself with all the ardour of his Hanoverian forebears. He even seemed to adopt the adage applied to the Bourbons, that the greatest aphrodisiac is variety. In short, his womanising was not so much the product of a permissive society as the custom of a regal dynasty.

Yet the dynasty itself was uncomfortably aware that the times were changing, and Charles became the key figure in a cautious attempt to update the royal image. The Queen's old press secretary, Sir Richard Colville, had believed that no news about his employer was good news; but he retired in 1968 and his Australian successor, William Heseltine, took the view that Her Majesty must be seen to be believed. Heseltine aimed to present the human face of the monarchy and, with the support of Prince Philip, the BBC produced a documentary entitled *Royal Family*. Containing intimate glimpses of lives hitherto kept reverently private (and afterwards criticised for letting daylight in upon magic), it was billed as the 'most exciting film ever made for television'. Charles played the juvenile lead, promoting the improved Windsor brand as well as acting as an advertisement for himself. Of course, Heseltine denied that the programme was 'a public relations exercise'.[69] But it was broadcast a few days before Charles's investiture as Prince of Wales and it was accompanied by a professional campaign to package and market him as a commodity. Thus he was sent to the University of Wales in Aberystwyth to drum up loyalty among the increasingly nationalistic people of the Principality, notably by learning a bit of their language. David Checketts, who was allowed to moonlight from royal service as non-executive director of a public relations company, coached Charles in question-and-answer sessions before interviews with carefully selected broadcasters and journalists. Moreover, the investiture itself, which took place at Caernarvon Castle on 1 July 1969, was specifically designed as a television spectacular. The Garter King of Arms, Sir Anthony Wagner, resisted the sacrifice of heraldry to publicity: 'I don't regard myself as part of show-business.'[70] Lord Snowdon, Princess Margaret's husband and the impresario of the investiture, urged: 'Garter darling, can't you be a bit more elastic?'[71]

Snowdon, who nicknamed Wagner 'Wanker', used his photographic expertise and his elevated station to ensure that the investiture made Charles, as the coronation had made his mother, a star of the small screen. Everything was done for the cameras, which topped each tower and battlement. A gigantic Perspex canopy, reminiscent of Henry V's tent at Agincourt but transparent to the lens, was erected over the proscenium on which the Queen invested the Prince with the symbols of his office – sword, coronet, ring, sceptre and ermine mantle. As Lord Snowdon later confessed and as Prince Philip's testy detachment suggested at the time, much of the ceremonial was spurious. It was less a pageant than a pantomime. It was a hotchpotch of invented tradition and romantic illusion calculated to burnish the crown, reflect lustre on the government and boost the tourist industry. Yet the various elements combined to make a scintillating display: the processions of scarlet uniforms, the fanfares of silver trumpets, the gold three-feathered insignia of the Prince of Wales, the silken banners decorated with tawny lions and red dragons, the green grass and the vermilion chairs, the 'vaguely Stone Age thrones' on their grey slate dais, and the cast of supporting dignitaries – bishops, peers, retainers, heralds, harpists, singers, bards and druids in white nylon robes. Prince Charles, wearing the blue uniform of the New Royal Regiment of Wales, flushed as he pledged allegiance to his mother and gave her a rare kiss of fealty. As he said in his address, read partly in Welsh, the ritual filled him with pride and emotion, taking place as it did 'in this magnificent fortress, where no one could fail to be stirred by its atmosphere of time-worn grandeur'.

Although some Welsh nationalists were stirred to protest, throwing eggs and even exploding bombs, most people in the Principality acclaimed their Prince. Crowds roared 'Good old Charlie.'[72] Commentators praised the Prince's dignified bearing, while noting the nervous grin of relief that he directed at his father as the ordeal came to an end. Welsh patriots welcomed Charles's tribute to their cultural heritage, including his droll salute to 'a very memorable "Goon"' – Harry Secombe. Charles responded so warmly to mass enthusiasm that, he declared, 'I woke up in the middle of the night waving my hand.'[73] Unaccustomed to adulation, he soon began to expect it, to require it. The poet laureate, Cecil Day-Lewis, dutifully called on God to bless the Prince of Wales, who commanded that John Betjeman too should compose a poem on the investiture. Betjeman rhapsodised over the ceremony, asserting that it brought eternity within reach and marked Charles's coming of age:

> You knelt a boy, you rose a man.
> And thus your lonelier life began.[74]

The subject of this fancy, who supposed that he had become a man in Australia, was not gratified. Nor were critics of Betjeman's loyal verse, which was indeed barely superior to Clive James's fawning doggerel. Maurice Bowra unforgettably parodied his friend Betjeman's effusions:

> Green with lust and sick with shyness,
> Let me lick your lacquered toes,
> Gosh, oh gosh, your Royal Highness,
> Put your finger up my nose,
> Pin my teeth upon your dress,
> Plant my head with watercress.[75]

Here was a donnish expression of the cynicism of the sixties, which would help to undermine public respect for Charles.

Indeed, the age of deference was dying. The *Royal Family* film was nicknamed *Corgi and Beth*. A satirical song entitled 'Carlo' (the Welsh version of Charles and a name usually given to dogs) became a hit; it lampooned the pidgin Welsh of 'Muckingham Palace' and urged serfs to join in the chorus of 'Carlo, Carlo, Carlo, he play polo with daddy'.[76] Five days after the investiture, the Rolling Stones gave a free concert in Hyde Park that attracted a crowd of 250,000, the same number as had gathered in Caernarvon. The group played to mark the death (evidently drug-induced) of its founder, Brian Jones, and the lead singer, Mick Jagger, heavily made up with lipstick, rouge and mascara, appeared in a frilly white dress and simulated masturbation and fellatio with his microphone. However stagey the performance, it seemed to epitomise the current spirit of rebellion that virtually bypassed but implicitly challenged Prince Charles. Furthermore the republican Rupert Murdoch was now a presence in Fleet Street and he had started to chip away at the pristine image of royalty traditionally presented by the press. The Duke of Edinburgh would damn him for undermining the sovereign institution but the Australian could justifiably retort that the royal family, by exploiting the media to puff itself, had opened the door to critical scrutiny. During the 1970s Roy Strong, director of the National Portrait Gallery, observed the erosion of monarchical mystique. How, he exclaimed, the 'royals must meditate on the vanishing magic'.[77]

In the afterglow of the investiture, Charles was little affected by snippets of scepticism. Although carping about 'the bloody press', he recognised that it had a job to do and that without good coverage there might be no cheers for royalty. As yet he did not share the almost pathological animus of his father and his sister towards journalists, whom they reviled as 'mosquitoes', 'pests' and 'bloody vultures'.[78] Indeed he tried to be polite to them and they considered him relatively genial. The Prince still laughed at puerile jokes: driving huskies, he said, 'just sleighed me'.[79] Formerly reckoned an ineffectual dimwit, he gained credit for completing his interrupted studies at Cambridge in 1970 with a lower second degree. He was admired for trying to make something of his position rather than being content to remain a mere figurehead. Moreover, he carried out his official duties with such evident dedication that some of his more bizarre encounters were not reported: when a woman told him on a walkabout that she had had a double mastectomy he said, 'I trust you feel lighter, madam.'[80] Such repartee was worthy of Prince Philip, yet Charles tried to show that he really cared about people. So heartfelt were his feelings about the Welsh that they scrambled his syntax: 'To know that somebody is interested in them is the very least I can do at the moment.'[81] In private, as in public, Charles won golden opinions. Lady Gladwyn described him as charming, humorous, artistic, diffident, benevolent, intelligent (but luckily not too clever) and sensitive (unlike his father). Roy Strong found him earnest, unsophisticated, prankish, thoughtful, kind and shy, and 'couldn't help being impressed by his sheer "niceness"'.[82]

Charles never seemed more amiable and well-intentioned than when embarking on the military career mapped out for him by his elders. It is true that he was, as only a Royal Highness can be, instinctively *de haut en bas*. While attending the Cranwell Royal Air Force College, the Prince remarked that his training programme was designed to teach him more about people, and when he switched to the Royal Navy, he said that it would give him 'a marvellous opportunity to get close to the ordinary British chap'.[83] (He apparently hit it off with this sort of chap because of his extensive acquaintance with butlers, chauffeurs and grooms.) Charles could also display his father's tetchiness when he felt unappreciated, dismissing as pointless and ill-informed the charge that he had entered a profession that trained for killing. Yet it was easy to see him as a Buchanesque hero – modest, plucky and chivalric. According to his own account, Charles believed in living dangerously and was stupid enough to test himself to the limit. He adored flying, although it was sometimes 'bloody terrifying'. He made a parachute jump (getting his legs briefly entangled in the lines) and went on a 'Tarzan' assault course with the Royal Marines. He embraced hardships afloat and liked being 'made to do ghastly things in force ten gales'. He dived in the Arctic and trekked in Kenya, all in a spirit of 'enlightened masochism'. His passion for the elite sport of polo was undiminished, though at this stage he did say that if his playing attracted serious criticism he might abandon it: 'People's susceptibilities count.'[84] In short, he did much to earn his reputation as a man of action – though he loathed being dubbed 'Action Man', which suggested his resemblance to a boy's uniformed doll made of pliable pink vinyl.

Yet there was something synthetic about the personality that Charles presented to his future subjects. The young Lionheart received elaborate police protection, particularly in his own principality. The daredevil pilot flew aircraft modified for safety and shadowed by RAF emergency services. The intrepid sailor was everywhere at sea. Charles spent some six years in the Royal Navy but he proved an indifferent officer. He was homesick and seasick. He was so cack-handed that a cursing Prince Philip banned him from his own boat. Charles barely mastered the science of navigation and once confessed that 'I appear even more useless than usual.' When he rose in 1976 to command his own ship, a tiny wooden-hulled minesweeper named HMS *Bronington*, the Admiralty had to provide him with an exceptionally proficient crew. But it did not prevent the Prince from getting into several scrapes. In truth he was bored by shipboard life, using his privileged position to escape from it as often as possible. Alternating between bouts of acute self-pity and furious self-assertion, he took his frustrations out on his personal staff. To a slapdash typist he raged: 'I am *fed up* with these mistakes which are thoroughly inexcusable. . . . If it happens again I shall *totally* lose my patience and will do something more drastic about it.'[85] But Charles himself made no sustained effort to excel in the navy, virtually admitting that he was a dilettante: 'I am one of those people who leaps from one thing to another.'[86] His most conspicuous nautical achievement was to grow a beard, which one loyal subject commended because it hid his weak chin. The aspersion rankled,

particularly as Charles was already so sensitive about his jug ears
– immortalised by the cartoonist Marc, who drew him on a mug
with a lug for the handle.

The Bible reading at the investiture had exhorted mortals to
'abstain from the passions of the flesh that wage war against your
soul',[87] and Charles was understandably anxious to conceal his
premarital amatory adventures. Celebrated as the word's most
eligible bachelor, he gave a convincing impersonation of a romantic
prince in search of a perfect princess. There was little pretence in
this, but it did disguise Charles's role as a sexual predator. His
great-uncle Lord Mountbatten famously encouraged him to play
the field, offering Broadlands for the purpose, and the Prince had
affairs with a string of aristocratic young women, known to the
press as 'Charlie's Angels'. He also conducted more fleeting liaisons
with girls of slender means. Not even his valet, Stephen Barry,
who bought Charles everything from condoms to the pancake
make-up he wore to hide hot flushes, could keep track of his
sexual slumming. When Barry, camp even by the standards of the
Queen Mother's queens, knew the owner of female underclothes
found in the Prince's four-poster, he had them laundered and
returned in an Asprey gift box; when the valet could not determine
her identity, he gave them to another member of the palace staff,
later confiding to a gossip columnist that sometimes 'this would
be a gentleman'.[88] Needless to say, both the priapic Prince and
the status-seeking doxies got something out of their brief encounters. Thanks to one inamorata, Zoe Sallis, he even took up Eastern
philosophy, yoga and vegetarianism, prompting his mother to call
him a fool. But Charles was an ungenerous lover, seldom giving
presents or sending flowers. And he was imperiously as well as
cynically exploitative. He summoned and dismissed sleeping partners as though they were odalisques . . . or polo ponies.

Charles was almost equally cavalier with his society mistresses,
who had to accept him on his own terms. When he snapped his
fingers they came running. When he departed on business or
pleasure they had to find their own way home. They learned of
their rejection from the palace telephone operator, who would

tell them that the Prince was unavailable – this sometimes happened, as with Davina Sheffield, Jane Ward and Sarah Spencer, because they attracted unwelcome attention in the newspapers. But male chauvinist and royal egotist though he was, Charles easily fell in love with well-bred young ladies. Clearly his most intense affair was with Camilla Shand. She rejoiced in being the great-granddaughter of the notorious Mrs Keppel, who had had the ear, and not only the ear, of Edward VII. Camilla was a horsey ex-debutante educated in a typically upper-class fashion – her first school was called Dumbrells, the r presumably being silent. Although not beautiful, she was exceptionally sensuous and shared the Prince's liking for bawdy and Goonish humour. Charles still went to bed with his teddy bear and believed that copulation should take place in the dark and in the missionary position. Camilla, who was said to be 'mind-bogglingly good' at sex, nannied him out of his inhibitions, apparently telling him to pretend that she was a rocking horse.[89] At one of the grand houses where they secretly met, the butler saw him with her 'up against a tree doing what Lady Chatterley enjoyed best'.[90] Camilla's very wantonness, however, seemed to disqualify her from marrying Charles, who shared his great-uncle's assumption that only a 'pure' girl could be the future queen. Thus Camilla became Mrs Andrew Parker-Bowles and Charles, while remaining friends with her, continued to sow his wild oats. He sowed with abandon. Mountbatten himself warned that the Prince was 'on the downward slope which wrecked your [great-]Uncle David's life and led to his disgraceful abdication and his futile life ever after'.

This was an apt caution, for since leaving the navy in 1977, Charles had failed to find a constructive way to fill his time. He was not amused, on entering civilian life, by a spoof advertisement that appeared in the *Daily Mail*: 'Situation sought: Prince, 29, degree, ex-Army, Navy, RAF, seeks employment. Will go anywhere, try anything once.'[91] Yet the joke was not far from the truth. Charles was nothing if not energetic, and he thrashed around for something useful to do. But to the intense annoyance of his father, who expressed his feelings in a stream of curt notes, the Prince of Wales lacked a sustained purpose. The endless charade of formal engagements induced in Charles a 'marked melancholy'.[92] He complained that people just wanted to see him, and he sometimes sacrificed duty to pleasure. He skimped on official engagements for the sake of skiing and polo, which, he claimed, kept him sane. But because of playing polo Charles arrived late at Sir Robert Menzies' memorial service and read the wrong lesson. It was, said one of his aides, an 'absolute disaster'.[93] Despite growing public disapproval, he also became more uncompromising about his addiction to blood sports. Killing animals, he asserted, 'doesn't mean that you don't appreciate them fully or want to conserve them'.[94] But when he took part in a boar hunt in Liechtenstein, the Royal Society for the Prevention of Cruelty to Animals dubbed him 'Hooligan of the Year'.

Charles did exert himself over the Queen's Silver Jubilee, a medley of loyal events that, he said, converted him to a belief in the monarchy for the first time. This was a singular confession to make after twenty-five years of the new Elizabethan era, not least because, according to *The Times*, Britons now habitually referred to the Crown in 'tones of half-patronising, half-affectionate mockery'.[95] Anyhow, Charles broadcast appeals. He attended Jubilee balls. He met community leaders, inspected guards of honour and unveiled plaques. He planted trees, on one occasion saying: 'Good luck, tree.' He promoted a Jubilee record in Australia, telling a television presenter who referred to 'your mum' that 'You mean Her Majesty the Queen.'[96] He asked John Betjeman 'to conjure up your muse' for the occasion and construct another of 'your masterpieces of scansion'.[97] However, he also presided over the Silver Jubilee Trust, which raised £16 million but turned out to have similar objects to those of the new Prince's Trust. Thus his two charities were in competition with one another, a muddle that prompted a characteristic explosion from the Duke of Edinburgh. His wrath was understandable, since well-advertised regal bounty played a perennial role in propping up the throne. It deflected criticism of sovereign extravagance and helped to justify lavish state subventions to the Queen and her family. Thus royals could be presented as public benefactors, just as locusts could be seen as a source of food. At a time when the tax exemption of Charles's huge income from the Duchy of Cornwall was being painstakingly concealed from parliament and people, his philanthropic endeavours were patently ham-fisted. They were a messy sweeping of crumbs from the rich man's table.

Charles dabbled in politics with equal insouciance. Indeed, the missives he sent to Westminster and Whitehall, expressing his views in increasingly shrill tones, earned him the title 'Prince of Wails'.[98] Subsequently the trickle of admonition became a flood and the subjects on which he wrote multiplied, ranging from nanotechnology to global warming. Politicians and bureaucrats were often irritated by his letters, which were vehemently incoherent. Despite his professed concern for the English language, Charles had a tin ear for words, alternating between hackneyed phrases and rococo flourishes, and mistaking effusiveness for persuasiveness. Although stubborn and dogmatic, he was too rambling and vacillating to make an effective campaigner. Like his great-uncle David, he was impatient with business routine and careless with official papers. As a courtier said, 'Charles starts things with great enthusiasm. Then he dithers and procrastinates, and he won't make up his mind.'[99] So his office was in a permanent state of chaos and he was slow to deal with replies from ministers and civil servants – sometimes they received no answer at all. Nevertheless they indulged the Prince, leading him to think that his opinions were significant in their own right. The Labour prime minister, James Callaghan, even invited him to a Cabinet meeting, asking how its current proceedings (actually stilted because of the royal presence) would have changed from those of George III's day. Charles responded with a wry smile, 'Well, then I would have been in your chair.'[100] Unable to occupy the seat of power, he was available for other situations and Callaghan tried to find him a worthwhile post. But the prime minister was snubbed by what an aide called this 'arrogant young man'.[101] As Lord McNally recorded, 'beyond a kind of general look-around' in Whitehall, the Prince did not display 'very much enthusiasm for doing a specific job'.[102]

Charles might not have been so aimless if he had received more sensible paternal encouragement. But the Duke found it impossible to control his exasperation with his son, who fiddled with his food and lagged behind when shooting. 'Move your bloody arse!' Philip would bark, to which Charles responded with nothing fiercer than a look of resignation.[103] The Duke was equally splenetic about Charles's habit of reading in bed: he should either sit up and read or lie down and go to sleep. Such decadent behaviour showed that his son was becoming an effeminate fop, as he had always feared – when invited to bring Charles to see the newly done-up Porchester House, Philip had retorted, 'Good God, no. We don't want him knowing about anything pansy like decoration.'[104] Actually Charles was interested in domestic decoration, as appeared when he bought Highgrove and endeavoured to make it the 'outward expression of my inner self'.[105] A sign of that ambition was the sardonic caption to a photograph on his desk that showed him walking one pace behind the Duke: 'I was not made to follow in my father's footsteps.'[106] Instead the Prince sought other father figures. The quest testified to his continuing insecurity at a time when he had never been more popular or acclaimed. In the opinion of *Woman's Realm* he was perhaps the most accomplished thirty-year-old in Britain, a 'twentieth-century Renaissance man . . . actor, sportsman, pilot, musician, artist, orator, academic, wit, sailor and future King'.[107] Although such verdicts buffed up Charles's gold-plated self-esteem, he remained at heart a lost boy in search of direction.

Like other princes, however, he was easily misled by charlatans. None was more fraudulent than Armand Hammer, the American oil magnate and art collector. He was notorious for unscrupulous commercial dealings and his companies were among the worst industrial polluters on earth. Suspected of being a Soviet agent, he was found guilty of making illegal contributions to President Nixon's final presidential election campaign. But Hammer created his own legend and used philanthropy, with some success, to buy respectability. He contributed millions of pounds to Charles's favourite charities, notably to the United World Colleges, founded by Kurt Hahn for the promotion of international understanding. He also whisked the Prince around by private jet, deluged him with presents and even laid on painting lessons to improve his wishy-washy watercolours – a contrast to his father's bold, bright daubs. Charles was '*enormously* touched' by Hammer's munificence and signed his letters, 'With warmest best wishes and everlasting gratitude'.[108] By way of further thanks the Prince proposed that Hammer should become the godfather of his first child, though this was eventually deemed inadvisable. However, in 1988 he did comfort Hammer when an explosion killed 167 men on the North Sea Piper Alpha oil platform, which was owned and badly maintained by Hammer's company Occidental. 'You must not blame yourself,' said Charles redundantly.[109] Later the Prince cooled towards the tycoon. But he was long in thrall to a man who had an unsavoury reputation at the time and who was subsequently exposed as one of the greatest confidence tricksters of the century.

Charles was equally taken in by his mentor Laurens van der Post, who did become a godfather to his firstborn. The South African, having won fame with his book *Venture into the Interior* (1952), had transformed himself from author into shaman. He preached salvation through mystical communion with the inner self, which incorporated the Great Memory, Jung's collective unconscious. Spiritual fulfilment was best accomplished, said van der Post, in the world of nature, uncontaminated by the materialism of a sick technological civilisation. This was a message, at once radical and retrogressive, that strongly appealed to Charles. He became a disciple of the messianic Afrikaner, who hailed him as a 'great Prince' and a future priest-king. Charles ventured into Kenya's Aberdare Mountains with van der Post, and later went on safari with him through the Kalahari Desert. In the wilderness, intoned his guide, the Prince could draw 'closer to the original blueprint and plan of life' and thus prepare for his redeeming role. Charles was not alone in being duped by van der Post

– Margaret Thatcher listened to him open-mouthed. But the sage was a patent fake. His mystagogy was part of a larger mythomania. Fantasy was his native element and lying, said a friend, 'seemed as automatic and necessary to him as breathing'. Van der Post invented his origins, his name, his early experiences and his expertise in Bushman lore. He concocted a heroic war record, promoting himself to colonel and claiming to have been called 'Lawrence of Abyssinia'. And he posed as a seer while being a satyr, sexually voracious enough to rape a fourteen-year-old girl entrusted to his care. Charles might have guessed that he was being gulled when *Private Eye* put bogus aphorisms into his guru's mouth – 'Only in the sea of silence can we find the fish of peace' – and had the hapless heir of sorrows answer, 'How very true.' But he was deluded by the ingratiating attentions of the older man, who sympathised with him for having been starved of 'spontaneous natural affection', provided some kind of psychoanalytical interpretation of his dreams and put him in touch with his true 'being'. Charles never lost faith in this false prophet, who had, in Lord Mountbatten's opinion, 'a Jesus Christ complex'.[110]

Mountbatten, who was the Prince's chief counsellor and 'honorary grandfather', knew whereof he spoke. As Supreme Commander in South East Asia during the war, he had gloried in the hosannas of a flock of acolytes known as the 'Dickie Birds', and as the last Viceroy of India he had felt 'endowed with almost heavenly power'.[111] Certainly Mountbatten had exercised more power than any other member of the royal family, and he had no difficulty in captivating the Prince of Wales. Handsome, charming and rich, he cultivated Charles's company and encouraged his confidences. In due course the Prince felt free to tell him anything, and he clearly found cosy chats with his great-uncle more congenial than his father's brusque memoranda. Mountbatten's progressive sentiments appealed to him, especially as they were alloyed with unfeigned devotion to the trappings of majesty – a devotion shared by Mountbatten's valet, who recorded that pulling off Queen Elizabeth II's gumboots at Broadlands was 'a glorious moment in my life'.[112]

The old proconsul's worldly advice seemed the quintessence of wisdom to Charles, whom he almost inveigled into marrying his granddaughter Amanda Knatchbull. Apparently the Prince did not see this as another dynastic plot hatched by a devious and ambitious schemer. He maintained, indeed, that Mountbatten was 'incredibly honest'.[113] This was an extraordinary misapprehension, particularly as most members of the royal family saw through 'Tricky Dickie'.[114] So did others subjected to endless embellishments of his legend. One senior lady-in-waiting refused to sit next to him at palace banquets, saying that if she heard 'one more account of how Dickie won the war, I'd scream'.[115] Anthony Eden, who also knew whereof he spoke, described Mountbatten as a congenital liar. General Sir Gerald Templer asserted bluntly: 'You're so crooked, Dickie, that if you swallowed a nail you'd shit a corkscrew.'[116] Yet Charles was spellbound by Mountbatten's 'unique personality'. He was correspondingly devastated by his death in August 1979 at the hands of IRA assassins, whom Charles called 'sub-human extremists'.[117] The Duke of Edinburgh thought his show of grief self-indulgent, especially as it made him late for lunch before their journey to receive Mountbatten's body on its return from Ireland. When Charles finally appeared, Philip upset guests and staff by baiting him in an attempt to put steel into his spine. As the son left the table in tears, the father remarked: 'Perhaps now he won't cry at the funeral.'[118]

No doubt Charles was also weeping for himself. The loss of one of the mainstays of his existence left him both unhappy and unbalanced. His misery accentuated his eccentricity. He became more prone to fads, banning mango ice cream, experimenting with herbal remedies, amassing varieties of honey. His moods swung sharply from warm affability to violent rage – like his grandfather George VI, Charles cursed footmen in public and threw things at them in private. He banged his fist on the desk in his dysfunctional office and demanded to know what was wrong with everyone. The Prince's need for support and reassurance grew. He sought David Hockney's opinion of his watercolours and urged on Tom Stoppard 'a most frightfully funny idea for a play' – about a hotel for people with phobias.[119] Charles invited approval by displays of humility and by paying himself back-handed compliments. He claimed, for example, in a conceit worthy of Mountbatten, that many people said after meeting him: 'Good Lord, you're not nearly as pompous as I thought you were going to be.'[120] His remoteness from mundane matters surprised even his servants. He did not know where the kitchens were in Buckingham Palace. When his father told him to put more than a miserly pound in the church collection plate and his valet gave him a £5 note, Charles, who had never seen one before, asked: 'What's this?'[121] He relied more than ever on his small circle of discreet friends, some of whom were prepared (as the old joke went) to lay down their wives for their future king. Camilla Parker-Bowles in particular provided him with rather more than a shoulder to cry on after Mountbatten's murder. She proved a more amenable mistress than Charles's latest lover, Anna 'Whiplash' Wallace, who refused to put up with his other dalliances. Such was his passion for Camilla that he scarcely bothered to hide their renewed liaison. In 1980 he even took her to the Zimbabwe independence celebrations, where their blatant flirting and fumbling amused some witnesses and appalled others.

Charles's parents were relaxed about the presence of a mistress but agitated by the prospect of a scandal. In such circumstances the customary solution was to marry off the erring prince with all deliberate speed. As it happened, Charles had already said that thirty was the right age for a person such as himself to take a wife, who must be chosen with care because their union would be for life and she might some day be queen. Now, moreover, it seemed that a suitable girl had caught his eye. She was Lady Diana Spencer, the youngest sister of his old flame Sarah and the daughter of the eighth Earl Spencer. Her family was linked to his by blood and old acquaintance: Charles's great-uncle had described Diana's grandfather as 'the world's biggest snob'.[122] Her close relations held court positions and, having been born at Sandringham (in 1961), Diana was familiar with the royal scene. She was the soul of empathy, commiserating with Charles over the loss of

Mountbatten and ingratiating herself with the Queen Mother. Visiting Balmoral, Diana seemed to share his love of country life and his reverence for nature. Significantly, too, she favoured intuition over intellect. Her mind was unblemished by education (Diana's most notable academic achievement had been to win a school prize for the best-kept guinea pig) and she presented Charles with a blank sheet on which to inscribe his ideas. Charming, giggling and ravishing, she was young enough to be sexually inexperienced. In the Prince's set virgins were as rare as mermaids and, according to the rusty canons of the Palace, a future queen must have no past. Camilla Parker-Bowles apparently encouraged Charles to see Diana as a winsome child fit to be moulded into a consort who would keep him young. Touched by Diana's obvious adoration, he termed her 'a perfect poppet'.[123]

Yet a moment's serious reflection should have been enough to show that she was anything but an ideal mate. From the time of Sarah, Duchess of Marlborough, matriarch and termagant, the Spencers had been a headstrong clan. The Queen Mother herself pronounced them difficult, perhaps reflecting on the seventh earl's scandalous treatment of the bones of his ancestors, which he cleared out of the crowded family vault in Great Brington church and incinerated. In 1969, Johnnie, the eighth earl, divorced his wife on grounds of desertion and, despite counteraccusations of cruelty, got custody of their four children. An unruly brood, Diana and her siblings, including her little brother Charles, feuded with a succession of wretched nannies. The domestic turmoil worsened when their father married Raine, Countess of Dartmouth, daughter of the novelist Barbara Cartland, whose throbbing romances coloured Diana's imagination. With some justice the young Spencers called their fearsome new stepmother 'Acid' Raine. Spoilt yet deprived, Diana wallowed in unhappiness. She was not just the casualty of a broken home but the victim of volatile emotions. Whether weeping, sulking, plotting or raging, she developed a will of quicksilver. After Swiss finishing school, where all she learned was skiing, Diana flitted from party to part-time job, mainly looking after young children. With the girls who shared her London flat she indulged in japes such as tele-phoning people with odd names or smearing friends' cars with flour and eggs. Even by the standards of 'Sloane Rangers', county women about town, Diana was painfully naïve. Nevertheless, she turned the pulp-fiction dream of marrying the Prince of Wales into a reality.

Predictably, Charles could not make up his mind about whether to propose to her. Friends warned him that Diana was unstable and intractable – they would later call her 'the mad cow'.[124] His sister Anne considered her a silly girl. He himself was perturbed by Diana's immaturity and vacuity – she disliked people who were wrinkly or brainy and her notion of using her head was to change her hairstyle. The couple shared few tastes, as her fanciful catalogue of what they had in common revealed: 'Music, opera and outdoor sports including fishing, walking and polo.'[125] He was unwilling to break with Camilla. On the other hand, Diana's allure was palpable. She gleamed like a film star. Although as thick as a plank (by her own confession), she was canny and funny, flirting outrageously and enjoying a dirty joke as much as he did. She possessed a coltish vivacity but assuaged his hurts with maternal tenderness. She seemed to comprehend the holiness of the heart's affections. In any case, it was the Prince's duty to perpetuate the dynasty. As Charles hummed and hawed amid an orgy of press speculation, his father intervened. With his usual finesse he wrote telling Charles either to ask for Diana's hand, which would please his family and the country, or to let her go. The Prince bitterly resented the Duke's letter, afterwards carrying it around in his pocket to show friends that he had been the victim of an ultimatum. Charles was indeed being jockeyed into matrimony, with the apparent collusion of his mother, who, a courtier would charge, paid less attention to mating her children than to mating her horses. As always, the Prince submitted to his destiny. He hoped for happiness and convinced himself that he was in love – 'whatever "in love" means', the aspirant philosopher-king would famously add in a television interview. On 6 February 1981, in the pale-green cocoon of the palace nursery, Charles asked Diana to marry him. She accepted at once and they sealed the betrothal with a chaste kiss.

The 'royal romance', intoned *The Times*, should 'give pleasure to all but the stoniest of hearts'. The bride-to-be was 'eminently suitable' and it was fitting that the Prince should embark on matrimony now that the monarchy was generally 'regarded as an exemplar of the family'.[126] This seemed a modest enough plaudit as public euphoria mounted over the impending nuptials. In truth, though, Charles's engagement was so forlorn that he might well have cancelled the wedding had there been no need to satisfy popular expectations. But to lead his subjects he had to follow them. So he quelled the doubts prompted by Diana's increasingly erratic behaviour. Incarcerated in Mabel Anderson's former apartments in Buckingham Palace to protect her from the media, she moped, fretted and wept. She complained of boredom and loneliness. She resented the Falklands War for diverting attention from her. She also lost weight, showing the first symptoms of bulimia, the psychosomatic compulsion to gorge and vomit that would plague her for years. Preoccupied with his own activities, including a tour of Australia, Charles saw Diana only about a dozen times before the wedding. He tried to sympathise with her, attributing her moodiness to nerves and stress. But a self-absorbed bachelor, prematurely middle-aged and accustomed to being the world's cynosure, was ill-equipped to solace her. Moreover, she resisted help, let alone counsel. When Robert Runcie, the Archbishop of Canterbury, talked of abstract ideas, he saw 'her eyes clouding over'. Even courtiers who tried to show her the ropes were amazed by Diana's encyclopedic ignorance, to say nothing of her preference for consorting with servants. As one shrewd observer noted, Charles himself was now 'seriously depressed'.[127] He seems to have had a final fling with Camilla, of whom Diana was insanely jealous. At any rate, he spent much of the night dancing with his mistress at the pre-wedding ball, at which 'Charlie's aunt', as Princess Margaret amusingly dubbed herself, attached a balloon to her tiara and his brother

Andrew dispensed a cocktail tastefully called 'A Long Slow Comfortable Screw up against the Throne'.

Yet nothing could dim the glory of the wedding, which Archbishop Runcie himself described as 'the stuff of which fairy tales are made'. It was a brilliant episode in the continuing royal melodrama, watched on television by 750 million people all round the world. London was a carnival in red, white and blue. The procession was a tableau from the Field of the Cloth of Gold. St Paul's was an alabaster rhapsody studded with gems. The ceremony was a masterpiece of pomp and circumstance. The bride, in her frothy wedding gown of ivory silk taffeta and antique lace, looked exquisite. The groom, immaculate in blue naval uniform and sash, was nervous and (like her) fluffed one or two lines. But the jubilation of the multitude outside, roaring and waving plastic Union Jacks, could be heard within the cathedral when Diana said: 'I will.' Everywhere parties celebrated the event, which seemed to mark an epoch in the life of the nation. It is true that some dissident voices were raised during Margaret Thatcher's summer of discontent, a time of high unemployment and urban riots. Writers such as Jan Morris and Patrick White condemned the extravagance and escapism of the wedding, 'a kind of rosy women's weekly romance to lull the more soft-centred of us, and distract us from reality'. Dame Edna Everage, alter ego of the comedian Barry Humphries, quipped that 'Charles's Di is cast'. Republicans boycotted the proceedings and hawkers sold T-shirts bearing the motto 'I hate Prince Charles'. But most Britons anticipated the fairy-tale conclusion, mentioned in Runcie's address, and hoped that the couple would live happily ever after.

The Archbishop was shrewd enough to add, however, that marriage was not the end: it was after the vows that 'the adventure really begins'.[128] Like many horror stories, it began brightly. There were moments of joy, and even, over the years, prolonged passages of cheerfulness. The Princess wrote that she could not have been happier or felt more wonderful during their honeymoon cruise on the royal yacht *Britannia*, an ocean-going palace that the Queen's family considered 'a necessity, and not a luxury'.[129]

Charles and Diana 'spent most of the time giggling and mobbing each other up'. They often watched a video of the wedding, which made them 'practically blub'. And Charles overcame her spasms of depression with 'patience and kindness'.[130] As her eating disorder intensified, however, his patience frayed. He was baffled by the malady. He was disappointed by Diana's inability to discuss his cherished current reading, van der Post's novels. Moreover, what she allegedly called his 'roll on, roll off'[131] sexual performances may have been as unsatisfying to him as to her – smelling as she did of vomit and toothpaste. Charles could not understand why Diana was (in her own argot) 'shitting bricks' over the prospect of their final honeymoon destination, Balmoral, and he was shocked by her loathing for it. Whereas he regarded this Highland sanctuary as the best place in the world, she found it a purgatory of stuffed-shirt dullness. She felt diminished by her husband's parents: 'He was in awe of his Mama, intimidated by his father, and I was always the third person in the room.'[132]

Charles became the victim of her anger and anomie. Increasingly she behaved, in the words of a royal cousin, like 'a bat from hell'. According to one account, Diana became so enraged by the sight of Charles kneeling beside their bed to say his prayers that she hit him over the head with the family Bible. On another occasion she ran after his Land Rover shrieking: 'Yes, dump me like garbage. Leave me on my own again. Run off and have lunch with your precious Mummy.'[133] In the words of a courtier, Charles was 'absolutely stunned by Diana. . . . He thought he was marrying a docile, compliant, sweet-natured, adoring girl. He woke up with a dominant, determined woman who did not hesitate to rant and rave if she wasn't getting her own way.'[134] Faced with tantrums resembling epileptic fits, Charles sought psychiatric help, calling in a Jungian friend of van der Post's named Dr Alan McGlashan. He could do nothing about the major source of her anguish. 'Obsessed by Camilla, totally,' explained Diana in her characteristic telegraphese. 'Didn't trust him, thought every five minutes he was ringing her up asking how to handle his marriage.' She had grounds for suspicion. Few of the gewgaws that preoccupy royalty loom larger than cufflinks – the Prince of Wales thought nothing of sending a valet halfway across the country to retrieve a forgotten pair. So Diana was incensed when Camilla gave Charles cufflinks decorated with entwined Cs, which he tried to palm off as 'a present from a friend'.[135]

By autumn 1981, however, Diana was pregnant and Charles enjoyed some respite from the rows. She now had an understandable reason to be sick and he displayed rare tenderness. They collaborated on refurbishing Highgrove and he accepted her fashionable choice of interior designer Dudley Poplak. Charles taught Diana to appreciate opera, while she smartened up his clothes and haircut. For some time he tried to accommodate her passions and prejudices, dropping old friends whom she disliked, sacking faithful servants who somehow offended her, even getting rid of his much-loved Labrador, Harvey, who had made messes on some of the finest carpets in Britain. Following the novel custom, Charles attended the birth of his son William, saying afterwards that 'I really felt as though I had shared deeply in the process.' Diana, who suffered from post-natal depression, later sneered that he only got off his polo pony in order to see the baby emerging from 'the engine room'.[136] In fact Charles exerted himself to be a progressive parent and to forge a loving family, taking an active part in William's infant rituals. This provoked a snort from the Duke of Edinburgh: 'You'd think that the Prince of Wales could find more gainful ways of employing himself than bathing his son, when the boy already has a nanny to do such monumental tasks for him.'[137] Diana herself used William, and later Harry (born in 1984), in renewed hostilities with Charles. Her excuse was that their upbringing, relaxed in T-shirt and jeans, should be as little like his as possible – whereas he remained viscerally royal, going so far as to design a special livery for the staff at Highgrove. However, Diana was as neurotically driven to attack her husband as to attack herself. This she did in a series of distressing incidents after William's birth, cutting her body with sharp implements and making apparent suicide bids.

Charles was distraught, bewildered by Diana's violent impulses

and harrowed by the domestic discord. He instigated more psycho-
therapy, but she would not endure it for long. Instead, in a wicked
parody of his penchant for alternative medicine, she would seek
salvation from every quack cure under the sun: aromatherapy,
reflexology, homeopathy, astrology, occultism, acupuncture, chiro-
practic, shiatsu, t'ai chi, crystal healing and colonic irrigation, the
last of which allegedly dealt with her inner rage. Nothing moder-
ated Diana's behaviour towards Charles, who rivalled her in
narcissism. He remained frigidly aloof when she scorned his artistic
interests and idealistic preoccupations. He ignored her when,
seeing him in gardening clothes, she asked: 'Who is getting the
benefit of your wisdom today? The sheep or the raspberry
bushes?'[138] He tried to maintain his dignity in the face of her
contemptuous nicknames, 'The Boy Wonder', 'The Great White
Hope'[139] and 'Killer Wales' – she also called the Queen 'Brenda'
(*Private Eye*'s alias) and the Duke 'Stavros'. Charles kept a stiff
upper lip when she mocked him for having done nothing to earn
the medals by which he set such store. But he did sometimes
retaliate, demanding to know why she was crying now or whether
her food would reappear later. He frowned on her horseplay and
refused to laugh at her jokes. He was stung by her outbursts of
obscene invective – Diana called him 'barking mad,'[140] 'fucking
selfish' and a 'pathetic old fart'.[141] 'Why the fuck can't you go
to work like every other husband,' she once screamed, 'and get
out from under my fucking feet?'[142] 'How dare you talk to me
like that!' Charles expostulated in another of their quarrels, during
which he apparently flung a bootjack at her. 'Do you realise who
I am?'[143]

He was galled still further when she upstaged him in public,
transforming herself from capricious harpy into a glamour idol
who entranced individuals, mesmerised crowds and dazzled the
Argus eye of the camera. Charles let his jealousy show, especially
on foreign tours, each one a matter of political moment, he insisted,
and 'not just a social junket'.[144] Personally outshone, he also
found that Diana put his charities in the shade. She espoused
increasingly headline-grabbing causes, such as care for victims of

AIDS and anti-personnel mines, while displaying an instinctive compassion for the sick and suffering that he could not emulate. Charles vented his ire on his staff. During a visit to Canada aboard *Britannia* in 1983, for example, he flew into a fury with his secretary, Michael Colborne, shouting and kicking the furniture. Colborne's crime had been to devote too much time to the Princess while neglecting the Prince – who afterwards apologised for his behaviour, though it led to Colborne's resignation. Charles also became more rancorous towards the press, which noted Diana's 'wobblies' and recorded the first sight of him with Camilla after the royal wedding, at the Vale of the White Horse Hunt in November 1981. He yelled at reporters, 'When are you bloody people going to leave me alone!'[145] It was a futile *cri de coeur* since the newshounds themselves were in full cry. They scented a whiff of despair, though they did not detect when first Charles sought refuge from his marital miseries inside (as he later put it) Camilla's trousers. He subsequently claimed that their adultery did not take place until his marriage had irretrievably collapsed. Diana, herself a consummate muckraker and spy, believed that it occurred at least as early as 1984, when she told Camilla: 'I know exactly what is going on between you and Charles. I wasn't born yesterday.'[146]

Charles pursued other forms of escape. As he recorded in a book about Highgrove, he made classical additions to the house but he put his heart and soul and back into the garden, pruning and raking and digging for both physical and spiritual exercise. Following the natural rhythms of the 'wheel of life', he wrote, 'I felt like a man with a mission.' The cultivation of the soil was a form of worship, and organic gardening, which respected 'complex, universal laws', bore a character that was 'almost sacred'.[147] No doubt Charles dwelt on all this in the tranquillity of his pseudo-Gothic pavilion at Highgrove, where he fled from connubial strife, lit candles and indulged in meditation. But meditating is to thinking as drowning is to swimming; and it is clear that the Prince, though he prided himself on feeling 'very strongly and deeply about things',[148] avoided strenuous mental exercise. This emerged in his speeches, which the *Economist* described as lightweight constructs full of 'random observations and clichés'.[149] It also appeared during business meetings, where his attention wandered and he gazed out of the window, particularly when the weather was fine. With the zeal of admirers of the Emperor's new clothes, courtiers reiterated that the Prince, and all other members of the royal family, worked very hard. A dispassionate glance at their daily routine might have dispelled the illusion. However, as a palace aide confessed, Charles's entourage used 'a lot of deceit'[150] to hide the fact that he spent so much time and energy on sport and leisure. He did, though, make increasingly contentious forays into public life. Perhaps this was because he felt so helpless about his private life. But he also felt impelled to promote his own brand of princely wisdom, an abstract version of his organically produced Duchy Original oatmeal biscuits.

Charles shared contemporary concerns about the decline of his mother's realm, fearing that it would become a fourth-rate country and 'motivated by a desperate desire to put the "Great" back into Great Britain'. Like his father, he found the attitudes of his compatriots 'unbearably exasperating'.[151] Particular bêtes noires were idle workers, obstructive trade unionists, intrusive bureaucrats and complacent business leaders. 'I like to stir things up,' Charles said, 'to throw a proverbial royal brick through the inviting plate glass of pompous professional pride.'[152] But the only proverbial royal bricks were the ones he dropped. His initiatives were rash enough to cause the resignation of his private secretary, Edward Adeane, after a blazing row. They were also sharply regressive, even by the antique standards that he cherished. The Prince, unlike the Duke, had no faith in a technological future. So his crusades were imbued with acute nostalgia for a feudal past – though national recovery could no more be achieved by a return to peasant farming than by a revival of jousting. As one commentator noted, Charles wanted to 'accelerate backwards'[153] most rapidly in the field of architecture.

In 1984, at a celebration in Hampton Court Palace to mark the 150th anniversary of the Royal Institute of British Architects

(RIBA), he initiated his campaign against modernist design by famously declaring that a scheme to extend the National Gallery in Trafalgar Square was like 'a monstrous carbuncle on the face of a much-loved and elegant friend'.[154] He grew more vituperative with the years. At least when the Luftwaffe destroyed British buildings, he said, 'it didn't replace them with anything more offensive than rubble'.[155] According to the style connoisseur Stephen Bayley, Prince Charles attached to avant-garde architects 'the sort of revulsion due to paedophiles'.[156] Certainly he damaged the careers of some, notably Richard Rogers, by using open and covert influence to sabotage plans that violated his traditionalist criteria. Yet the Prince's principles made about as much sense as the Athanasian Creed. For example, his rubric that new buildings must be in keeping with their surroundings would have precluded the construction of St Paul's Cathedral, a luminous, numinous gem that must at all costs be preserved, Charles affirmed, in its current setting.[157] He said that Dharavi, one of the largest slums in Mumbai, was superior to Western architecture as a model for housing people in the developing world because of its 'underlying intuitive grammar of design'.[158] Naturally his denunciations of glass boxes and steel dustbins, hideous creations of an arrogant elite, won him support in the salon and the saloon bar. But to his chagrin, many professionals dismissed the forms he advocated – Greek pediments, Etruscan columns, Roman porticos – as at best neoclassical pastiche and at worst the architecture of authoritarianism. In due course Charles retaliated by building a model town named Poundbury on Duchy land near Dorchester. It was widely derided as a pretentious hybrid: 'the Parthenon meets Brookside'.[159] The town's regulations, which included a ban on satellite dishes and ball games, were evidently a product of Georgian paternalism tinged with green fascism. Poundbury had its defenders, but Dorset folk called it 'Charlieville'.

Prince Charles admired King George III and shared his salient characteristic, high-minded pig-headedness. Having scrupulously opposed all innovation apart from trying to revive the Crown's defunct prerogatives, George had been, as Walter Bagehot said, a 'consecrated obstruction'. Charles was equally sure that he was on the side of righteousness, which sanctioned, if it did not sanctify, his obstinacy. But his convictions were never sustained by exertions and all too often his projects ended in embarrassment. Charles's architectural magazine *Perspectives* quickly collapsed. His Institute of Architecture, which aimed to provide an alternative form of professional education focusing on buildings that 'appeal to the human heart',[160] proved a costly fiasco. It failed to win formal approval from the RIBA, and after internal ructions it was subsumed into the Prince's Foundation for the Built Environment. This charity also had a chequered history. Recently, for example, having accepted fees to advise developers about model urban communities in Scotland, it objected to a local planning decision that permitted only low-density housing in a national park.[161] As critics pointed out, there was an obvious conflict between the Foundation's commercial interests and its ecological objectives.

Lucre otherwise tarnished Charles's reputation as a green prince. To the shock of villagers in Newton St Loe, he backed a recent plan to build 2,000 houses on a neighbouring environmentally friendly farm owned by the Duchy, which reportedly stood to make £100 million from the deal.[162] The Duchy has supported schemes (opposed respectively by English Heritage and the Cornwall Wildlife Trust, of which, ironically, the Prince is patron) to impose a multimillion-pound ferry terminal on the historic seafront area of Penzance and to construct a housing estate on an animal sanctuary outside Newquay. It has also sanctioned the cultivation of non-native Pacific oysters in the Helford River, thus blighting a special area of conservation and posing 'a serious threat to the local habitat'.[163] Furthermore, many of the products Charles sold turned out not to be strictly organic after all, and some appeared to deserve their nickname, 'Dodgy Originals'. Edzard Ernst, Professor of Complementary Medicine at Exeter, described the Duchy's herbal tincture containing dandelion and artichoke, which was advertised to help 'eliminate toxins', as 'outright quackery'. 'Products like these are a dangerous waste of money,' he said. 'Charles is exploiting people during hard times.'[164]

During the mid-1980s, as the Prince increasingly sought relief from domestic mayhem via outside activities, he caused offence in high places. The Queen was indignant when she learned of his plan to attend a papal mass in the Vatican and, much to his annoyance, nipped this ecumenical enterprise in the bud. The prime minister fumed about his scheme to forge closer links with Middle Eastern countries by personal contact with their royal rulers, and insisted that diplomacy should be conducted through official channels. Regarding Charles as a complete 'wet', Margaret Thatcher resented his support for traditional methods of primary education and complained to the Palace when, with inner cities in mind, he spoke in America of a 'divided Britain'.[165] Since her policies favoured the rich at the expense of the poor, he had a point. But the more apt his criticisms were, the more Charles was accused of unconstitutional interference. Since Britain has no written constitution, the degree to which royal influence can legitimately be exerted is a matter of opinion based on precedent, some of it invented. Plainly, though, Charles himself was divisive when the *raison d'être* of constitutional monarchy is to unify. It was hard to see how a partisan prince could become a neutral king. So Charles was wrong even if he was right. His strictures on stubble-burning and the New English Bible, and indeed on some modern buildings, were doubtless sound; but they gave gratuitous offence to, respectively, farmers, clerics and architects. His sympathy for those out of work did credit to his heart, but it recalled his great-uncle David's commiseration with unemployed South Wales miners, which seemed a challenge to Stanley Baldwin's government shortly before the abdication. Charles provoked a brutal response from the ultra-Tory Norman Tebbit, who said that his dangerous political intervention on behalf of the jobless was understandable, since he himself had 'got no job'.[166]

As Margaret Thatcher's premiership drew to its close, however, most people did not take the Prince of Wales that seriously. *Private Eye* satirised his woolly idealism, giving him this catchphrase to sum up the horrid realities of the contemporary scene: 'It really is appalling.' The popular press, which charted his retreats back to nature, portrayed him as a tree-hugging loon who would sit cross-legged on the throne wearing a kaftan and eating muesli. It mocked Charles's half-baked transcendentalism, typified by his feeling that 'deep in the soul of mankind there is a reflection as on the surface of a mirror, of a mirror-calm lake, of the beauty and harmony of the universe'.[167] It poked fun at his inconsistencies: the conservationist drove a gas-guzzling Aston Martin; the simple-lifer loved luxury yachts; the apostle of duty was devoted to skiing. Despite losing a friend in a fatal accident off-piste at Klosters in 1988, Charles later threatened to spend his whole life on the slopes if fox-hunting was outlawed at home. Yet the public, which still generally regarded him with fond respect, was indulgent about his crotchets. Fits of pique were the prerogative of princes and added to the gaiety of nations. Furthermore, Charles's eruptions identified him as his father's son, though he was more magnanimous than the Duke. The Prince was burdened, as one commentator wrote, 'with a hyper-sensitive conscience', which impelled him to intervene 'on a range of oddball issues'.[168] But only those involved felt much hostility to him on that account. What did it matter if Charles was, as the novelist Julian Barnes said, an 'odd fish'?[169]

It did matter when popular opinion turned against the Prince as his marriage disintegrated. Attempts were made to conceal the process, and media lackeys such as Sir Alastair Burnet obligingly declared that the royal partnership worked. But Charles's body language told a different story: on television he looked tortured, squirming, grimacing and referring to Diana as 'another person'. In private, too, he could hardly bear to mention his wife by name: 'It's agony to know that someone is hating it all so much. . . . It is like being trapped in a rather desperate cul-de-sac.'[170] Their mutual antipathy became ever more apparent as they led increasingly separate lives, Charles at Highgrove, Diana at Kensington Palace. In 1987 the press reported that he spent well over a month at Balmoral, away from his wife and children. Evidently he endured severance from the boys to avoid emotional upset: on one occasion William exclaimed, 'I hate you, Papa. I hate you so much. Why do you make Mummy cry all the time?'[171] Charles tried to preserve the decencies. He and Diana travelled separately but changed into one car so that they could arrive together when taking the eight-year-old William to prep school at Ludgrove. Characteristically, Charles subjected his own sons to boarding discipline despite his ordeal at Cheam, to say nothing of the verdict of one distinguished old boy that Ludgrove was 'a Belsen of the spirit'.[172] But he felt their pain. In 1992 Charles told his grandmother: 'It very nearly finished me off completely, seeing those two pathetic little figures standing in the drive waving forlornly as I drove away.'[173] Perhaps he thought that they would benefit by removal from the domestic cockpit, where his temper battled against their mother's temperament. Once, when berating the butler for revealing his whereabouts to Diana, a puce-faced Charles stamped his foot and screamed: 'I am the Prince of Wales and I will be king!'[174] It was no help to the children, Highgrove staff thought, that both parents were 'off their rockers'.[175]

As it became harder to hide the breakdown of his relationship with Diana, Charles was especially incensed by her manipulation of the media. She secretly briefed sympathetic journalists, who portrayed him as a selfish spouse, which was true, and an indifferent parent, which was false. She used her good causes to steal his thunder, generating publicity through stunts such as shaking hands with lepers or hugging sick infants – the smartest of all fashion accessories. On joint tours she totally eclipsed him, not least by posing in front of the Taj Mahal alone – apart from a huge posse of photographers. And when she made a semi-official visit to Egypt on her own in May 1992, newspapers reported that her aircraft, financed by the tax-payer, went via Turkey to take Charles and a party of friends on one of his many holidays. The Prince of Wales increasingly allowed his vexation with her to show. But at a time when the marriages of his sister Anne and his brother Andrew were on the rocks, he evidently thought it vital to preserve his own. So he turned a blind eye to Diana's adulteries while pursuing his affair with Camilla, whose husband Andrew, himself not notorious for monogamy and once Silver Stick in Waiting to the Queen, seems to have been equally complaisant. Charles even behaved politely to Diana's most virile lover, her 'riding instructor' Captain James Hewitt, although he was (as she herself later acknowledged) 'about as interesting as a knitting pattern'.[176] Driven by her daemon, however, the Princess brought the whole edifice of her marriage crashing to the ground. By devious means she confided in a minor royal hack, Andrew Morton, who in June 1992 published a sensational account of her failed union entitled *Diana – Her True Story*. It was, of course, her *own* story. But it plausibly told how an unfeeling and unfaithful husband had 'crushed her spirit'.[177] The book generated a wave of ill-feeling towards Charles, whose unfitness to be king was widely canvassed. The *Economist* said that many feared he had 'a bug in his software'.[178] A tabloid cartoon showed Charles saying to his plants, 'I need hardly tell you how worried I am about my wife's state of mind.'[179]

Soon afterwards the press published the transcript of an intimate telephone conversation between Diana and another lover (James Gilbey, an upper-class car salesman, who called her Squidgy) in which she expressed aversion towards her husband's 'fucking family'[180] and proposed to make a dramatic escape from married bondage. It is still not clear who was responsible for the original tape-recording, though the finger of suspicion points at rogue agents of the state. But there is no doubt that Charles was shocked and humiliated by the revelation of his cuckoldry. He stopped taking the newspapers and wandered round in a daze, tormented by having made such a gross marital mistake and sometimes calling unannounced at the houses of friends for counsel and sympathy. Even the Duke of Edinburgh commiserated with him. The Duke also suggested to Diana that her conduct had driven Charles back into the arms of Camilla, whom he had earlier left at 'a considerable sacrifice' to himself. If this was hardly calculated to reconcile the royal couple, the ducal mediator did at least tell Diana that a man in his son's position was silly to risk everything for a mistress, and that 'I cannot imagine anyone in their right mind leaving you for Camilla.'[181] By this time, however, Charles and other members of his family had concluded that Diana was mentally deranged. Indeed, she was 'bloody crazy'[182] and completely out of control. So, towards the end of what Queen Elizabeth famously described as her *annus horribilis*, which culminated in a fire at Windsor Castle and a decision that the sovereign should pay tax, the separation of the Prince and Princess of Wales was officially announced. According to the prime minister, John Major, there was no constitutional reason why Diana should not eventually be queen. The public was unconvinced, and in Charles's view, his mad wife had to be 'written out of the script'.[183]

In January 1993, when the recording of a telephone conversation between the Prince and his mistress was published, he himself seemed about to be written out of the script. The so-called 'Camillagate tape' of their long-distance tête-à-tête was advertised as 'six minutes that could cost Charles the throne'.[184] Opinion polls showed that a third of the population considered him unfit to be king. Some proposed excluding him from the succession (in favour of William) on the grounds that he had broken his marital vows and therefore could not be trusted to keep his coronation oath. Of course, as Charles himself said, he was not the first Prince of Wales to have had a mistress. But he was the first to have an adulterous dialogue broadcast to the nation, replete with sexual intimacies ('I want to feel my way along you') and gusts of vanity ('your great achievement is to love me').[185] He was also the first to circulate, albeit involuntarily, a quip about his apotheosis as a tampon. This made Charles a global figure of fun. A British cartoon showed the Prince's plants begging him to 'Talk Dirty to Us!'.[186] An American television show, *Saturday Night Live*, featured a sketch in which Mick Jagger, dressed as a footman, presented a Camilla impersonator with a box of tampons on a silver salver. Italians called Charles Prince Tampacchino. Curiously enough, he toyed with the idea of going to live in Tuscany, giving up everything and capitulating to malign fate. Never in his adult life had Charles been so mortified. Never had his well-developed *amour propre* been so battered. Never had he succumbed to such gloom and self-pity. As an aide said, 'He has hit rock bottom.'[187] To a wondering world, the Prince of Wales looked like a busted royal flush.

He literally flushed when, emerging from self-imposed isolation to take part in his first public engagement after Camillagate, a man in the crowd shouted: 'Have you no shame?'[188] However, Charles did not flinch. As he showed during an apparent assassination attempt in Australia the following year, the Prince was as doughty as any of his Hanoverian forebears. Encouraged by friends, he tried to behave as though it was business as usual. This actually meant refining his role as a solo performer and detaching himself as far as possible from Diana. Charles doggedly concentrated on routine duties such as tours to promote trade; but the glamour was lacking and he griped that people deliberately chose 'to ignore the things I continue to do day in, day out'.[189] Just as Diana had Kensington Palace 'cleansed' of her husband's 'negative energy'[190] and then feng-shuied and refurbished, Charles purged Highgrove of all traces of his wife. He banished the clutter of soft toys and pink sofas in favour of marble tables, red curtains, tapestry covers and hessian basket-weave carpets – when Dudley Poplak saw the new decor, he said that Charles was withdrawing into the womb. However, the Prince could not so easily rid himself of the Princess. She and the press were obsessed with one another, and scarcely a day passed without coverage of her antics, liaisons, clothes or causes. She haunted him. When Charles asked why so few photographers met him at Klosters, he was told that the rest were in Nepal with his wife. Most journalists took her side against him. 'How dare they say this about me?' he would exclaim, his face contorted with pain, his fist slamming the table. 'Oh, bloody hell, these bloody people! Why don't they leave me a-bloody-lone?'[191]

Charles fought fire with fire, resorting to counterpublicity. He failed to appreciate the merits of reticence, as exemplified by his mother. The Queen confined herself to platitudes on principle, never saying anything of the slightest interest about any subject whatever, let alone about royalty itself. The Prince assumed that by explaining himself in fascinating detail he would infallibly win popular sympathy. Thus in 1994, to mark the twenty-fifth anniversary of his investiture, he cooperated with Jonathan Dimbleby, who produced a television programme about his life and an authorised biography. Both were eminently deferential, as befitted a son of the original Gold Microphone in Waiting. But the film was notable for Charles's strangulated confession of infidelity:

> Mrs Parker Bowles is a great friend of mine . . . And I think also most people, probably would, would, realise that when your marriages break down, awful and miserable as that is, that, so often you know, it is your friends who are the most important and helpful and understanding and encouraging – otherwise you would go stark, raving mad. And that's what friends are for. [192]

Dimbleby's book caused still more horror in Buckingham Palace since it dwelt on the emotional deprivation that Charles had suffered at the hands of a distant mother and a bullying father. Moreover, the Prince's appeal for understanding backfired in the country at large. His revelations were widely condemned and they fed a growing mood of republicanism, expressed in national newspapers. They also prompted retaliation. Having scrubbed grass stains from Charles's pyjamas after another al fresco encounter with Camilla, his valet, Ken Stronach, washed the Prince's dirty linen in public. Diana plainly intended to take the whole man to the cleaners. In a well-rehearsed interview on BBC television, broadcast in June 1995, she blamed her husband for the ruin of their relationship – 'there were three of us in this marriage, so it was a bit crowded' – and hoped that his uneasy head would never wear the crown.

Despite her reliance on schmaltz, fantasy and psychobabble, despite even her admission of adultery with Hewitt, Diana gained overwhelming public support and Charles was correspondingly vilified. However, he held back retaliation against his wife for the sake of the children, who were increasingly discomfited by their mother's frenetic behaviour. Instead, with the Queen's approval, he initiated divorce proceedings. After much legal wrangling and financial haggling, Diana agreed to sacrifice her title of Royal Highness and to accept a settlement of some £17 million plus other perquisites. By August 1996, Charles was free to wed Camilla, whose marriage had also been dissolved. But to persuade his family and his future subjects to accept her was a daunting task. During the last year of her life Diana still dominated the headlines, whether as saint, sinner or psychopath. Whatever her role and whatever attempts Charles made to diminish it, she was a star. Beside such vivid beauty, to quote the coarse simile of Mohamed Fayed, father of the Princess's last lover Dodi, Camilla was 'like something from a *Dracula* film'.[193]

The car crash that killed Diana and Dodi on 31 August 1997 also destroyed any immediate prospect that Charles might make his mistress his wife. Indeed, his tearful reaction to the news was that he himself would become the prime scapegoat. In a panic he telephoned his new 'spin doctor', Mark Bolland: 'They're all going to blame me, aren't they? What do I do?' What Charles did was to fly to Paris and bring back Diana's body for a quasi-state funeral, giving the impression that he acted decisively while his parents dithered and the populace indulged in an extraordinary paroxysm of grief. It is true that the Queen, hidebound by protocol and anxious to insulate her grandsons at Balmoral, was sadly out of touch with the national mood. But Charles was shattered by viewing the corpse of the mother of his children and did little more than fuss about trivia, such as her lost gold earring. As a palace insider said, 'Charles was like a wet weekend at Balmoral. He was pole-axed by guilt, and any suggestion that he was taking charge is ridiculous.'[194]

At the funeral, he gave way to other emotions. In particular Charles was incensed by the address of Diana's brother, Earl Spencer, who decried the bizarre style of life the Princess had been forced to adopt and pledged that her 'blood family' would ensure that William and Harry were not stifled by tradition but could 'sing openly' as she had planned. Charles was outraged by the hypocrisy of this declaration: Spencer hardly knew his nephews and was scarcely a paragon of familial virtue himself. Even more maddening was the fact that his rhetoric sparked off a vast catharsis: crowds listening outside Westminster Abbey applauded and many in the congregation followed suit, among them the young princes. Charles was restrained from lambasting Spencer, whom he envied for having come into his inheritance so early. Instead, the Prince of Wales devoted himself to nurturing his motherless boys, to restoring his battered public image and to reconciling the world to the prospect of a Queen Camilla. Deploying warmth, charm, courtesy, pertinacity and self-deprecating humour, he eventually succeeded in all three projects. But he also suffered major setbacks. These stemmed partly from a royal bump of conceit that grew with age, a swelling desire to impose his opinions because they were his. Inevitably these leaked. Few were as undiplomatic as his views during the handover of Hong Kong: his remark that the uncomfortable club-class aircraft seats he had to suffer signified 'the end of Empire'; his 'exasperated sadness' at the decommissioning of *Britannia*; and his description of the Chinese leaders as 'appalling old waxworks'.[195]

More injurious still, at a time when the Duke of Edinburgh was making modest efforts to prepare the monarchy for the new millennium, the Prince of Wales put himself (said Tony Blair's press secretary, Alastair Campbell) 'at the head of the forces of conservatism'.[196] Charles took William hunting even though two-thirds of the population supported a law to ban the sport. Arguing that hereditary peers had so much to offer, he opposed reform of the House of Lords. Like a latter-day Colonel Blimp, he blustered about the cost of living and the European Declaration on Human Rights. In the interests of military tradition he protested against the Ministry of Defence's proposal to stop importing bearskins for use by Guards regiments. He promoted ecotowns and campaigned against genetically modified crops, an initiative that so angered the prime minister that he raised the matter with the Queen, though, Campbell recorded, Blair 'seemingly didn't push too hard'.[197] At any rate Charles was unmoved, secure in his mimic court where he maintained an intricate system of segregation according to rank. To visit Highgrove, Campbell wrote, was to take 'a journey so far back in time it felt extra-planetary'.[198]

Charles was the Sun Prince. Around him orbited a host of satellites: secretaries, equerries, butlers, valets, chefs, housekeepers, chauffeurs, grooms, gardeners. He even acquired his own personal harpist. Queen Elizabeth herself found such Edwardian extravagance grotesque, but in his private realm Prince Charles prided himself on doing things well. He fretted endlessly about details, writing his retainers busy little notes. 'This sponge is dry. Please see that it is watered immediately.'[199] 'Please make sure all the lights are off.'[200] 'A letter from the Queen must have fallen by accident into the wastepaper basket beside the table in the library. Please look for it.'[201] Unsurprisingly, Charles's little kingdom was the scene of intrigue, toadyism, sleaze and vendetta. As in medieval times, flunkeys nearest their royal master wielded the greatest influence and reaped the richest rewards. Charles's valet, Michael Fawcett, was a notable beneficiary. According to an equerry of the Queen Mother's, Fawcett, who shouted and screamed at other members of staff and was 'an absolute bloody nightmare to work for . . . somehow managed, with the trust and full knowledge and cooperation of the Prince, to build up a huge power base which threatened the whole employee structure within St James's Palace'.[202] Prince Albert's admonition to his eldest son might have been coined for Charles: 'try to emancipate yourself as much as possible from the thraldom of abject dependence . . . on your servants'.[203]

Charles's dependence was such that when he broke his arm playing polo, Fawcett held the specimen bottle for what tabloids inevitably called 'the royal wee'. This bizarre detail emerged during 2002, the Queen's Golden Jubilee year, which should have been a triumph. But in the spring Charles's grandmother died, having outlived his aunt Margaret by just six weeks. And after a summer of Jubilee celebration (during which the Prince of Wales hailed the sovereign's five decades of achievement in a speech beginning, 'Your Majesty – Mummy . . .') came an autumn of regal humiliation. This stemmed from the trial of Princess Diana's butler, Paul Burrell, who was accused of stealing hundreds of her possessions. He was acquitted after the Queen told Charles that she remembered Burrell telling her that he had taken the items for safe-keeping. Critics suspected that the monarch had intervened to prevent Burrell or, worse still, Charles and William, from going into the witness box. Testimony given on oath might have done the monarchy incalculable harm. As it happened, a number of damaging stories were published after the trial, Burrell himself cashing in on the public eagerness to know what the butler saw. A 'mafia of gay royal servants'[204] was supposedly responsible for various misdemeanours, though Charles dismissed a valet's allegation of homosexual rape as 'downstairs gossip'.[205] However, it was impossible to deny that the gifts with which Charles was deluged were sometimes used to compensate his badly paid staff. He himself was quoted as saying, 'There's a very good, gold wedding ring here which someone in the office might find useful.'[206] Often such items were sold by the Prince's closest factotum, who was nicknamed 'Fawcett the Fence'.[207] An internal inquiry blamed the Prince's entourage for ineptitude rather than corruption. Journalists were less generous. Anthony Holden wrote that Charles's household 'sounds like a cross between Ancient Rome and the back of Del Trotter's truck'.[208]

If all this spoilt the Queen's Golden Jubilee, it also marred Charles's propaganda campaign to transform Camilla from hated other woman to respected member of the royal family. Nevertheless, he persevered. Through staged public appearances, choreographed charitable endeavours and orchestrated reports in the mass media, Camilla was gradually established as Charles's consort. In 2003 she became acknowledged chatelaine of Highgrove. Both sets of children were reconciled to the arrangement. Queen Elizabeth and the Duke of Edinburgh reluctantly came to terms with the fact that their baffling eldest son was bent on making an honest woman of Camilla. But the awkwardness of his position was highlighted at their wedding, in April 2005. It could not be held in a church since Camilla had a living ex-husband. Nor could it take place at Windsor Castle, as Charles had planned, because of licensing difficulties, and it had to be transferred to the Guildhall at Windsor. Even so, questions were raised about the validity of the civil ceremony, and Charles's parents did not attend it – the Queen presumably because she could not, as Supreme Governor of the Church of England, be seen to countenance divorce. She did, however, appear for the subsequent blessing at St George's Chapel, demonstrating her acceptance of the Duchess of Cornwall – as Camilla had become, avoiding the trap of adopting Diana's title.

As for Charles, entering his sixties and soon the oldest Prince of Wales in history, he was at last happily married. He settled down to wait . . . and wait, hoping to inherit an earthly throne before he inherited a heavenly one. Naturally he became impatient. Encouraged by unctuous courtiers and obsequious friends, he dispatched more 'Black Spiders', pressed for an executive role, cultivated his garden, proselytised for his idiosyncratic ideas and intervened ever more urgently in architectural matters. For example, he thwarted a 'Brutalist' plan to develop the Chelsea Barracks site, describing it as part of a 'gigantic experiment with the very soul of our capital city'.[209] In short, Charles went backwards into the future. Yet there was little appetite on the part of politicians or people to stop him in his tracks, let alone to advance William in his stead. On the contrary, the Freedom of Information Act was modified in 2010 to allow the many government ministers summoned by Charles to conceal the content of their talks, and even the fact that they had taken place. And it subsequently emerged that he could impose a secret veto on legislation where his own interests (notably his £700 million property portfolio) were concerned. His elder son, meanwhile, was urged to concentrate on royal procreation. As his father crassly remarked when William's engagement to Kate Middleton was at last announced, 'They have been practising long enough.'[210] Charles himself, once ridiculed as an absurd anachronism, was often now saluted as a 'passionate and prescient Prince'.[211] He burnished this image through the media, notably in a recent television documentary about Sir Hubert Parry, identifying with the composer on various counts and describing him as a 'complex man with a mind of his own'.[212] Even Camilla, who had previously attracted brickbats, was now deemed 'a brick'.[213]

The Prince of Wales had become the embodiment of a royal myth that seemed impervious to assaults of reality, immune to disenchantment, exempt from reason. In addition to the scandals that discredited the royal family as the guardian of British morality, the new Elizabethan age witnessed the destruction of buttresses that had traditionally supported the monarchy. The loss of empire subverted the old social hierarchy and made nonsense of an honours system so reliant on imperial titles, OBE, CBE and so on. The Commonwealth, with the sovereign at its head, was eclipsed by the European Union, in which she played no substantial part. Reform of the House of Lords undermined the hereditary principle. The advent of other cultures and religions marginalised the monarch's role as defender of the established faith. Yet however irrelevant or anomalous a king or queen was in a democracy, republican logic had yet to prevail over royalist sentiment. Thus Rupert Murdoch's organs, which mirrored public opinion, did not follow the lead of liberal newspapers such as the *Guardian* in coming out for an elected head of state. What Prince Charles's career demonstrated was that, even in twenty-first-century Britain, the more things changed the more they stayed the same. The country, despite the radical velleities of the 1960s, was reluctant to countenance any fundamental transformation. New Labour was old Toryism writ large. Royalty, however tarnished its crown, retained an atavistic hold on the national imagination.

Margaret Thatcher

Few public figures have been loved and loathed as fervently as Britain's first female prime minister. Margaret Thatcher practised her own form of divide and rule, polarising society during a term of office that lasted from 1979 to 1990 – longer than that of any twentieth-century man. She aroused passionate devotion among those convinced that she had reversed the spiral of post-war decline and brought about a national renaissance. She inspired visceral revulsion among those who thought that she had done her best to dismantle the welfare state and re-create the two nations of Victorian Britain – rich and poor. Admirers hailed her as 'Battling Maggie', the heroic Amazon who defeated General Galtieri's invading forces in the Falkland Islands and crushed Arthur Scargill's striking miners at home, whom she branded 'the enemy within'.[1] Detractors called her 'Attila the Hen',[2] a vicious termagant who antagonised her European and Commonwealth partners and, by imposing harsh measures of economic and social discipline in England, provoked bloody urban riots. For some her achievements were unsurpassed: lower direct taxes, privatised state concerns, incapacitated trade unions, emancipated capitalism and shattered socialism. Others saw her monuments as derelict factories, cardboard cities, dole queues, the poll tax, the big bang, chauvinism and authoritarianism. The faithful, wrote one journalist, welcomed Margaret Thatcher with screaming euphoria, 'as if she were a rock star or a sporting hero'. Unbelievers, notably three million unemployed, chanted: 'Maggie, Maggie, Maggie – out, out, out.'[3]

Margaret Thatcher's character and appearance also came in for adulation and execration. Of her industry, energy, ability and bravery there could be no doubt. She worked with furious concentration, hardly noticing when her children played music at full blast and staying awake into the small hours to read papers or write speeches. She had an incomparable mastery of detail, often memorised by means of mnemonics and deployed with the forensic skill of a trained tax barrister. She revelled in argument, dominating others through force of personality and articulating views that were as pellucid as her china-blue eyes. Margaret Thatcher had an adamantine faith not only in her rightness but in her righteousness. In her crusade to restore British greatness, she possessed what one of her advisers called 'a manic sense of mission'.[4] Such zeal made her the flail of colleagues, civil servants and opposition politicians, most of whom were at first inclined to patronise her. They were further intimidated by her aura of power – power radiating from electric-blue suits and orthodontically enhanced smiles, from a lustrous casque of blonde hair and a handbag wielded like a mace. Yet power, as Henry Kissinger unforgettably remarked, is the ultimate aphrodisiac, and some were struck by Mrs Thatcher's sex appeal. She could be flirtatious, and the raffish junior minister Alan Clark was entranced by her ankles. Kingsley Amis had amorous dreams about her. His fellow novelist Anthony Powell found the prime minister physically attractive (though 'her voice would jar a duchess')[5] and thought her appearance justified President Mitterand's oft-quoted comment that she had the eyes of Caligula and the lips of Marilyn Monroe. Rather surprisingly, the historian A. L. Rowse was also attracted to the Iron Lady, saying that he 'would like to rape her'.[6] Margaret Thatcher was the chief object of erotic fantasy in the armed services during the Falklands War. Furthermore, psychiatrists reported that she now held the pre-eminent position, hitherto reserved for the Queen, in the minds of severely demented people.

Sane critics, however, condemned the prime minister as cold, reactionary, dictatorial, small-minded and humourless. Nothing demonstrated Mrs Thatcher's lack of human sympathy more explicitly than her assault (for which she at once apologised) on do-gooders who 'drool and drivel [that] they care'.[7] Despite a genuine concern for individuals, she never commiserated with the unemployed or the homeless en masse. Indeed, she seemed to blame them for their plight. And she suggested that its alleviation was better achieved through private endeavour than public provision, which (as Victorians liked to say) made dependents 'moral cripples'.[8] Thus she sapped the noble ideal of collective responsibility for social well-being that went back at least to the Edwardian age. Then her hero Winston Churchill had championed state aid for 'the left-out millions',[9] whereas she herself famously declared that 'There is no such thing as society.'[10] If Mrs Thatcher rationed compassion, her will to power was unbridled. She had sublime confidence in her own judgement and her determination to inflict it on others amounted to an obsession. To get her own way she could be rude, beguiling, petulant, coquettish, hysterical and altogether unreasonable. Of course males were quick to accuse her of feminine irrationality, to say that she 'argued like a woman'.[11] Colleagues complained that she could not think systematically. Speech-writers found her mode of composition 'madness'.[12] This was because she tried too hard and had no natural feel for words. Her emphases were often subtly wrong and (like Rupert Murdoch and Prince Charles) she stumbled over the personal pronoun, unforgettably proclaiming: 'We have become a grandmother.'[13] Although capable of flashes of wit, she had no real sense of humour. Her file entitled 'Ideas: funny' was painfully thin, though it did include Kipling's verse about the female of the species being 'more deadly than the male'.[14] Jokes for Margaret Thatcher, as for Edward Heath, were no laughing matter. Those written on her behalf had to be laboriously explained. Irony was lost on the Iron Lady. Moreover she let slip embarrassing double entendres. Visiting a destroyer in the Falklands, she asked a sailor about the recoil of a naval gun on deck: 'Can this thing jerk you off?'[15]

As Mrs Thatcher's acolytes hardly needed to emphasise, much of the animus against her stemmed from a combination of snobbery and misogyny. Tories were not alone in preferring patricians to plebs, and most of her countrymen found it hard to accept women in positions of authority. Mrs Thatcher was despised as a bossy arriviste, a shrill governess who had risen above her station. Immaculately groomed, she seemed intent on disguising her modest origins behind floral hats, pearl necklaces and tailored suits. She spoke like an elocution lesson, mouthing right-wing platitudes with fundamentalist vehemence. 'My God, she is like the chairman of my women's committee,' said a Conservative MP, 'but writ hideously large.'[16] Party grandees were especially disdainful. When Sir Edward du Cann invited Margaret and Denis Thatcher to his smart house in Lord North Street, he likened their manner to that of a couple coming to be interviewed for a job as 'housekeeper and handyman'.[17] And when she curtly sacked Christopher Soames from her government in 1981, he behaved, the prime minister said, as though he were being dismissed by his housemaid. Left-wing intellectuals were still more contemptuous: Jonathan Miller, who found Mrs Thatcher 'repulsive in almost every way', excoriated her 'odious suburban gentility'.[18] Academics stigmatised her as a first-class philistine and (as one Oxford scientist superciliously put it) 'a perfectly good second-class chemist'.[19] The metropolitan elite deplored her vulgarity. Even pop singers echoed the enmity, dreaming of 'Margaret on the Guillotine' or hoping to 'tramp the dirt down'[20] on her grave.

Still, it cannot be said that hostility to Mrs Thatcher was based simply on atavistic prejudice. Her opponents sincerely believed that she and the doctrine named after her – Thatcherism – were doing irreparable damage to the social fabric of Britain. Even liberal-minded Conservatives were perturbed by the 'cancerous'[21] effect that high unemployment was having on the body politic. They feared that the much-vaunted 'enterprise culture'[22] was destroying the soul of the community. They warned that ideals of selfless service were being vanquished by a philosophy of cut-throat competition, that the old Tory spirit of *noblesse oblige* was being eradicated by the brassy principles of laissez-faire. The aged Harold Macmillan, once Mrs Thatcher's venerated patron, gave the most sardonic expression to these views. He jibed that the party of landowners now belonged to estate agents, and that in the cabinet Old Etonians had given way to Old Estonians – a crack at Thatcherite ministers of east European origin. He also said that her government's policy of privatising public assets to fund current expenditure was like 'selling the family silver' to pay the butler's wages.[23] Macmillan had always been the advocate of moderate, inclusive, one-nation Disraelian Conservatism – the Middle Way. This was anathema to Mrs Thatcher. She told Jim Prior, a colleague who espoused it: 'Standing in the middle of the road is very dangerous; you get knocked down by the traffic from both sides.'[24]

Margaret Thatcher scorned compromise, regarding it not as a key element in the democratic process but as a betrayal of moral and intellectual integrity. She gloried in being a 'conviction politician' and described consensus as a renunciation of values, beliefs and policies 'merely to get people to come to an agreement'.[25] Moreover, she demanded the same commitment from her ministers, asserting before the election of 1979 that she could not 'waste time having any internal arguments'.[26] In office, of course, she did just that. Seldom listening, and interrupting constantly, the new prime minister indulged in such frantic squabbles that by 1980, according to Prior, 'She hasn't really got a friend left in the whole Cabinet.'[27] Outside the cabinet, Mrs Thatcher was noted for her resolution. As early as 1975, a journalist on the *Daily Mirror* christened her the 'Iron Maiden'[28] (a medieval instrument of torture), and the following year a Soviet army newspaper dubbed her the 'Iron Lady',[29] a nickname initially rejected as a slur but quickly adopted as an accolade. She was cheered to an echo when she rejoiced in her own inflexibility – 'You turn if you want to. The lady's not for turning.'[30] Whether this was clear-eyed strength of purpose or blinkered intransigence, Mrs Thatcher appeared to embody an adamantine consistency. Rather than be suspected of dithering, she rejected canons of tolerance and habits of conciliation that had long been the staple of British life. Indeed, she condemned Tory moderates as wishy-washy 'wets' – an adolescent taunt favoured by Young Turks in her entourage such as Patrick Cosgrave. Mrs Thatcher, whose mentality was essentially sectarian, theorised as little as she temporised. An ideologue without ideas, she was interested in forging dogmas not in fostering concepts. The high priestess of monetarism preferred bigotry to ambiguity. The evangelist of capitalism made judgements in black or white. The messianic leader seemed as constant as the northern star.

Actually she was more like a wandering asteroid, with a diverse composition and an uncertain trajectory. Despite her hard-line image, she was enough of a pragmatist to equivocate, to dissimulate and to deviate. She admitted that government was often a matter of 'shades of grey'.[31] And it turned out that being a 'conviction politician' was as much about politics as about convictions. Notwithstanding her brains, Mrs Thatcher was a creature of emotion. One official said that he had at first thought her all head and no heart but concluded that 'she was all heart and no head'.[32] Although a hanger and flogger who deplored the permissive trends of the 1960s, she was indulgent towards moral lapses and sexual peccadilloes. Although a paladin of free enterprise, she disapproved of financial speculators, declined to become a 'name' at Lloyd's, rejected a national lottery and frowned on credit cards. She was a dirigiste opponent of big government who attacked rival centres of power – the civil service, local councils, professional associations, trade unions, Eurocracy. She was an ardent monarchist who curtsied to the Queen so deeply as to cause comment, even mirth. Yet the prime minister referred to 'my troops' and excluded the royal family from the victory parade after the Falklands War, taking the salute herself in the manner of some latter-day Boadicea. Above all, Margaret Thatcher was a traditionalist with a passion for reform. In the words of an early aide, Matthew Parris, who found her a bundle of contradictions: 'Nobody I have encountered in politics had a firmer belief in doing certain things simply because they were the done thing

– an instinct hard to reconcile with her root-and-branch radicalism.'[33] She was indeed a radical Tory, a politician whose revolutionary impulses were at odds with her conservative beliefs. She prided herself on the paradox, applauding critics of her own ministers at party conferences and claiming to be 'the rebel head of an establishment government'.[34] How can these conflicting elements in Margaret Thatcher's personality be explained? What was the true nature of the Iron Lady, a lady who never admitted to mutability let alone to base metal fatigue?

Any assay must start in the Grantham grocer's shop owned by Margaret's father, Councillor Alfred Roberts, where her character was forged. Roberts's own forebears had been Northamptonshire shoemakers, members of a workforce notorious for both Nonconformity and radicalism. He embraced the one but not the other. Having left school at thirteen and risen in the retail trade, he became a pillar of Grantham's Wesleyan Methodist church and an independent member of the local council – in other words, a Conservative (though with vestiges of liberalism). As the proprietor of a small store-cum-post office in a humble district of the Lincolnshire market town, he and his wife Beatrice, née Stephenson, formerly a self-employed dressmaker, were embodiments of dissenting respectability. They worked almost all the hours God made and devoted nearly all their leisure to religion. Thus Margaret, who was born above the shop on 13 October 1925, four years after her sister Muriel, was raised in a sternly industrious and pious household. The business was a family enterprise, run on penny-pinching lines. Margaret assisted with it from an early age, serving customers (who were never given credit) and learning the virtues of honesty, responsibility, frugality and thrift. She also attended her father's chapel, enjoying the music, studying the Scriptures at Sunday school and acquiring a knowledge of good and evil. As she later wrote, 'Our lives revolved around Methodism.'[35] There was inevitably a tension between the lauding of spiritual values Margaret heard from the pulpit and the imperatives of getting and spending she witnessed at the counter. It was not easy to harmonise the chink of the collection plate with the ringing of the till. Yet, as has often been observed, Protestantism and capitalism can combine in a creed affording transcendent ethical certainties. John Wesley himself had urged Christians to labour diligently in order to grow rich, for if 'those who *gain* all they can, and *save* all they can, will likewise *give* all they can, then the more they will grow in grace'.[36] Based on this notion, Margaret subsequently enunciated a new beatitude: blessed are the wealth creators, for only they can afford to bestow charity. Her upbringing taught her to reconcile God and Mammon, to lay up treasure on earth as well as in heaven.

There are even hints that she was tempted to worship the golden calf. As a girl, Margaret seemed to resent the strict austerity imposed by her father, which included a Sabbath ban on dancing and playing snakes and ladders. She yearned for more stylish clothes than those sewn by her mother. She evidently disliked the family's spartan living conditions, typified by the outside lavatory (or, to use her later euphemism, facility). She was entranced by the silver screen and irked by Puritan restrictions on her visits to the cinema. A trip to London dazzled her. By contrast she found incessant chapel-going 'too much of a good thing'.[37] Moreover, her autobiography suggests that she felt her parents were narrow-minded and provincial. Her mother hardly features in it, and her father, who rose to be alderman and mayor, emerges as little more than a personification of high principles. Nevertheless, Margaret was a dutiful daughter. At home she imbibed improving maxims: cleanliness is next to godliness; politeness costs nothing; waste not, want not; a stitch in time saves nine; the devil makes work for idle hands; if a man will not work he shall not eat.[38] At Kesteven and Grantham Girls' Grammar School she excelled at her studies and took pains to ensure that her efforts won their due reward. Even as a wartime adolescent she was determined to escape from lower-middle-class existence in the Midlands, from that section of society that Sir John Seeley had described as sunk in 'dead-level, insipid, barren, abject, shop-keeping life'.[39] She persuaded her father to pay for elocution lessons, saying: 'Daddy, one has got to speak properly.'[40] She specialised in chemistry, knowing that 'science was the coming thing'.[41] And she took a crash course in Latin to try for an Oxford scholarship at the age of seventeen, just missing it but earning a place at Somerville College. Here a fellow undergraduate described her as 'a plump, neat, solemn girl with rosy cheeks and fairish hair curled flat on her head'.[42] Margaret was not popular, being seen as prim, boring and manipulative – she tried to impose her own opinions without regard for those of others. She was also deemed insincere because of what another contemporary called her 'elocutiony, actressy way of talking'.[43]

There was nothing artificial about her ambition, however, nor about her flinty resolve to make the best use of her talents in the political arena. Of course, Oxford was a male preserve and she was excluded from the Union because of her sex. She later implied that she had been one of the stars in the undergraduate firmament, shining brightly with other future cabinet ministers, such as Tony Crosland, Tony Benn and Edward Boyle. In fact, only the last of these was a friend, and she herself was a peripheral figure, callow, serious, unsophisticated, something of a prig. Yet she studied the art of platform speaking, and during the 1945 election she intoned Tory clichés as though she meant them. Aged only nineteen, she rallied voters to Winston Churchill's cause with a series of imperious demands: Germany must be punished, Russia must remain a friend and the British Empire (then on the eve of dissolution) 'must never be liquidated'.[44] At Oxford Margaret rose majestically to the top of the only political organisation open to her, becoming president of the University Conservative Association. In 1946 she attended her first Conservative party conference, at Blackpool, where she formed an almost mystical bond with the Tory faithful – to paraphrase Sir Geoffrey Howe's observation, she would listen to 'our people' as Joan of Arc listened to her 'voices'.[45]

Having gained a second-class degree, Margaret found work as a research chemist in a plastics company near Colchester, where she was called variously 'Duchess', 'Snobby Roberts' and 'the future Prime Minister'.[46] Her leisure was entirely devoted to politics. And at another party conference, in 1948, she met the chairman of the Dartford Conservative Association, which led to her selection as its prospective parliamentary candidate for what was a safe Labour seat. Two years later, having changed jobs to lodge in the constituency (where the landlady described her as 'a chatterbox'),[47] she fought in the election campaign, at twenty-four the youngest woman to do so. Attending a Conservative fete, she was buoyed up when a fortune-teller looked into her pearls (always thereafter deemed lucky) and predicted: 'You will be great – great as Churchill.'[48] On the hustings, of course, Margaret extolled Churchill's own 'prophetic voice'. She echoed his denunciation of communism abroad and 'soul-less socialism' at home. And she urged that, at the centre of their Empire, 'this proud island race' should 'recreate a glorious Britain'.[49] A dauntless speaker and a dynamic organiser, she roused local Conservatives from their defeatist attitudes and astonished observers by her wholly unreasonable faith in victory. She did win golden opinions but, while increasing the Tory vote, she lost decisively in 1950 and again the following year.

By then she had become engaged to Denis Thatcher, general manager of his family's paint and chemicals company. A bluff thirty-six-year-old divorcé in search of a wife, he had given her lifts in his Jaguar and taken her out to meals and entertainments. She had been told by the MP for Maidstone, Sir Alfred Bossom (whose name Churchill had mocked for being neither one thing nor the other), that to get on in politics she needed a husband and children. Denis was mad about sport and Margaret was wholly committed to her vocation, so they had little in common. In fact theirs was a union of convenience, not so much a marriage as a merger between his wealth and her ambition. The wedding ceremony took place on 13 December 1951 at Wesley's Chapel in London's City Road, which was far too Anglican for Alfred Roberts, who evidently frowned on the profane and bibulous Denis and afterwards receded into the background of his daughter's life, to be cherished as an icon. In an early exhibition of power dressing and upward mobility, Margaret wore a brilliant blue velvet costume with a matching ostrich-feather hat, modelled on Georgiana Duchess of Devonshire's outfit as painted by Gainsborough. The new Mrs Thatcher was seasick en route to Madeira, but Denis managed to combine a couple of continental business trips with their honeymoon, which he described as 'quite pleasant'.[50]

Her marriage was a career move, not an alternative career. Writing in the *Sunday Graphic* 'at the dawn of the new Elizabethan era',[51] she asserted that, like the young Queen, women were perfectly capable of caring for a family and doing a professional job. Mrs Thatcher seemed to accomplish both with consummate efficiency, cooking, keeping house, reading for the bar and in August 1953 producing twins, Mark and Carol. Born prematurely, by Caesarean section, they prompted their father to exclaim: 'My God, they look like rabbits. Put them back.'[52] They were certainly a handful, but Denis had no trouble paying for a full-time nanny. Their mother rationed her attention to them, focusing on her new work as a fledgling tax lawyer with what Carol later called 'impenetrable tunnel vision'.[53] Margaret never remembered to wave to the twins when she left home, and she even neglected Denis, flatly refusing to consort with his mother. Moreover, she seemed to resent her domestic commitments, entitling the relevant chapter in her autobiography 'House Bound'. Naturally she loved both her offspring; but she was besotted by Mark, whose ineffable stupidity and insatiable cupidity only became evident with age. During their childhood, her overwhelming priority was to get into parliament. She honed her broadcasting skills, cultivated her contacts and applied unsuccessfully to several constituencies. At last, after a fiery performance, Mrs Thatcher was chosen for Finchley, a true-blue middle-class district of London. She was delighted to overcome 'anti-woman prejudice'[54] in what had boiled down to a contest between racial and sexual discrimination – her predecessor complained that 'We've got to choose between a bloody Jew and a bloody woman.'[55] At the general election of 1959, Margaret Thatcher won the seat with a huge majority.

This was the first election in which television played a crucial role, and to advertise Conservative prosperity Harold Macmillan improved his image, wearing more stylish suits, getting a smarter haircut and having his teeth straightened. This example Mrs Thatcher would follow as prime minister, though even as a young MP her appearance was impeccable, stimulating one journalist to describe her as the 'most beautiful Tory flogger'.[56] Having brains and guts as well as looks, she was clearly marked out for preferment. But she also possessed that special quality prized by Napoleon, luck. In 1960 she won second place in the ballot for Private Members' Bills, which gave her the chance to make her mark in the statute book. She plumped for a measure to prevent local government from censoring reports of its proceedings. This was an odd choice, since she had little interest in press freedom and supposedly revered her councillor father. But when Mrs Thatcher prepared the bill, with the aid of civil servants who disliked her abrasive manner, she revealed her 'low opinion of local authorities, their members and officials'.[57] She hoped that publicity would expose their misconduct but, modified by the government, her bill proved a mess. Nevertheless, her maiden speech, in which she introduced it, was a triumph. In 1961, Macmillan appointed her parliamentary secretary at the Ministry of Pensions and National Insurance. Here she challenged colleagues and antagonised officials, usually correcting and occasionally tearing up letters they drafted for her. She devoured raw data and crunched numbers like acid drops, spitting out statistics in the Commons and once bringing the House down by declaring, 'I have the latest red-hot figure.' Roguish members praised her vital statistics. Others treated her with a galumphing chivalry that, in this noisy male club, she was happy to exploit. No feminist, she deployed feminine charm and won promotion as a token female.

In her autobiography, Margaret Thatcher wrote that the path to political power during the 1960s lay through the middle ground. No aspiring leader could afford to be branded a reactionary, and the Conservative party was 'obsessively worried about being out of touch with contemporary trends and fashions'.[58] Here was doubtless a retrospective justification of her balancing act during a decade that she subsequently damned for its decadence. Sometimes Mrs Thatcher must have been astonished at her own moderation. During Harold Wilson's premiership, she reversed her opinion on the merits of a short, sharp birching. She supported the legalisation of abortion and homosexuality. She even voted to ban hare coursing. However, she continued to favour hanging, disagreeing with Denis on this topic but sharing his right-wing outlook on matters such as nationalisation, immigration, trade unionism and law and order. As she rose, he seems to have suffered some kind of psychological collapse, compounded by business worries. Apparently it was resolved when he sold the family firm and reconciled himself to ploughing his own furrow while Margaret reached for the stars. The new Conservative leader, Edward Heath, tried to keep her out of the shadow cabinet on the ground that 'once she's there we'll never be able to get rid of her'. But her fitness for promotion was undeniable, and in 1967 he made her shadow minister of power. Later she was given the transport portfolio, and later still, realising Heath's worst fears, that of education. In the shadow cabinet she was loquacious and pertinacious. A colleague recalled: 'How she talked! And she certainly irked the Leader. Instinctively he seemed to bridle at her over-emphasis.'[59] Heath, a carpenter's son who failed to refine his vowel sounds, never warmed to the grocer's daughter, whose fluting accents were said to resemble 'some devilish Roedean water torture'.[60]

What struck observers was the contrast between Margaret Thatcher's peaches-and-cream exterior and the pugnacious, robotic quality of her intellect. At times she appeared winsome and demure, but her words were sharp as needles and her default state was one of aggression. Strife was the medium of her existence, her salamander's fire. Like the Suffragette leader Emmeline Pankhurst, she was distinguished above all by 'the sublime and terrific violence of her soul'.[61] This became manifest in the Department of Education and Science when, after the unexpected Conservative victory at the polls in 1970, Ted Heath put Mrs

Thatcher in charge of it. She hated its 'self-righteously socialist' ethos and disliked officials who were convinced that they could 'create a better world'.[62] She even tried to remove their chief, Sir William Pile (who found her both inflexible and driven by detestable passions), maintaining that his left-wing wife made him a security risk. She was also keen to sack teachers, and she infuriated subordinates, who sneered at her banal mind, by fussing over the tiniest details. Few could have been sorry when their boss provoked a hurricane of adverse publicity in 1972 by abolishing free school milk for children aged from eight to eleven. The public chanted 'Margaret Thatcher – Milk Snatcher'.[63] The press pilloried her as 'The Lady Nobody Loves', lacking the milk of human kindness. The *Sun*, later her most hysterical cheerleader, asked if she was human. She was upset by the furore and concluded that she had 'incurred the maximum of political odium for the minimum of political benefit'.[64] She expected to be dismissed, not least because Labour backbenchers catcalled, 'Ditch the Bitch.'[65] But Ted Heath was content to keep Mrs Thatcher at the cabinet table, sitting where he could not see her – two places to his right, with the aptly named Sir Burke Trend, who leaned forward to take the minutes, between them.

The controversy enhanced her reputation for toughness and insensitivity. She refused to buckle under the assault, some of which was spurious – Labour had already stopped the provision of free milk to secondary school children, yet one opposition MP denounced her as the government's 'most mean and vicious member'.[66] The ordeal burnished her brazen panoply. Moreover, the critics were fickle, and soon she was earning headlines such as 'The Mellowing of Margaret'.[67] She won plaudits for other policies: support for the Open University (which was cheap to run), raising the school leaving age to sixteen (a long-projected measure) and planning free nursery education (frustrated by budget cuts after the 1973 oil crisis). There was a suspicion, which embarrassed her later, that she had been domesticated by the high-spending education department. Under Mrs Thatcher's Labour predecessor, Anthony Crosland, it had promoted the establishment of comprehensive schools and, despite her insistence on the value of parental choice, she permitted local authorities to proceed with this policy at a swifter rate. She also spurned a national curriculum (which she would later impose), with the assertion that a minister should not have power over ideas. And she supported heavy expenditure on school buildings. All told her performance was 'solid, respectable and unspectacular', as might be expected from an almost archetypal, somewhat right-wing Tory lady who worked hard but had no realistic expectations of becoming leader of her party. This was an American assessment, based on a lunch Mrs Thatcher had with a US diplomat in May 1973. He was struck by her steely self-confidence and her frank verdicts on colleagues, whom she invariably judged by the criterion of cleverness despite her own 'anti-intellectual bias'. Thus she admired the 'brilliant, versatile' Sir Keith Joseph but said that Peter Walker, though able, lacked a 'first-class mind'. She respected Sir Geoffrey Howe despite his willingness to compromise, and wondered if he would overcome 'this weakness'. Michael Heseltine, she observed, 'had everything it took in politics except brains'[68] – though it was more of a disadvantage in the Tory party to be thought too clever by half.

In public and in private, however, Mrs Thatcher professed to be a keen adherent of Edward Heath. Their personal antipathy occasionally surfaced in cabinet, where she once remarked that most men had too high an opinion of themselves, and he was not above telling her to shut up. But she seldom hinted at their political differences, which were real. In foreign policy she looked to America and backed Israel, while he single-mindedly took Britain into the European Economic Community. At home she was uneasy about giving government help to 'lame duck' enterprises, whereas he feared rising unemployment and sought industrial conciliation. She put her faith in the operation of the free market, whereas he, performing an abrupt volte-face to counter inflation in 1972, introduced a statutory prices and incomes policy. Margaret Thatcher sympathised with the views of the Tory maverick Enoch Powell on monetarism (he thought it a pity that she didn't understand them) and on the contentious subject of immigration. Eccentric, charismatic and apocalyptic, Powell had been sacked by Heath in 1968 for prophesying racial conflict if the flow of coloured immigrants was not stemmed. His famous 'rivers of blood' speech, which referred to 'wide-grinning piccaninnies'[69] and blacks pushing excreta through white letter boxes, had certainly been inflammatory. It inspired dockers to march to Westminster in his defence. And it provoked a liberal backlash, including satire as well as savage indignation.

Mr Enoch Powell
Always carries a trowel,
To dispose of the faeces
Pushed through his letter box by members of an alien species.[70]

Thereafter, as Mrs Thatcher observed, Powell 'commanded influence without power'.[71] This she regarded as ruination. Notwithstanding his suggestion that she should have resigned over Heath's 'U-turn' and her subsequent musings on the subject, she stayed firmly in office and kept her eye on the main chance. Like another clever fool, the historian A. J. P. Taylor, Enoch Powell said she could never succeed, certainly not with that accent and those hats.

However, Heath's failures were palpable. He had presided over a prolonged economic crisis during which miners' strikes had led to states of emergency, three-day working weeks and the lights going out all over Britain. And voters, encouraged by the defection of Powell from the Tory ranks, gave Heath a dusty answer when he went to the country in February 1974 on the question of 'Who governs Britain?'.[72] Moreover, Harold Wilson held a second general election that autumn, which confirmed Labour's tenuous grip on power. Stubborn and ungracious, Heath behaved as if he had a permanent lien on the party leadership. But disgruntled Conservative MPs secured a contest for it, even though they had no clear candidate. Margaret Thatcher, who had improved her own position as shadow environment minister and now took on the formidable Chancellor Denis Healey, backed her friend and mentor Sir Keith Joseph. Like Powell, though, Joseph was brilliant but unsound, sailing under a huge spread of intellectual canvas but lacking a bottom of good sense. In October 1974 he gave a speech saying that 'our human stock' was threatened by too much breeding in 'social classes 4 & 5'.[73] Thereafter the prophet of monetary continence was mocked as the champion of mass contraception, 'Sir Sheath'. Lord Hailsham concluded that he was 'dotty'[74] and a younger Conservative, Chris Patten, dubbed him the 'Mad Monk'.[75] Healey said he was a mixture of 'Hamlet, Rasputin and Tommy Cooper'.[76] The lacerated Joseph withdrew, deciding that he did not possess the stuff of which leaders are made. So in November Margaret Thatcher put herself forward in the name of their brand of enterprise Toryism. When she told Heath, he was variously reported as saying, 'If you must' and 'You'll lose.'[77]

Most people thought that she hadn't a hope, including her husband, who said that she must be out of her mind. Her chances were not improved when the press revealed that she had advised pensioners to stockpile tins of ham and sardines as a hedge against inflation. The milk snatcher was damned as a food hoarder. Behind the wholesale moralising appeared the crass retail mind. Moreover Margaret Thatcher, married to a millionaire, seemed to be quite out of touch with the budgets of the poor. She was shocked by the onslaught but determined that, unlike Keith Joseph, she would not be broken. So she presented herself as a prudent housekeeper and continued with her campaign, skilfully run by the war hero Airey Neave. It succeeded because at this stage she looked to be an emollient alternative to Heath, whom many Conservative MPs were resolved to depose at any cost – an attitude he considered 'absolutely mad'.[78] In the first ballot, held on 4 February 1975, she defeated him by 130 votes to 119. The former Home Secretary Reginald Maudling rushed round parliament muttering, 'The Party's taken leave of its senses. This is a black day.'[79] Other heavyweight members of Heath's cabinet, such as William Whitelaw, James Prior and Geoffrey Howe, entered the race. But

Mrs Thatcher had built up too much momentum. 'My God!' exclaimed a Tory vice chairman after the second ballot was cast a week later, 'The bitch has won!'[80] Conservatives were amazed that she had triumphed over the runner-up (Whitelaw) by 67 votes and perturbed that the party was now in thrall to an exceptionally wilful female. She was ecstatic about her elevation – a colleague, Norman St John-Stevas, called it the assumption of the Blessed Margaret. She gloated over the feeble showing of her rivals. Observing from the Labour front bench, Barbara Castle wrote that Mrs Thatcher, 'the best man' the Tories had got, looked radiant. 'She is in love: in love with power, success – and with herself.'[81]

High on the afflatus of victory, she became ever more domineering. She quickly decided that 'I shall have to take most of the major decisions myself.'[82] She bullied subordinates, who found her 'shrill, prickly, combative, opinionated and bourgeois'.[83] She harangued journalists, transfixing them with an icy blue gaze and stabbing points home with her index finger. She hectored industrialists, one of whom protested: 'I would not mind being treated as a schoolboy if only she would put me in the 6th form. But I do mind being put in the 4th.'[84] Appearing supremely indifferent to what others thought of her personally, she was even capable of rebuking William Whitelaw for not mastering his brief. Nevertheless, he served as faithful deputy to 'that awful woman' (his term), earning in due course her most notorious double entendre: 'Every Prime Minister should have a Willie.'[85] There are no friends at the top, but she had precious few allies. Some senior Conservatives remained loyal to Heath, who barely disguised the disdain he felt for this preposterous usurper. Others could not bear the rule of a woman, particularly a woman who was not a lady. Francis Pym complained that they had a corporal at their head and not a cavalry officer. Tory wits called her Hilda or Heather. When Mrs Thatcher told the shadow cabinet that she had been unimpressed by President Jimmy Carter but that sometimes the job could make the man, Maudling reminded them of Churchill's remark: 'If you feed a grub on royal jelly, it will grow into a Queen bee.'[86] If any body manufactured that substance, it was the Tory rank and file, who paid homage to her at annual party conferences. She drew strength from their communion, overcoming a deep fear of failure (confided to her daughter Carol) and confirming her sense that she was the incarnation of Conservatism. More and more, indeed, she became 'conscious that in some strange way I was instinctively speaking and feeling in harmony with the great majority of the population'.[87] In the words of her future Chancellor, Nigel Lawson, this state of mind was 'part of the hubris that led to her nemesis'.[88]

For the moment, though, Mrs Thatcher found being leader of the opposition purgatory. Heath remained an angry, taurine presence behind her. She could only commend his campaign to confirm Britain's adherence to the European Community (EC) in the 1975 referendum, even though it sidelined her. But on at least one occasion his open rancour prompted her to exclaim: 'The bastard, the bastard, the bastard!'[89] Across the Commons floor she faced first a coruscating Harold Wilson and then a beaming James Callaghan, both of whom eclipsed her. Patronised by the latter, she sounded like a nag and a scold. Even in economic debates Mrs Thatcher did not shine, for she approved of the financial stringency imposed by Denis Healey, who (while privately considering her brighter than Heath) said that her homilies on inflation had all the 'intellectual distinction of a railway timetable'.[90] She assuaged her frustration by incessant activity outside the chamber, testing her minions to breaking point and, as Matthew Parris wrote, bustling about with 'small steps, like a partridge conscious of pursuit but unwilling to break into an undignified flap'. With equal vigour she toured the country, descending on hapless citizens like an avalanche. She spoke with tongues of flame and her eyes burned with 'that icy fire which seemed to inhabit her the moment she was on display'.[91] As Lord Hailsham acknowledged, Margaret Thatcher was 'extremely good at walkabouts & meeting the public'. Yet he and other members of Heath's old guard, such as Christopher Soames and Lord Carrington, hated her aggressive style and resented the impression she gave that the Conservatives were 'an extreme right-wing party'.[92] They hankered to replace her, even to bring back Heath. The irony is that for all her sound and fury at the time, and for all her later attempts to claim that she was thwarted in her efforts to inaugurate a radical programme, she took care to adopt the standard Tory policies of her predecessor. Healey said she was 'Heath in drag';[93] Soames called her 'Ted with tits'.[94] Admirers retorted that she was 'Heath with balls'.[95]

'Thatcherism' was not a coherent philosophy and it did not spring fully armed from her head, let alone from her privy parts. It was a set of expedients – monetarism, privatisation, trade union regulation and so on – developed piecemeal over years, more by accident than design. It was not a revolutionary doctrine since, as Matthew Parris said, Mrs Thatcher was intellectually cautious, given to making 'bold, simple statements of the obvious'. Its purpose was to change things in order that they should remain the same. In this sense, Parris remarked, the Tory leader was 'a reactionary of the most glorious sort'.[96] She did not grab the epoch by the scruff of the neck and bend it to her will; rather she let the epoch grab her. She did not make waves, she rode them. She was an opportunist, the supreme beneficiary of time and chance. Nothing worked more to her advantage than Callaghan's failure to go to the country in the autumn of 1978, when he might have defeated her, and the subsequent 'winter of discontent'. This was caused by trade unionists going on strike against the government's counterinflationary limit on pay. Among them were lorry drivers, railway workers, ambulance men, refuse collectors and grave-diggers. To be sure, journalists and broadcasters grossly exaggerated the chaotic state of snowbound Britain. Nevertheless, parts of the country presented a lurid spectacle. Rubbish piled up in the streets of London, cancer patients were denied entry to hospitals in the Midlands and corpses lay unburied on Merseyside. The situation was aggravated by violent secondary picketing and the callous attitude of some union officials – one said that 'if people died, so be it'. During the general election, which Callaghan called in the spring of 1979 after losing a

Commons vote of confidence, Margaret Thatcher therefore stiffened her stance against organised labour. Yet although she spoke with evangelical fervour, her message was milk and water.

It was the familiar recipe of sound money, free enterprise, tax cuts, strong defences, family values, law and order, improved social services, less state interference and more property-owning democracy. To match this bland content, Mrs Thatcher's advisers tried, with some success, to soften her style. Her instinct was to fight the good fight and to shoot from the hip, as when she declared, in the manner of Enoch Powell, that Britons felt 'swamped by immigrants'.[97] Her public relations adviser, Gordon Reece, gave her a less bellicose, more sympathetic image. He made her smile more and act less obviously. He fluffed her hair and deepened her voice to a husky contralto. He raised her necklines and lowered her hems. He dispensed with her hats and put her in pastel shades. Reece, for whom the new term 'spin doctor' might have been coined, discouraged Mrs Thatcher from appearing on serious current affairs radio and television programmes. Instead he directed her towards inane 'chat shows' such as that hosted by the disc jockey Jimmy Young. Similarly he concentrated on the tabloid newspapers rather than the broadsheets, conjuring up favourable 'photo opportunities' and 'sound bites'. Warily, she even censored herself. Mrs Thatcher was strongly opposed to coal mining in the beautiful Vale of Belvoir, which she had loved since childhood: 'I know this area *yard* by *yard*. Only a *Philistine* could think of mining there.'[98] But she refused to publicise her feelings for fear of offending industry (and later sanctioned pits in her juvenile paradise). Writing for the *News of the World*, she first threatened to make union wreckers 'walk in fear', then changed the phrase to 'run for cover'.[99]

Like Eliza Doolittle, Margaret Thatcher acquired a glossy veneer; but it was liable to crack under stress, exposing the coarse grain beneath. Her natural truculence would keep breaking through, especially when she was challenged. Thus she harried anyone in the shadow cabinet who queried her 'strong moral crusading positions'. She vowed to 'finish'[100] an assertive BBC political commentator. She exploded when party hierarchs proposed that Heath should appear at her last press conference before the ballot. 'Scared rabbits!' she cried. 'How *dare* they!'[101] In the event, Labour (assisted by organised labour) lost the election, and on 4 May 1979 Mrs Thatcher became prime minister with a comfortable majority of 43 seats. Before entering No. 10 she prayed for the cameras, supposedly in the spirit of St Francis: 'may we bring harmony' where there is discord, truth where there is error, faith where there is doubt and hope where there is despair. If the call for harmony was Franciscan, the other pleas were uttered more in the spirit of Savonarola. Not for the last time, her wholesome public persona was overtaken by her daemonic inner drive. Or, to put it in Freudian terms, Mrs Thatcher's superego was often at the mercy of her id.

Modestly disclaiming any comparison between herself and Lord Chatham, Mrs Thatcher nevertheless began her memoir, *The Downing Street Years*, by quoting the famous boast attributed to him: 'I know that I can save this country and that no one else can.'[102] She confessed to sharing that conviction and, indeed, there was another similarity between the two prime ministers. Both made elaborate obeisance to their sovereign, Chatham bowing so low before George III that courtiers could see the tip of his hooked nose between his legs. Despite their shows of homage, however, neither self-styled saviour of the nation was popular in Buckingham Palace. Margaret Thatcher was nervous and obsequious in the presence of Queen Elizabeth, who wondered why she always sat on the edge of her chair and was flippant about her propensity to faint in the vicinity of royalty. When the prime minister asked if she should ensure that her clothes did not clash with the Queen's, she was told that Her Majesty did not notice what other people wore – a patent snub from someone who could spot a sartorial solecism at fifty paces. Plainly the monarch resented the arrival of 'that woman',[103] as she sometimes termed the prime minister. Mrs Thatcher was a second queen in the hive and she occasionally smacked of Elizabeth I. When security forces stormed the terrorist-held Iranian embassy in 1980, she reminded the Cabinet Secretary of Queen Bess at Tilbury. A Foreign Office mandarin said that her favourites came and went 'like Essex and Raleigh'.[104] Impressed by her regal bearing on the global stage, where she talked of 'my government' and referred to herself as 'we', newspapers dubbed her the Deputy Queen. Insiders joked that the initials MTFS, which stood for Medium Term Financial Strategy, really meant Margaret Thatcher for Sovereign. But it was not the aping of royalty that worried Queen Elizabeth II, so much as the killing of sacred cows. Not only might Mrs Thatcher's divisive policies disrupt society, but her attack on archaic vested interests could logically include the Palace. Yet stuffy, snobbish and effete though the prime minister found the court, she revered the monarchy. It was a bastion of order, tradition, hierarchy, discipline and patriotism – her strongest conservative values. It was also one of several breakwaters that checked and channelled her radical urges – she would not privatise the Post Office because it was the 'Royal Mail'.[105]

Another breakwater was her first cabinet, which was an amalgam of 'wets' (Prior, Soames, Pym, Hailsham, Peter Walker and Ian Gilmour) and 'drys' (Joseph, John Nott and, at the Treasury, Howe). Across the Atlantic President Carter's Security Adviser Zbigniew Brzezinski reckoned that the balance Mrs Thatcher had struck indicated that she was now 'cooler, wiser, more pragmatic' than the 'dogmatic lady' they had met the previous autumn, though patience would still be needed to deal with her 'hard-driving nature and tendency to hector'.[106] This was not a bad assessment as far as it went. Later Mrs Thatcher would suggest that she spent the first two years of her premiership struggling to free herself from the sink of saturated Toryism. At the time, however, she pursued a timid course, imposing only mild curbs on trade unions, permitting huge wage inflation and assisting 'lame ducks' such as the doomed car manufacturer British Leyland. Indeed she privately acknowledged that her government was following 'a conscious softly-softly-catchee-monkey policy'.[107] Yet she had grave doubts about this approach and behaved as though it were being foisted on her by traitors within the cabinet and the civil service. The latter she often treated as a nest of left-wing vipers. Almost at once Mrs Thatcher instructed the head of a government think-tank, which she soon abolished, to '*Look at your people!*' '*Look* at them, Prime Minister?' he quavered. 'You know what I mean. *Reappraise them!* I know the sort of people you've got in your team!'[108] She might heed and even respect well-informed officials who politely stood their ground. But she ruined the career of one who responded angrily to her ill-informed barracking: 'Prime Minister, do you really want to know the facts?'[109] In cabinet she talked incessantly – ninety per cent of the time, according to one estimate – and seldom allowed others to complete a sentence. She was a hopeless chairman, advancing her own views first, blaming others for her mistakes and turning discussions into disputes. Meetings often became a shambles, wrote an adviser, as Mrs Thatcher railed at her foes in a 'mood of confused frenzy'.[110]

Some of her excesses stemmed from a need, or a desire, to master a cabinet of males. But ministers were personally enraged by her conduct, perhaps because it unmanned them as the lords of humankind, perhaps because gentlemanliness inhibited them from tit-for-tat retaliation. Some did stand up to the Iron Lady, though one aide complained that nobody told her when she was talking nonsense. Others tried to win her round, using such animal magnetism as they possessed – by her own confession she liked being made a fuss of by chaps, and she was especially susceptible to the allure of tall, dark men. Still others sulked or made jokes about 'Her Malignancy'[111] and the 'Immaculate Misconception'.[112] 'Wets' variously oozed and leaked. Mrs Thatcher inveighed against them, insisting on the need for cabinet confidentiality and declaring that she always adhered to it herself, though she actually leaked like a drain. The main conduit of such disclosures was her ferociously loyal press secretary Bernard Ingham, whose alleged capacity for 'backstabbing colleagues of the Prime Minister'[113] belied her reputation for plain dealing. Still, she was not above blasting those around her for lack of fortitude, and she noted severely that 'Dry rot begins with wetness.'[114] Particularly offensive was her habit of slating ministers' papers well before she had finished reading them. As Howe said, they were driven to choose between submission and defection. And this produced, according to Gilmour, the most divided cabinet in Conservative history. In the long run Mrs Thatcher's ill-treatment of colleagues would prove fatal both politically and metaphorically – as early as 1980 she confessed to intimates that she couldn't live without being prime minister.

She worsened the current rift by forming a cabal of true believers in monetarism, a creed that promised to bring economic salvation in the form of low inflation by restricting the money supply. The trouble was that no one understood the theory and it did not work in practice, largely because the money supply was almost impossible to manage or even to measure. Gilmour characterised monetarism as 'the uncontrollable in pursuit of the indefinable'.[115] With lumbering facetiousness, Heath termed it 'the Dogma that Barked on the Right'.[116] Observing not only the squeeze on borrowing and public spending and the erosion of manufacturing industry but also the growth of indirect taxation and unemployment, Denis Healey described the doctrine as 'sado-monetarism'.[117] Having promised not to turn, the Iron Lady bent. As Britain plunged further into recession in 1981, she allowed Howe to relax monetary constraints while taking severe budgetary measures to reduce government debt. Focusing narrowly on the state of the national cash register, she rejected Keynesian investment policies for a regimen of corner-shop niggardliness. Watching the jobless total rise to a figure reminiscent of the hungry thirties, the 'wets' damned it as 'the economics of the madhouse'.[118] In a letter to *The Times*, 364 economists said that raising taxes and cutting expenditure would deepen the depression and provoke civil strife. Margaret Thatcher was not moved. She believed that the deflationary shock would transform British attitudes, and she put her faith in the redemptive effects of the struggle for financial survival. 'Economics are the method,' she said, 'the object is to change the soul.'[119] As the gulf between rich and poor widened, not least because she had linked old age pensions to prices instead of earnings, a conversion of sorts did indeed take place. The summer of 1981 saw an unprecedented outbreak of rioting in cities such as London, Liverpool, Leeds and Manchester. It seems to have been caused by unemployment, social deprivation and racial tension. But the prime minister blamed criminals for the 'saturnalia'[120] of violence. Witnessing the destruction of property in Toxteth, she reserved her sympathy for 'those poor shopkeepers'.

As it happened, Mrs Thatcher was duly able to claim that she had initiated an economic miracle. After the budget of 1981, output expanded, strikes abated and her chief enemy, inflation, beat a retreat. Prosperity increased, especially in the City, and house prices boomed. However, the recovery was mainly caused by a revolution in the business cycle and a drop in global commodity prices, soon assisted by North Sea oil revenue and the sale of state assets. The prime minister maintained that under her auspices British industry had been restructured, to which Sir Ian Gilmour retorted with indignant hyperbole that the process was similar to the restructuring of Coventry by the Luftwaffe. In fact the country had lost a fifth of its industrial capacity in the two years since Mrs Thatcher came to power. Britain was so ill-equipped to compete with foreigners that by 1983 the former workshop of the world began for the first time to import more manufactured goods than it exported. To add to this grim picture, economic growth remained unimpressive and in 1987 Britain's gross national product fell below that of Italy. Despite the prime minister's rhetoric about financial discipline, she never got government expenditure under control and inflation surged again (to eleven per cent) before she left office, to her intense chagrin.

Worse still, unemployment continued to rise during the mid-1980s, its effects painfully visible on city streets – almost every doorway in London's Strand served as a dormitory for the homeless. Rupert Murdoch told Ian Gilmour that nowadays nobody cared about unemployment. Margaret Thatcher cared enough to trim it statistically – or fiddle the figures – on twenty-two separate occasions. In more ways than one, therefore, her Department of

Employment was as aptly named as George Orwell's Ministry of Truth. However, her priorities were clear. She considered that joblessness was a price worth paying to defeat inflation, an 'insidious moral evil'[121] that destroyed savings and prevented long-term economic growth. She also believed that business benefited from a shake-out of labour (not least because long dole queues cowed trade unions) and that most of those out of work were feckless. Unemployment benefits shrank in real terms during the 1980s, but she reckoned that they remained substantial enough to encourage sloth. She told the Secretary of State for Industry, 'I think we will have to go back to soup kitchens.' 'Soup kitchens, Prime Minister?' he gurgled. 'Take that silly grin off your face,' she replied. 'I mean it.'[122]

Mrs Thatcher's conduct of foreign affairs was equally harsh. Lord Carrington did his best to soften it by exploiting the sexual chemistry between them, and for a time, at least, he thought her 'very nice as a human being'.[123] On the whole, though, she regarded British diplomats as decadent quislings. In an attempt to prevent the Foreign Office serving the interests of foreigners, she ruled that the word 'compromise' must never appear in its briefing papers, which had to be couched in the rhetoric of 'battle and victory'.[124] Battle and victory were certainly what she had in mind while negotiating to reduce Britain's excessive financial contribution to the EC. By sheer pertinacity she won a rebate, though to her fury it was less than she had demanded. But Mrs Thatcher's success was gained at the cost of alienating her European colleagues. While arguing with them about 'our money', she once invoked 'my fish' and 'my oil' and finally exclaimed 'My God', to which an anonymous voice responded: 'Oh, not that too!'[125] The French president Giscard d'Estaing, whom she considered more Olympian than patrician, was especially offended by the antics of the grocer's daughter. When he came to Downing Street she seated him opposite full-length portraits of Wellington and Nelson – much as, during the war, General de Gaulle had been accommodated in Waterloo Place, off Trafalgar Square. Even at home, however, the prime minister could be put out of countenance. Despite supporting Israel, she greeted its leader Menachem Begin reluctantly because of his terrorist past, only to have him accuse her of being 'responsible for the death of two million Jews'[126] – because Britain had not bombed the railway lines to Auschwitz. She was profoundly disheartened by their meeting.

Much more positive was her response to Zimbabwe-Rhodesia, where a white minority led by Ian Smith clung to power with the help of a black faction, in the teeth of opposition from nationalist guerrillas loyal to Robert Mugabe. Mrs Thatcher instinctively sided with her own kith and kin, though she was discreet about her prejudice. Her gut reactions were probably expressed by Denis, who roared with laughter when Australian journalists said that CHOGM (Commonwealth Heads of Government Meeting) stood for 'Coons Holidaying On Government Money'.[127] *Private Eye*'s satire on this boozy, blimpish Little Englander was none too broad, as became evident after the Thatchers were persuaded to prove that they could take a joke against themselves by attending a theatrical version, *Anyone for Denis?* Through gritted teeth the prime minister afterwards hailed it as a marvellous farce, while her husband, mistaking an actor who had played a stage policeman for the real thing, complimented him and his ilk for sorting out 'fuzzy wuzzies going on the rampage down in Brixton'.[128] Newspapers in Zambia, where a Commonwealth conference offered hope of breaking the Rhodesian deadlock, certainly branded Margaret Thatcher a racist, and she prepared for her arrival in Lusaka by donning dark glasses, convinced that acid would be thrown in her face. Carrington pooh-poohed the idea and she soon found herself in the welcoming arms of Kenneth Kaunda, who made bold to dance with her. Thus encouraged, and with no alternative in sight, she accepted Carrington's view and announced that Britain was wholly committed to genuine black majority rule in Rhodesia. Africans were euphoric. According to the *Daily Telegraph*, they would not have been surprised to see her home-bound aeroplane 'drawn skywards by cherubims'.[129] The decolonisation procedure was agreed in London and confirmed by an election in Zimbabwe in April 1980, which Mugabe won. Margaret Thatcher fretted over the result. She grieved as another nail was driven into the imperial coffin. Watching television pictures of the Union Jack being lowered in Salisbury, the Iron Lady wept.

She would shed more tears over another vestige of Empire, the Falkland Islands; but until the Argentine invasion in April 1982 her eyes were so fixed on domestic woes that she could barely see the distant scene. The previous autumn Mrs Thatcher had reshuffled her cabinet, flushing out the wettest of the 'wets' in a purge that one of them, Norman St John-Stevas, called 'the night of the long hairpin'.[130] John Nott was appointed Minister of Defence to make the spending reductions that his predecessor, Francis Pym, had resisted. Nott imposed huge cuts on the Royal Navy, decommissioning two aircraft carriers, some thirty frigates and destroyers, and the Antarctic spy and survey ship HMS *Endurance*. Even these did not satisfy the prime minister, who was supposedly committed to a well-armed Britain. She secretly briefed against the hapless Nott, eventually pronouncing him a victim of second thoughts, 'a mixture of gold, dross and mercury'.[131] What she failed to recognise was that the naval emasculation indicated a lack of will to reject the hoary Argentine claim to 'Las Malvinas' now being pressed by General Galtieri's military junta. With astonishing carelessness, moreover, she had sent other signals conveying the same message to Buenos Aires. The Nationality Act (1981), which was mainly designed to deny Hong Kong Chinese right of abode in Britain, also excluded 800 Falklanders, nearly half the population. And on sorties to the South Atlantic Nicholas Ridley, a Thatcherite junior minister, had made no bones about her government's desire to shed, by hook or by crook, the burden of these bleak colonial relics. He plainly shared Denis Thatcher's view, expressed on a post-war visit, that the Falklands were 'miles and miles of bugger all'.[132]

So Mrs Thatcher, who had much in common with Neville Chamberlain as a democratic dictator, conducted a foreign policy of appeasement from a position of weakness. She maintained

British sovereignty over the Falklands as the islanders wished, fearful that the Tory right wing would rebel if they were sold down the River Plate. But unlike Callaghan, who had sent a naval force south in 1977, she did nothing to deter Argentine aggression. Responding to newspaper warnings, she said in March 1982 that 'we must make contingency plans'.[133] But no action followed and she was taken completely by surprise at the end of the month when signals intelligence revealed that Galtieri's troops were about to land. Having virtually encouraged the invaders, she now proposed to fight them on the beaches. Consciously modelling herself on Churchill, she insisted that the Argentine forces must be made to withdraw for the sake of Britain's honour and prestige as a nation. To that end she supported the fire-eating Admiral Sir Henry Leach, who offered to assemble an armada that could reach the Falklands in three weeks. 'Three weeks? You mean three days,' replied the prime minister, who was ignorant about military matters and, as Nott observed, correspondingly 'impressed by men in uniform'.[134] 'No, I mean three weeks,' said Leach. 'The distance is 8,000 nautical miles.'[135]

With the diplomats Mrs Thatcher was more belligerent. She accepted the resignation of Carrington (who anyway, said Stevas, 'couldn't stand "that woman" a moment longer')[136] and berated his successor, Francis Pym, for recommending 'conditional surrender'.[137] She was equally robust with President Reagan's peace-seeking, chain-smoking, language-garbling envoy, General Alexander Haig. According to the diary kept by one of his team, Jim Rentschler, 'La Thatcher is really quite fetching in a dark velvet two-piece ensemble with gros-grain piping and a soft hairdo that heightens her blond English coloring.' But she rejected Haig's suggestions as woolly and Chamberlainite, explained that her candour was only possible because the Americans were such close friends ('with everyone else we're merely nice!') and refused to ease naval pressure on the Argentines. 'Unthinkable, that is our only leverage, I cannot possibly give up at this point, one simply doesn't trust burglars who have once tried to steal your property! No, Al, no, absolutely not, the fleet must steam on!'[138] The

Americans, who blamed Britain for its previous vacillation over the question of sovereignty, now dithered themselves over whether to conciliate the anti-communist junta in Buenos Aires. Reagan, Margaret Thatcher's ideological soulmate, eventually backed America's long-standing ally. Even after hostilities commenced at the end of April, though, he continued to plead for a negotiated settlement. Thatcher retorted, 'I didn't lose some of my best ships and some of my finest lives, to leave quietly under a ceasefire without the Argentines withdrawing.'[139] Talking to her on the transatlantic telephone Reagan sounded, in Rentschler's opinion, 'even more of a wimp than Jimmy Carter – "Well, I know I'm intruding on you, Margaret, you see, Margaret, uh . . . Yeah . . . uh . . . well . . . uh . . . uh."' However she was diplomatic as well as downright, reaping the priceless reward of American aid and intelligence. But she understandably concluded that the poor dear president had nothing between his ears. While envious of his charm, she was, indeed, astonished by his stupidity.

The prime minister also had to keep her less staunch colleagues in line and to rally the nation as a whole. Cabinet ministers worried that recovering the Falklands would either prove impossible or incur a huge butcher's bill. As Rentschler noted, Whitelaw's 'Falstaffian joviality has been replaced by obsessive nail-biting'.[140] Overwrought and overbearing, Mrs Thatcher herself agonised over the inevitable bloodshed. Indeed her famous exhortation, directed at television reporters, to rejoice at Britain's first success was an expression of relief that it had been achieved without casualties. But it was widely understood as an incitement to jingoism – Tony Benn thought her 'an absolutely Victorian jingoist'[141] – and no doubt it did inflame a vengeful mood already fired by Rupert Murdoch's *Sun*. So did her hostility to the BBC, which tried to remain impartial while being harried by what one journalist called the Ministry of Defence's 'brain police'.[142] So did Mrs Thatcher's fierce defence of the sinking of the Argentine cruiser *General Belgrano*, at a cost of 323 lives, compounded by her false assertion that it 'was not sailing away from the Falklands'.[143] And so did her chauvinistic speeches: the war 'awoke in Britain a fantastic pride of country', she said, enabling it to find a new role that consisted of 'upholding international law and teaching the nations of the world how to live'.[144] Like her self-aggrandising manner in cabinet, such rhetoric seemed vindicated by the success of British arms – Argentine forces surrendered on 14 June. An exultant people hailed it as her triumph. The response of massed Conservatives reminded one minister of the Nuremberg rallies. Winston Churchill's eponymous grandson lauded her resolute leadership. Enoch Powell said that the Iron Lady's metal had been tested and found to be 'ferrous matter of the highest quality'[145] – a tribute that was framed and hung in her office. An admiring Mick Jagger called her 'Iron Knickers'.[146]

The Falklands War was the making and the breaking of Margaret Thatcher. It provided her with a fascist enemy who was easy to hate and relatively easy to beat. The resulting euphoria not only obscured the cost, 255 Britons killed and billions spent, but also the incongruity of fighting for islands that her government did not want. Winning lifted the prime minister, who had plumbed new depths of unpopularity, to a pinnacle of public esteem. It confirmed her courage and enhanced her stature. It transformed her from party politician into national leader, recognisable all round the globe. It expunged the humiliation of Suez and dissolved her compatriots' secret fears, she said, that 'Britain was no longer the nation that had built an Empire and ruled a quarter of the world'.[147] It validated her tough domestic policies and secured her hold on power for the foreseeable future. On the other hand, the war fostered a sense of self-exaltation that would eventually bring about Mrs Thatcher's downfall. It dramatised her Manichean view of the world as a scene of perpetual conflict between good and evil; and it cast her in a messianic role, leading the legions of light against the forces of darkness. Taking the salute at the Mansion House as members of the task force paraded through the City of London and the crowd sang 'Rule Britannia', she was transfigured. Clad in martial garb – broad-brimmed white hat with navy ribbon, navy blue suit and white gloves – she radiated vainglory. This pageant was her apotheosis. It sanctified a heroic egotism and aggravated a raucous intolerance of dissent. Unlike Churchill, Margaret Thatcher showed no magnanimity in victory. She spat blood (Denis's expression) when churchmen included Argentina in their prayers. She sacked Pym immediately after the 1983 election, surrounding herself with so many acolytes that her cabinet meetings were said to be a 'weekly festival of sycophancy'.[148] She also looked for new foes to conquer.

Nothing better indicated that Margaret Thatcher's *amour propre* was mutating into *hypertrophie du moi*, if not *folie de grandeur*, than her craving, immediately after the Falklands War, to hold Hong Kong by force against the might of Red China. Britain's last major colony was due to revert to Beijing in 1997 and she was eventually persuaded that the Communist leader Deng Xiaoping could take it with a telephone call. Her plea that British administration (but not sovereignty) should nevertheless be extended in order to maintain the prosperity of Hong Kong literally fell on deaf ears. What the aged Deng did hear from that 'stinking woman', however, prompted a volley of untranslatable curses. In Hong Kong Mrs Thatcher reiterated Britain's case, provoking further fury from mainland 'Chinamen'.[149] She was weaned away from using that term, but her speech, which conjured up fears of a clash between British imperialism and Chinese nationalism, precipitated an economic crisis in Hong Kong. As *The Times*'s correspondent wrote, 'Seldom in British colonial history was so much damage done to the interests of so many people, in such a short space of time by a single person.'[150] Actually all she did was to prolong negotiations over what the Prince of Wales would wittily call 'The Great Chinese Takeaway'.[151] When agreement was reached, in 1984, with Deng undertaking that Hong Kong's capitalist system would continue under Communist rule, the prime minister praised his compromise as a 'stroke of genius'. But, as appears from her memoirs, she resented having to bow to the inevitable, let alone kowtow to an 'overwhelmingly superior power'.[152]

At home, luckily for her, the prime minister faced an enemy

whom she could trounce even though she was his intellectual inferior. Michael Foot was a man of letters who had inadvertently strayed into Westminster and, to everyone's surprise including his own, succeeded Callaghan as Labour's leader. Foot was as much champion of the left as Mrs Thatcher was of the right, and his advent had led to the defection of prominent Labour figures such as Roy Jenkins, who formed a centre coalition of Social Democrats. They failed to take advantage of the polarised state of British politics, particularly since the prime minister presented them as the mould and herself as the mould-breaker. But they lamed Foot, whose unpopular policies (unilateral disarmament, withdrawal from Europe, enhanced trade union power) Mrs Thatcher reviled. Privately regarding her as a terrible woman, he responded courteously in public. For though Foot was a powerful orator, he was also, she acknowledged, a gentleman. With her flawless coiffure she looked like a lady, whereas he wore a 'donkey jacket' at the Cenotaph and resembled an 'unemployed navvy'. *Private Eye* nicknamed him Worzel Gummidge, whereas she was known as the Leaderene.

Foot's campaign in the general election, which Mrs Thatcher called in the spring of 1983, was a shambles, while hers was run like a military operation. She did experience a few setbacks. One contributor to a BBC phone-in programme exposed her deception over the *Belgrano*, which prompted conspiracy theories as well as a play by Steven Berkoff featuring her as Maggot Scratcher. Several subordinates proved lukewarm and she openly slapped them down. And at a Conservative rally the comedian Kenny Everett shouted, 'Let's bomb Russia! Let's kick Michael Foot's stick away!'[153] Happily Mrs Thatcher detected that this was a joke, and she inveighed against one of her harassed speech-writers, Ronnie Millar, who said that it was in bad taste. Millar saw himself as her impresario (though she once crouched behind a sofa to avoid him) and proposed that she should star in a mood piece for the final party political broadcast. 'No! No!! No!!!' she raged, her bouffant hairdo exploding, adrenalin pumping furiously beneath an importunate blue dress. 'I want facts not moods. Facts,

facts, facts . . . Facts about housing, facts about the economy, facts about the NHS, more nurses, more doctors, more dentists! More of everything!'[154] For the prime minister, as for any prima donna, tantrums behind the scenes were apparently inescapable preliminaries to a virtuoso performance on stage. On polling day, 9 June, her daughter Carol asked how, when other leaders had been exhausted by such campaigns, she managed to look 'younger and prettier'. Mrs Thatcher replied that it was because the job suited her: 'it's the job I most want to do in the world'.[155]

A landslide victory was her mandate to go on doing it. The Conservatives won an outright majority of 144 seats, and so, in the Commons at least, Mrs Thatcher became the strongest Tory leader since Lord Salisbury. Her new cabinet was largely created in her own image. She made Nigel Lawson Chancellor, having come (as she cattily wrote in her memoirs) to share his high opinion of himself. He was, indeed, extremely clever but their relationship would founder on both policy and personality. Lawson turned out to be his own man, capable even, in a meeting marred by her interruptions, of telling her to shut up – which she blushingly did for at least twenty minutes. Mrs Thatcher appointed Geoffrey Howe Foreign Secretary, mauling him relentlessly and with so little retaliation that he seemed to resemble the dead sheep to which Denis Healey had famously likened him – until, so to speak, the worm turned. Typically, when a waitress at Chequers spilled food over Sir Geoffrey, the prime minister ignored him and comforted her. Part of Mrs Thatcher's animosity stemmed from the fact that she had wanted the handsome and devoted Cecil Parkinson at the Foreign Office; but he made his secretary pregnant during the election campaign, which surprised the prime minister, who could not understand how he had found the time. Other Thatcherites got preferment, though they all disappointed her in the end. Leon Brittan became an embarrassment as Home Secretary. Having elevated John Gummer* to chair the party as

---

* Gummer was a loyal Thatcherite at the time, extolling the morality of the Poll Tax and weeping at the Lady's departure. But he was also loyal to Edward Heath and John Major when they were in No. 10.

a kind of nightwatchman, she complained that he seemed to go to sleep on the job. She promoted Nicholas Ridley, though he was as much addicted to indiscretions as to cigarettes. And she advanced Norman Tebbit, who was menacing enough to be known, even in Downing Street, as 'the Chingford Strangler'.[156] But in due course Mrs Thatcher found it hard to quell the suspicion that she might be his next victim.

Although her hand-picked second-term team soon proved to be divided, demoralised and leaky, she pursued the policies outlined in the Conservative manifesto, or, as it was nicknamed, the Maggiefesto. The trade unions were further regulated, while the City was deregulated, banks gaining a freedom they would eventually exploit with disastrous consequences. Tax changes aimed to stimulate enterprise by rewarding them that had and penalising them that had not. Thus mortgage holders, whom Mrs Thatcher called 'our people', continued to benefit from tax relief despite the rocketing value of their properties. The sale of council houses proceeded apace, whereby the prime minister hoped to increase the number of self-respecting Tory voters. But she did so by depleting the stock of good public housing (the only kind tenants would buy), leaving behind sink estates. Privatisation accelerated, its purpose being to release nationalised industries from the dead hand of the state and to create a share-owning democracy. Both intentions were partially realised, though large investors gobbled up most of the stock and private monopolies pursued profit more voraciously than public services. Still, there was no denying the improved efficiency of such organisations as British Telecom, British Gas and British Airways. The last was run by Lord King, whom Ridley described as the sort of businessman Mrs Thatcher admired, 'a tough and determined bully, and very successful'.[157] She had a weakness for self-made millionaires. Indeed she measured worth by wealth, the grocer's scale of value. As Norman St John-Stevas told the journalist Hugo Young, 'what she is most interested in is money. She is absolutely fascinated by people who have made vast amounts of it . . . There is no doubt, he says, that is her dominating drive: the thing by which she judges people.'[158] Similarly the prime minister gauged national well-being in terms of private affluence. She disregarded the public squalor, the decay of state enterprises, the epidemic of avarice and the dismal mean-spiritedness associated with it, an attitude hard to reconcile with the Christian charity she professed.

Evidently the iron had entered into her soul and, as new difficulties arose, she got as little sympathy as she gave. Despite having proclaimed that the health service was safe with her, Mrs Thatcher presided over fresh spending cuts, for which she was censured on all sides. She found it difficult to fulfil her pledge to abolish the Greater London Council, and at County Hall, across the Thames from the Palace of Westminster, a billboard displaying the capital's unemployment figures long stood as a defiant reproach to the prime minister. In October 1983 she was also reproached for her refusal to condemn Reagan's invasion of Grenada, a Commonwealth country. This seemed a rueful acknowledgement that the Iron Lady was plastic in the president's hands, as proved to be the case again three years later when she permitted American aircraft to bomb Libya from British bases. Her nation's abject dependence on the United States was further emphasised by the deployment of cruise missiles, with Reagan's senescent finger on their trigger, at the Greenham Common RAF base. Mrs Thatcher was outraged by the 'women's peace camp' established outside its perimeter, which won a surprising measure of popular respect. She tried various tactics to disperse the protesters and to discredit the Campaign for Nuclear Disarmament (CND), even using MI5 to dish 'dirt' on it.[159] As a fan of Frederick Forsyth's thrillers, she was, in Nigel Lawson's words, 'positively besotted'[160] by the security services. And if their 'intelligence' was apt to be corrupted by stupidity, fantasy or fraud, she herself saw subversion everywhere. The prime minister's passionate efforts to eradicate it, not least in and through the secret agencies of the state, exposed nothing so much as her autocratic temper.

Subversion was particularly rife, she believed, in the ranks of organised labour. So early in 1984 she prohibited employees at the Government Communications Headquarters (GCHQ) from belonging to a trade union, claiming that otherwise they would have divided loyalties. Thanks to what Howe called Mrs Thatcher's '"all or nothing" absolutist instinct',[161] she rejected any compromise, displaying a tragic inability to appreciate that Conservatives did not have a monopoly of patriotism. Nor would she accept that there was any justification for whistle-blowers such as Clive Ponting, a civil servant who revealed the truth about the *Belgrano*, and Cathy Massiter, an officer who disclosed that MI5 had been tapping the telephones of CND and civil rights organisations. In fact, after a jury acquitted Ponting on the grounds that he had acted in the public interest, the prime minister amended the Official Secrets Act to eliminate that defence, a change widely denounced as despotic. She was similarly adamant over *Spycatcher*, Peter Wright's notorious account of how MI5 operatives had 'bugged and burgled' their way across London at the state's behest.[162] Mrs Thatcher's futile struggle to ban his book at home when it was available overseas not only made her look foolish but vastly increased its sales. Still, perhaps intentionally, she did kill the canard that no woman can keep a secret. And at least her line had the merit of consistency. As early as 1978 she had felt 'some disquiet' over James Callaghan's expressed intention to authorise the publication of Professor Harry Hinsley's 'carefully sanitised' volumes on *British Intelligence in the Second World War*. Surely it was inadvisable to divulge what we knew, let alone how we interpreted it. Her rule, she told Callaghan, was 'never admit anything unless you have to'.[163]

Singularly blessed in her foes, however, Margaret Thatcher now had to confront a genuine subversive against whom she could marshal the full apparatus of the state, overt and covert. He was Arthur Scargill, president of the National Union of Mineworkers (NUM), a Marxist ideologue whose avowed purpose was to overthrow her democratically elected government. This was far from being an impossible dream: the miners had not only toppled Edward Heath, they had forced Mrs Thatcher to back down over proposed pit closures in 1981, a humiliation that cut her to the quick. Convinced that Scargill would again mobilise them as shock troops in a class war, she built up coal stocks at power stations and prepared for battle. In March 1984 he gave her a crucial advantage, calling a strike (over the closure of uneconomic pits) when the demand for coal was weakest and refusing to hold a national ballot, which fractured the miners' unity. Some kept working, for which they were attacked by militants and extolled by Mrs Thatcher: 'Scabs?' she cried. 'They are lions!'[164]

In fact, as the strike grew more bitter, violent and protracted, becoming the longest in English history, the prime minister tried to maintain the fiction that it was essentially a dispute between the NUM and the National Coal Board (NCB). However, advised by Peter Walker at the Department of Energy, she determined strategy throughout. Matching Scargill in strength of conviction, she refused to let the NCB broker a compromise. She appeased other trade unions, some of which threatened to assist the NUM. Inveighing against mob rule, she supported the police to the hilt as they clashed bloodily with massed pickets. And according to a few disaffected employees at GCHQ, she personally authorised the security services to mount 'a large-scale "Get Scargill" operation' involving surveillance, infiltration and assorted dirty tricks.[165] Mrs Thatcher had no need to discredit Scargill, who, as a ranting revolutionary backed by foreign dictatorships, effortlessly accomplished the task himself. On the other hand, the credit she won for defeating him was largely eroded by her failure to show the slightest sympathy for the destitute families and deprived communities of strikers who were forced back to work in a doomed industry. Opponents saw her as a crazed harpy preying on her own people. And even devotees were dismayed by her boasts about having 'seen off'[166] the miners – whom Harold Macmillan, in his memorable maiden speech to the House of Lords, called 'the best men in the world'.[167]

She had taken an equally hard line against jailed members of the Provisional wing of the Irish Republican Army (IRA) who went on hunger strike in support of their demand to be treated as political prisoners. Like Churchill faced by a fasting Gandhi, she would not give in to moral blackmail. Indeed, she later privately insisted that no one remembered the names of any of the ten inmates who starved themselves to death except the first, Bobby Sands. Yet the blood of martyrs is the seed of terrorism. And just as the conflict with the miners was at its height, a vengeful IRA tried to see her off permanently. On 12 October 1984, it blew up part of the Brighton hotel in which she was staying for the Conservative party conference. The explosion killed five people and injured others, including Norman Tebbit, but the prime minister behaved with exemplary sangfroid. She recognised it as an assassination attempt and told a distressed secretary, 'Don't worry, dear, it's only a bomb.'[168] Mrs Thatcher was certainly shaken, later that night praying beside her bed; but the next morning she gave a fighting speech to the conference. In it she lumped her anti-democratic adversaries together and proclaimed that the decisive battle was between 'extremists and the rest'.[169]

The following year, urged to pursue peace by the Foreign Office and the White House, she did conclude an Anglo-Irish agreement. But Protestant Ulster resented the licensed interference of Catholic Eire in its affairs, and Dublin did little to help London thwart the IRA, whose atrocities punctuated Margaret Thatcher's premiership. Her robust response, which could hardly have been unaffected by the slaying of her close political friends Airey Neave and Ian Gow, let alone by the Brighton bombing itself, gave rise to charges that she sanctioned a 'shoot-to-kill' policy. Suspicions hardened as a police investigation into official homicide was stifled in murky circumstances. Then in 1988 a British special forces unit shot three unarmed IRA men who were planning to detonate a car bomb at a military parade in Gibraltar, a trio of killings that the Irish historian Tim Pat Coogan described as government-sponsored 'murder'.[170] Such allegations were routinely denied, but the prime minister harmed her cause by damning circumstantial television reports and banning the broadcasting of extremist voices. This led to a media pantomime in which actors dubbed the words mouthed by IRA spokesmen, while the public wondered what Mrs Thatcher could hope to suppress by such a bizarre form of censorship.

Having survived the bombers, she almost fell victim to a crisis that blew up quite unexpectedly inside her own cabinet. It was precipitated by her Defence Secretary, Michael Heseltine. Dynamic and ambitious, he was popularly known as Tarzan – thanks in part to a cascade of auburn hair, which he sometimes combed in public, to the outrage of Willie Whitelaw. Whereas Conservative snobs sneered at Heseltine as a parvenu who had to buy his own furniture, Mrs Thatcher dismissed him as glamour without substance. But there was no denying his ability to rouse the Tory faithful, who waxed ecstatic during his conference speeches. To quote the actor Noel Picarda, playing the part of a drunken peer in a satirical revue: 'You can shay what you like about that fella Heseltine – he can't half find the party's clitoris.' The Iron Lady was unmoved by Tarzan's bravura performances, regarding him as a rival and preferring not to see him in the flesh. Towards the end of 1985 they clashed decisively over the question of how to save Britain's last helicopter manufacturer, the ailing Westland company. Heseltine wanted to merge it into a European consortium, which would have a large local market. Mrs Thatcher favoured a more solid bid from the American firm Sikorsky, which Westland itself preferred, as did Leon Brittan at the Department of Trade and Industry (DTI). The argument raged in cabinet, soon becoming personal. When Heseltine tried to raise the Westland issue yet again, she stopped him because it was not on the agenda. 'Don't interrupt me,' he said. 'That's the position,' she declared. 'I'm sorry.' He rejoined, 'You're not in the least sorry.'[171] Both were livid. In private he called her 'the old cow'.[172] In the presence of officials she spat out the order, 'Get Heseltine!'[173]

There followed a vicious subterranean struggle. While Heseltine spared no pains to muster journalistic and other support for his Westland proposal, No. 10 tried to discredit him through off-the-record briefings. It was a technique familiar to all Mrs Thatcher's ministers. As Heseltine later wrote, he saw many good people broken by her Downing Street machine, with its refined 'techniques of character assassination: the drip, drip of carefully planted, unattributable stories that were fed into the public domain, as colleagues became marked as somehow "semi-detached" or not "one of us".[174] Thus on 6 January 1986, the Solicitor General's opinion (requested by Mrs Thatcher) that there were 'material inaccuracies' in a letter about Westland written by Heseltine appeared in the newspapers. The phrase was leaked by the DTI's press officer, Colette Bowe, who apparently demurred until told by Bernard Ingham: 'You'll ******* well do what you're ******* well told.' Ingham denied this, but Leon Brittan subsequently confirmed that such a damaging disclosure would never have been made without 'express approval from Number 10'.[175] And it is hardly conceivable that Ingham acted without the prime minister's consent, something she briefly conceded but quickly repudiated. At a cabinet meeting three days later, she insisted that all statements from ministers about Westland should first be cleared with the cabinet secretary, Sir Robert Armstrong. Declaring that if this was the way her government was to be conducted he no longer wished to be part of it, Heseltine swept from the room. As he later wrote, 'I could not accept such a gagging order.'[176]

Mrs Thatcher had anticipated, perhaps even contrived, his resignation, for she was ready with a replacement, George Younger. She found it harder to mount a defence of her conduct in the House of Commons, wondering if she would still be prime minister by the end of the debate. However, she 'brazened it out',[177] wrote Tony Benn, claiming to know nothing of the leak and saying that the DTI had acted in good faith with 'cover from my office'.[178] Famed for her tight administrative control, she plainly realised that this account would not stand up to incisive examination. For a moment Neil Kinnock, Foot's successor as Labour leader, seemed to corner her and, as Alan Clark recorded, 'you could see fear in those blue eyes'.[179] But Kinnock was not known as 'the Welsh Windbag' for nothing, and he gave vent to a piece of oratorical flatulence that hurt no one except himself. Margaret Thatcher despised him as a vacuous poseur and their personal correspondence was notably acrid, each questioning the other's integrity. Kinnock accused her of being 'melodramatic', and she said that he had damaged the 'relationship which ought to exist between the Prime Minister and the leader of the Opposition'.[180] However, she gained enormously from his political ineptitude, crowing in her memoirs that he never let her down. Subsequent speakers in the debate did lay bare her equivocations. David Owen, the Social Democrat leader, derided her for setting up a formal inquiry into the leak when she herself must have been 'fully involved in the whole affair'. Roy Jenkins denounced a government sunk deep in 'the bog of deceit and chicanery'.[181] Mrs Thatcher survived, as Nigel Lawson said, by the skin of her teeth. But she lost another minister, Leon Brittan, whom Heseltine trapped into misleading parliament. And the Westland imbroglio exposed dishonesty at the heart of Mrs Thatcher's government. It pitted the Iron Lady's image with spots of moral rust.

She was shocked and chastened by the episode. After the resignation of Brittan, whose golden silence was supposedly bought with the promise (not kept) of a swift return to high office, Mrs Thatcher could hardly take in Lawson's budget plans and spoke with 'the automatic responses of a zombie'.[182] She held longer cabinet meetings and for a time became less voluble. She relied more on dependent officials such as her smooth private secretary Charles Powell and her rough press supremo Bernard Ingham. The latter, though, continued to interpret Mrs Thatcher to the media in his own splenetic and xenophobic fashion, making her seem more contumacious than she usually was. Yet she apparently felt impelled to live up to his representation. This was particularly damaging in relation to the Commonwealth, which wanted to impose economic sanctions on South Africa in the teeth of her resistance. In fact hers was the standard British policy (first formulated by Attlee's government) of trying to kill apartheid by kindness. It was even advocated by the progressive MP Helen Suzman, whom Mrs Thatcher admired despite the fact that her Labrador bit the prime minister on the ankle.

The assault caused widespread satisfaction, for Mrs Thatcher not only snarled at Commonwealth leaders but snapped at supporters of the African National Congress (ANC), which they all regarded as a liberation movement and she denounced as 'a typical terrorist organisation'.[183] She seemed less intent on dismantling racial discrimination in South Africa than on pandering to populist prejudice at home. Her stand threatened to break up the Commonwealth, to the intense dismay of its crowned head. On 20 July 1986, the *Sunday Times* made a huge splash with revelations of Queen Elizabeth's feelings. It reported that she found the prime minister's entire political approach, whether towards the miners in Britain or the non-whites in South Africa, 'uncaring, confrontational and socially divisive'. Based on indiscreet briefings from the royal press secretary, who would doubtless have heard the Queen's perennial complaint that the prime minister 'won't listen',[184] the story earned a palace denial that was the hallmark of its authenticity. Mrs Thatcher, whose ratings in the opinion polls dropped sharply, was said to have been 'knocked sideways by it'.[185] But she concealed her vexation and concluded sagely that the Queen (unlike the ultra-Thatcherite Queen Mother) was the kind of woman who would vote for the SDP – in sum, a royal 'wet'.

Nothing helped Mrs Thatcher to recover from such domestic setbacks more than her triumphs abroad, especially in the Soviet Union. She prided herself on having early spotted Mikhail Gorbachev as the man to do business with, and in the spring of 1987 she accepted his invitation to visit Russia. With characteristic thoroughness she took expert instruction. She bought a smart new wardrobe, dressing up as a kind of Aquascutum tsarina. Its crowning glory was the black fox-fur hat in which she arrived, and throughout her stay, according to the British ambassador, the prime minister 'looked like a million dollars'.[186] On television she spoke with awesome candour, championing nuclear-armed capitalist democracy. On walkabouts she displayed theatrical glamour, captivating ordinary citizens. She also struck sparks off Gorbachev, each talking vociferously and interrupting one another freely. Their mutual attraction prompted obscene jokes in the Kremlin and a risqué remark in the Commons – the Leader of the House once explained that he was deputising for Mrs Thatcher because she had decided to 'make herself available to Mr Gorbachev'.[187] She achieved no diplomatic breakthrough in Russia. Indeed, the Iron Lady was hostile to initiatives such as Ronald Reagan's 'Star Wars' programme (though she professed to support it) that upset the traditional East–West balance of terror. Yet in private she would subsequently claim to have made a historic contribution, through leadership of the Anglo-American alliance, to the collapse of the Soviet system: 'Roosevelt and Winston defeated fascism; Ron and I defeated communism.'[188] The modesty of this assessment is on a par with its accuracy, so perhaps the Muscovite adulation went to her head. At any rate, even her admirers were increasingly prone to ask whether 'our dear PM has gone bananas'.[189]

If so, Labour supporters must have wished that she would bite Neil Kinnock. Of course he could not match her vote-winning coup in Russia, whereby she virtually won the British election of June 1987 before it started. But he made sterling efforts to compete on home turf, where the Tory campaign was confused, jumpy and lacklustre, reducing her at times to hysteria. Kinnock's young director of communications, Peter Mandelson, had a particularly keen eye for matters on which Margaret Thatcher was vulnerable. Among them he listed: the 'political Jihad' she waged against enemies within her own party; 'her obsessional hatred of the public sector and her fawning affair with what became known, in Edward Heath's words, as the "ugly and unacceptable face of capitalism"'; her 'insistence that Thatcherite purity is the only measure for promotion in the civil service'; and the misuse of her private office, which had been 'gruesomely apparent during the Westland scandal'.[190] Another scandal that might have hurt the prime minister concerned the rumoured payment of huge commissions to her son on a forty-billion-pound arms deal she had negotiated with Saudi Arabia. When Mark, a failed accountant whose sudden wealth has never been explained, asked what he could do to help with his mother's election campaign, Bernard Ingham characteristically replied: 'Leave the country.'[191] Moreover, Mrs Thatcher made gaffes of her own, telling one interviewer that she hoped to 'go on and on',[192] an aspiration full of vague menace.

Yet she was a model of clarity beside Kinnock, whose television appearances mercilessly exposed his propensity to talk fluent nonsense. Her implacable leadership contrasted with his cheerful inexperience. He prescribed unpalatable remedies such as the closed shop and unilateral disarmament, whereas she trumpeted rising living standards and the rude health of the economy. Prosperity even permitted increased investment in social services, she bragged, disregarding her own strictures on public expenditure and her instinctive aversion to the welfare state in her eagerness to dent Kinnock's caring image. However, as Tory commentators themselves complained, her appeal was essentially materialistic. Even her espousal of Victorian values sounded like an advertisement for selfishness rather than self-help, a plea for private enrichment as opposed to public generosity, a glorification not of Pickwick but of Gradgrind and Merdle. Margaret Thatcher was the hierophant of the acquisitive society. She sanctified individual wealth in a decade when hippies had given way to yuppies – young, upwardly mobile professionals who sincerely wanted to make pots of money. As Auberon Waugh wrote, she preached a gospel of 'Salvation through Greed'.[193] At a time when ten million people were living below the poverty line, it attracted a still greater multitude of disciples. Dashing in her navy and white check suit, Mrs Thatcher trounced Kinnock at the polls, winning an overall majority of 102 seats in the House of Commons. She thus became the first person since Lord Liverpool, in the early nineteenth century, to serve a third successive term as prime minister.

During the first meeting of her new cabinet, held on a hot day, Mrs Thatcher sharply interrupted Sir Geoffrey Howe's elucidation of foreign affairs: 'Please open the window. We can't have people falling asleep.'[194] Doubtless she was irritated by Howe's delivery, which was so soporific that he was nicknamed 'Mogadon Man'. But by this time almost everything about the assiduously torpid Foreign Secretary provoked her. She compared him to a blancmange and occasionally screamed at him like a fishwife. Her rudeness amazed one senior adviser, Ferdinand Mount, who concluded that, although always heroic, she was 'intolerable often, vindictive, even poisonous sometimes'.[195] These characteristics became even more pronounced after her hat-trick at the ballot box. In toxic moods Mrs Thatcher made clear the disdain she felt for nearly all her ministers. Unblushingly she told Kenneth Clarke, 'The trouble with you is that you talk too much.'[196] 'I thought so,' she said to David Mellor on finding that he had not practised in Chancery, 'Not clever enough.'[197] She seemed to think that victory not only licensed discourtesy but conferred infallibility. Her confidant Woodrow Wyatt noted the prime minister's evident conviction that 'nothing she does is wrong or open to doubt'.[198] And according to an oft-repeated but apocryphal story, she began one speech with the words: 'As God once said, and I think rightly . . .'[199] Still, the Iron Lady was surprisingly tender towards toadies, among them Wyatt himself, whom she ennobled. She promoted the undistinguished John MacGregor soon after he embarrassed fellow MPs in the Commons tea room by flattering her outrageously, a performance she observed without expression. Mrs Thatcher's worst traits made her hard to like as a woman and to endure as a leader. As Douglas Hurd confided to a journalist in 1987, 'Her style and method remain a chronic problem for the government.'[200] But personal antipathies were not by themselves enough to bring her third term to a premature end.

The prime minister's cabinet and party were divided over a number of key issues, on which she was determined not to yield. The most important of these concerned Britain's relationship with the EC, which brought her into conflict with both Howe and Lawson. For the sake of political prestige and financial stability, they wanted closer integration with Europe, to be achieved especially by joining the Exchange Rate Mechanism (ERM), the precursor of a single currency. But as the Labour party moved towards the EC, Mrs Thatcher backed away from it, indulging her Poujadiste aversion to foreign neighbours: the French were selfish and pusillanimous; the Italians were so badly governed that it was natural they should prefer to be ruled from Brussels; the Germans were very Germanic, none more so than Chancellor

Helmut Kohl, whose taste for pig's stomach she disgustedly recalled. Actually her opposition to an increasingly federal EC (which she had sanctioned by signing the Single European Act in 1985 but memorably denounced at Bruges three years later) was a matter of shrewd calculation as well as innate prejudice. She believed that the European Commission, the EC's executive body, was bureaucratic and undemocratic. Moreover, it undermined British sovereignty – and thus her power. She objected to a 'social charter' protecting workers' rights, as proposed by the Commission's president Jacques Delors, because it would hobble free enterprise. She fought a long rearguard action against the ERM on the ground that sterling must find its own level and that no one could 'buck the market'.[201] This statement, at odds with her active desire for a strong pound and her tacit assumption that the market was only right when it behaved as she wished, angered Lawson. He used interest rates to align the pound with the Deutschmark as a preliminary to joining the ERM – keeping her in the dark about this manoeuvre, or so she implausibly claimed. Alone in the cabinet, moreover, he was not afraid to raise his voice to the prime minister, especially when she interrupted him with irrelevant points to show off her command of detail. The rift between them presaged her downfall.

It grew deeper as Mrs Thatcher decided that Lawson was essentially a gambler and he concluded that her most pronounced third-term characteristic was recklessness. Certainly they both continued to foster an unsustainable consumer boom. When the stock market suffered its largest fall in a single day, on Black Monday, 19 October 1987, Lawson slashed interest rates to stimulate growth.[202] And in his budget of March 1988, which according to the prime minister signalled the death of socialism, he cut taxes by £6 billion. Nearly half this bonanza went to the top five per cent of wage-earners, while, during a decade when the number of children in poverty tripled, child benefit was frozen. The opposition condemned 'a budget for the greedy paid for by the needy'.[203] Margaret Thatcher claimed that everyone would rise on the tide of prosperity, though she also believed that privation stimulated exertion. What she found was that easier credit and more cash boosted imports, increased the trade deficit and debauched the currency. Ironically, the apostle of thrift now presided over a huge borrowing and spending spree. As Lawson struggled to control inflation and reduce demand by raising interest rates, recession loomed and the Thatcherite economic miracle soon seemed little better than a conjuring trick. In 1989, the prime minister's disillusionment with the chancellor was exacerbated by his attempt, with Sir Geoffrey Howe, to force her to set a date for joining the ERM. They threatened resignation; she called their bluff, while simultaneously giving ground. Incensed by their 'cabal', 'ambush' and 'blackmail',[204] she plotted revenge.

Meanwhile Mrs Thatcher was suffering from a calamity of her own making. She launched as the 'flagship'[205] policy of her third term a reform of the local taxation system, which was then based on the rentable value of property. Instead she introduced a 'community charge' levied on each adult, which immediately became known as the 'poll tax'. Her motives were characteristically mixed and her expectations were sadly disappointed. The reform was morally desirable, she felt, because the domestic rates system had victimised house-owners, especially those on low incomes, whereas now everyone would be responsible for financing local services. It was politically advantageous, she hoped, because voter-payers would check or punish high-spending Labour councils. She would not acknowledge, however, that the poll tax was far less equitable than the rates. It fell harder on millions more people, many of them poor, and cost dukes the same as dustmen. As moderate Tories themselves warned, 'The Poll Tax is fair only in the sense that the Black Death was fair.'[206] Lawson alone among the cabinet seriously opposed it, arguing that the poll tax (unlike the rates) was difficult and expensive to collect. However, nearly all his colleagues believed that it was an impending disaster. The prime minister allowed amendments, preferring to call them adjustments. Yet with a sense of invincible rectitude, she clung to the principle. It seemed to be the quintessence of Thatcherism, though critics also recalled that another such impost had sparked off the Peasants' Revolt. As resistance to the Iron Lady's levy mounted, culminating in a serious London riot on the eve of its coming into force there on April Fool's Day 1990, she sank ever lower in public esteem. With such a captain on the bridge, Tory MPs agonised over their electoral prospects – not least when she visited the tea room to listen to their concerns and did nothing but talk. As Michael Heseltine said, the poll tax gnawed at their vitals. Many concluded that Mrs Thatcher should go down with her flagship.

It was as though Nelson had become a Jonah. In the past Margaret Thatcher had taken full advantage of her own good fortune, but during the last years of power, luck seemed to desert her and she lost her touch. As if reflecting her new accident-proneness, Britain was afflicted by a series of lethal disasters between 1987 and 1989, among them the sinking of the cross-Channel ferry *Herald of Free Enterprise*, the King's Cross fire, the destruction of the Piper Alpha oil rig in the North Sea, the Clapham rail crash and the crowd crushing at the Hillsborough football stadium. The prime minister evinced a real but remorseless sympathy for the victims, so much so that wits claimed to carry a card saying that if injured they did not wish to be visited by her – the same joke as was made about Princess Diana. In fact the Iron Lady was not always at her best with those who suffered: she apparently ticked off relations of people who had died in the *Herald of Free Enterprise* for smoking in the crypt of Canterbury cathedral after the memorial service. Moreover, as the name of that vessel suggests, the chapter of accidents could plausibly be attributed to the deregulation of capitalism (and the corresponding strangulation of state enterprises such as the railways) for which she was responsible. Tory callousness was epitomised by her most ardent ministerial supporter, Nicholas Ridley, who made a flippant reference to the shipwreck, for which he had to apologise. In 1990, a final piece of political incorrectness forced his resignation: the self-confessed former 'federast'[207] told an interviewer that giving up British sovereignty to a German-dominated European Community was as bad as giving it up to

Hitler. This damaged Mrs Thatcher, who patently shared Ridley's saloon-bar sentiments. Opposing German reunification, she said: 'We've beaten the Germans twice already, and now they're back!'[208]

Further harmful episodes took place. Many of the prime minister's key policies prompted opposition, notably the flotation of the electricity and water industries. These were obvious public utilities, and seventy-two per cent of the population objected to their privatisation. According to the contemporary cliché, Mrs Thatcher would try to sell the air next – though to her embarrassment, she could not sell the nuclear industry because of the cost of decommissioning the power stations. There was an outcry, too, over the plan to auction commercial television licences to the highest bidder irrespective of merit, and she was forced to introduce a quality criterion. Civil rights campaigners protested about her attacks on the BBC, about her scheme (eventually aborted) to introduce identity cards for football games, about her addiction to official secrecy. On the subject of open government, no mind was more tightly closed. Mrs Thatcher did not hesitate to conceal her support for covert arms sales to Iraq, for example, the source of a scandal that would blight her reputation for probity. Before that, she and her colleagues stumbled from one crisis to another: over child support, student loans, the pursuit of war criminals, the contamination of eggs by salmonella. Equally debilitating were the prime minister's frequent skirmishes with lawyers, doctors, teachers and members of other professions, which she saw as the rotten boroughs of modern Britain. As always, she wanted less government, more choice and market discipline, but she could not resist laying down the law herself.

She even confessed to making public statements in order to win private arguments with unconvinced ministers. Typically she tried to prescribe what should go into the national curriculum for schools. Acknowledging that she was no historian, Mrs Thatcher was adamant that the history syllabus should reflect her own view of the past as a patriotic pageant of great figures and glorious events. She obviously recalled from school that here was a classic swot's subject, one lacking analytical content but full of names and dates to be learned by rote. Frequently the prime minister was thwarted and occasionally she was insulted, as when Oxford denied her an honorary degree as a protest against cuts in funding higher education. Increasingly, though, she was ridiculed. Viewers jeered at her anti-litter campaign, when, awkwardly accompanied by the chain-smoking Ridley, she tore through St James's Park in front of the television cameras, picking up bits of rubbish that had been carefully dropped for her in advance. She was widely mocked as hyperactive, narcissistic and 'slightly off her trolley',[209] a mad governess bent on talking you to death. Aides would warn visitors that she was 'Daggers today' – an abbreviation of Dagenham, they would explain, 'one stop short of Barking'.[210] The cartoonist Steve Bell pilloried her as a dishevelled harridan jabbering at the doorway of No. 10, 'and in the words of St Francis of Assisi: "cock-a-doodle quack-quack mooo-moooo baa-baa business as usual"'.[211] The satirical TV puppet show *Spitting Image* notoriously lampooned her as a carnivorous cross-dressing tyrant with a cabinet full of vegetables.

Or, to cite another contemporary metaphor, Mrs Thatcher was a tigress among hamsters. Her strength and their weakness kept the Iron Lady in office well beyond what the British media called her sell-by date, thus postponing what a German newspaper called the *Thatcher-Dämmerung*. Febrile in good times, she was strikingly resilient in adversity, when she continued to dominate discourse and overawe ministers. If Alan Clark is to be believed, indeed, she exercised a mesmeric hold over them. In his diary he wrote that 'when she spoke of her determination to go on, and her blue eyes flashed, I got a full dose of personality compulsion, something of the *Führer Kontakt*'.[212] Perhaps she galvanised herself with hormonal supplements as well as vitamin pills, royal jelly and electrically charged hydrotherapy. Edwina Currie, the junior health minister who was forced to resign over the salmonella scare, thought so:

If that lady isn't on HRT, I'm a monkey's uncle. She is round and soft and sexy, very female indeed. It was hard to remember she's sixty-four . . . she's fizzing, in a controlled, deliberate, disciplined way. Still throwing off wild remarks, chucking around her prejudices, waiting for people to argue with her . . . She points a lot, and when she talks the creepy skin on her neck goes pink and blows out a bit. I kept thinking of a turkey which does the same when showing off.[213]

At any rate, every setback seemed to confirm Mrs Thatcher's faith in her immanent rightness and to feed her desire to make others share it. Chris Patten, probably the most liberal member of the cabinet, and thus saddled with the task of implementing the poll tax, found her style 'unbelievably wearing'. Having lost an argument in committee, he said, she invariably 'reopens the matter, picks apart what has been agreed, gathers informal groups to rediscuss it, finds numerous ways of twisting and turning to get her view back on top'.[214] As the prime minister made clear, she was resolved to remain on top.

Even when sinking to previously unplumbed depths in the opinion polls, she remained buoyant. She was heartened by the devotion of courtiers in her bunker, as Nigel Lawson put it, referring to the likes of Charles Powell and Professor Alan Walters, her economic adviser. Her spirits were lifted by cheering crowds on foreign visits. In Poland, for example, where she boldly defended the Solidarity trade union movement, Mrs Thatcher induced the kind of rapture normally reserved for the Pope or the Madonna. Moreover, she was able to represent the disintegration of communism in Russia and eastern Europe as a vindication of her creed. Similarly she claimed that her policy of not imposing comprehensive economic sanctions on South Africa paid off when, in 1990, President F. W. de Klerk lifted the ban on the ANC and released Nelson Mandela. These were momentous events and Margaret Thatcher saw herself as a historic catalyst, the midwife of destiny. Admittedly, not everything abroad substantiated her vision. In the United States she had to eat 'humble pie' on learning that the new president, George Bush, was 'exasperated by my habit of talking nonstop about issues that fascinated me'.[215] As Paris celebrated the bicentenary of the French Revolution, an event she deplored in the manner of Lady Bracknell, spectators shook their fists at her car, to the amusement of watching gendarmes. However, like Joan of Arc and General de Gaulle, Mrs Thatcher drew her inspiration from within. She felt herself to be a heaven-born leader, providentially elected to redeem her people. So she did not hesitate to follow her own instincts, identifying with the general will and distancing herself from the Tory front bench. Sometimes she scarcely veiled her antagonism towards cabinet colleagues. One complained that she was the only prime minister who 'moonlighted as leader of the opposition'.[216]

In the cabinet reshuffle of July 1989, she punished Sir Geoffrey Howe for his part in trying to make her join the ERM and lit a fuse that would set off a fatal revolt. Howe had once been a 'comfortable slipper', she said, but now he had 'become an unpleasant old boot'.[217] So she not only discarded him as Foreign Secretary but let it be known that his new title, Deputy Prime Minister, was a meaningless courtesy. As a further humiliation, she deprived him of both his grand official residences, obliging him to move into a flat off the Old Kent Road – an imbroglio that prompted newspapers to dub him 'Sir Geoffrey Houses'. He fumed like a waking volcano. Meanwhile Mrs Thatcher made it clear that she had lost confidence in Nigel Lawson and his unravelling economic policies. He complained that no chancellor had been more 'systematically undermined': week in and week out Bernard Ingham dripped 'poison' to the press, and she now relied on advice from Alan Walters, who told tales in the City.[218] In October 1989, Lawson demanded that she should sack Walters. When she refused in order to preserve her authority, the chancellor resigned – as did the hopelessly exposed Walters himself. Interviewed on television, Mrs Thatcher appeared jittery: she reiterated that Lawson's position had been unassailable and claimed not to know why he had gone. Ignoring suggestions that she faced a crisis in her premiership, the Iron Lady intimated that she was willing to carry on indefinitely by popular acclaim. She looked to a bright future with her new lieutenants: the personable John Major as Chancellor of the Exchequer, the cool Douglas Hurd as Foreign Secretary and, to her delight, the right-wing David Waddington at the Home Office. Moreover, the suave Kenneth Baker was now party chairman, possessing not only what were euphemistically described as 'presentational skills' but also, according to Chris Patten, the essential quality for the post: meretriciousness. Yet the *fin de siècle* atmosphere was palpable, and Baker himself would acknowledge that the early months of 1990 were for Mrs Thatcher's government 'an almost unmitigated disaster'.[219]

If the poll tax was a running sore, the rift over Europe was a hole in the heart of her administration. John Major persuaded the prime minister to agree to the ERM but after such a prolonged struggle that, having repeated that she would join when the time was right, she joined when the time was wrong – in October 1990, a period of deepening debt, spiralling inflation and worsening recession. However, her virulent hostility to the Community was all too evident at the European Council meeting in Rome shortly afterwards, where she broke ranks with cabinet colleagues by utterly refusing to countenance monetary union. She papered over their differences in her formal report to the House of Commons. But during subsequent questions she was egged on by anti-Europeans such as Ridley – with characteristic effrontery he condemned the intransigence of the other eleven states in the EC and congratulated her for isolating them. She reacted with maenadic force, repudiating Jacques Delors' federal aspirations: 'No. No. No.'[220] This performance, compounded by a final tongue-lashing in cabinet, precipitated Geoffrey Howe's resignation. It could hardly have come at a worse time, as catastrophic by-election results confirmed the opinion surveys and Michael Heseltine was poised to challenge her for the party leadership. Mrs Thatcher was unrepentant. On 12 November she attended the Lord Mayor's Banquet in a majestic outfit – Tudor cloak and black velvet gown with high collar and pearls. As one journalist wrote, 'She looked like Mary Queen of Scots on her way to the scaffold.'[221] But she put on a singular show of bravado. 'I am still at the crease,' she said, 'and though the bowling has been pretty hostile of late . . . [it's] going to get hit all over the ground. That's my style.'[222]

The following day Howe demonstrated in his resignation speech to the Commons that the somnambulistic style could be more devastating than the histrionic. With infinite politeness he conducted a public execution, garrotting Mrs Thatcher, as it were, with a silken cord. First he dismissed her claim that there was no issue of substance between them: if his critics were to be believed, he was 'the first minister in history who has resigned because he was in full agreement with government policy'. Then he deprecated her 'nightmare image' of a continent full of malign people scheming to extinguish British democracy and identity. Her representatives in Europe could not negotiate against such 'background noise'. Indeed, he added, memorably turning the prime minister's cricket metaphor against her, 'It is rather like sending your opening batsmen to the crease only to find, the moment the first balls are bowled, that their bats have been broken before the game by the team captain.'[223] Finally Howe said that by isolating Britain in Europe she was taking serious risks with the future of the nation, to which he owed his first loyalty. Others, he concluded, might consider where their loyalties should lie. Mrs Thatcher, who had sat stony-faced through an oration she later characterised as Howe's 'final act of bile and treachery',[224] realised that he was activating a leadership contest. The next day Heseltine announced his candidacy and at once began to canvass support, as one Tory wrote, 'like a child molester hanging around the lavatories and waiting to pounce on people'.[225] By contrast Mrs Thatcher made Heath's mistake, standing on her dignity and trying to conduct business as usual.

Thus her week-long campaign was managed so badly that many senior Tories were not even asked to help – one growled, 'I'd have got the old bat in.'[226] And ironically, the prime minister was attending a conference on European cooperation in Paris when she heard the news that she had just failed to defeat Heseltine by enough votes to prevent a second ballot. Mrs Thatcher at once announced that she would contest it. Back in Britain, she found that her parliamentary support was disappearing, and Denis himself said, 'Don't go on, love.' But she felt that no one else could quell inflation and combat Iraqi aggression in the Middle East – an issue on which she had warned President Bush not to go wobbly. 'I fight on,' she told journalists. 'I fight to win.'[227] That evening, however, she talked individually to her ministers, most of whom promised their support, feared that she could not win and wanted to spare her the humiliation of defeat. It was a formula she interpreted as smiling, mealy-mouthed betrayal. What it meant, though, was that unless Mrs Thatcher withdrew from the race in favour of more popular candidates such as Douglas Hurd and John Major, she risked losing to Michael Heseltine, who would wreck her legacy. Pale and sick at heart, she repeated insistently, 'I am not a quitter, I am not a quitter.'[228]

Despite this, she decided that there was no alternative. The following day, 22 November 1990, Mrs Thatcher tearfully informed the cabinet that she was going, and issued a resignation statement to the press. It was greeted with widespread jubilation. Strangers hugged one another as if a dictator had been overthrown. Londoners whooped, Mancunians roared, Glaswegians danced in the streets. But there were many pockets of sadness: Margaret Thatcher's staff wept; the *Sun* newspaper grieved; despondency gripped Peterhouse, Cambridge. On the telephone Cecil Parkinson told Heseltine that many people were saying that he had committed regicide, only to be asked: 'Reggie who?'[229] In the Commons that afternoon, the prime minister opposed a motion of no confidence with such pluck and verve that even Tories who had knifed her could scarce forbear to cheer. The spectacle disgusted loyalists, and one MP, urging her to cancel the resignation, shouted: 'You could wipe the floor with the lot of 'em.'[230]

Instead Mrs Thatcher prepared for the end. She ensured the succession of John Major, later absent-mindedly explaining her choice to the third runner, Douglas Hurd: 'he was the best of a *very* poor bunch'.[231] And on 28 November, wishing Major luck, saying that he would surely be a great prime minister and struggling to keep her mascara dry, she left Downing Street. As the car reached her new home in a gated community in Dulwich, reporters asked what she would do now. 'Work,' she replied. 'That's all we have ever known.' Of course she would hardly be joining the ranks of the unemployed, which had swollen so grossly during her premiership, but she did find the experience of losing her job heart-breaking. Rupert Murdoch said that she was 'absolutely shell-shocked, but if I'd lost everything, so would I be'.[232] John Major saw the pain 'etched on her face'.[233] Ronnie Millar wrote that she was so hurt by her rejection that 'it was as though someone had pushed her off the planet'.[234] Charles Powell said that after quitting No. 10 'she never had a happy day'.[235] The loss of office was, as she had anticipated, a kind of death.

Mrs Thatcher seemed to crumple physically under the shock. Sympathisers reckoned that without power she was a shadow of her former self, while foes likened her to a vampire deprived of blood, though still requiring a stake in the heart. Yet she gained in acerbity and was no less 'omniloquent', to use Douglas Hurd's term. She railed against the Tory Judases who had defeated her as the socialists never could. Feeling wronged, deserted and dispossessed, she slowly adopted the vendetta mentality of Edward Heath, who had greeted her downfall with a resonant 'Rejoice! Rejoice! Rejoice!'[236] Mrs Thatcher's bitterness was aggravated by the myriad inconveniences of impotence: she lacked an address book and a typist, could not operate the telephone or the washing machine. Furthermore, Denis continued to go out and enjoy himself while she now stayed at home – a place she had memorably defined as somewhere you go when you have nothing better to do. However, she soon organised a staff and started taking renewed draughts of her 'secret elixir', work. Without it, she confessed, 'I would have gone mad'.[237] She embarked on an arduous series of farewell and lecture tours abroad, attracting honours and making millions. Soon, too, she moved from Dulwich to be nearer the centre of affairs. She eventually settled into a Belgravia mansion, setting up an office nearby. It was situated in Chesham Place, just opposite the German embassy, where she could keep a beady eye on the old enemy.

She was also desperate to exert a continuing influence on public affairs. Before leaving No. 10, Mrs Thatcher had said that although she would not be pulling the levers, 'I shall be a very good back-seat driver'. However, she was not satisfied by giving directions and hankered to grab the steering wheel. She was correspondingly disappointed when President Bush telephoned for a friendly chat rather than for advice, and when John Major refused to become 'son of Thatcher'.[238] On the contrary, he proved in some ways to be an undutiful heir, promoting Heseltine, scrapping the poll tax, espousing compassionate conservatism and aspiring to be at the heart of Europe in a country at ease with itself. Within months she was sniping at him and his grey, second-rate, consensual government. The compulsion to carp was irresistible, though she complained of being gagged by loyalty: 'I am the only woman in the country who hasn't got freedom of speech, except for privately among friends.'[239] Inevitably her remarks were reported, as she must have intended. They incensed John Major, who thought her loopy and wanted her isolated and destroyed. But she was so determined not to be an irrelevance that she had to be a nuisance. Like any fading diva, she craved the limelight. At the Tory party conference in 1991, Mrs Thatcher basked in a huge ovation, receiving what Chris Patten mordantly called 'the applause of those she would have led to electoral disaster'.[240] Still keen to beat Labour, though, she did not steal Major's thunder on the podium. And she muted criticism of the Maastricht Treaty on European Union, which was abhorrent to her despite Major's opting out of the single currency and the social provisions. But when he did win a small majority at the polls in April 1992, Mrs Thatcher went to the House of Lords and prepared to ply the baronial handbag.

She took the first of many windmill swipes before even assuming her seat. In the bombastic tones that now distinguished most of her utterances, she proclaimed that there was no 'such thing as Majorism' but that 'Thatcherism will live'. However, she warned that Major's government would have to be 'jolly careful' not to 'undo what I've done'. [241] She thought that its appeasement of the EC posed the most serious threat to her legacy. Having lectured the new chancellor, Norman Lamont, like a small boy in shorts, she privately exulted when, as a result of the financial crisis in September 1992, he was forced to withdraw from the ERM. And she campaigned sulphurously against ratification of the Maastricht Treaty. Selectively amnesiac about her own role in opening the federal door, she argued that it would turn the Community into a tightly centralised super-state. Her baneful interventions aggravated the Conservative schism over Europe and made life almost impossible for her successor. Admittedly she hushed Denis when he shouted drunkenly in the Carlton Club that Major was awful, weak, hopeless and 'should be got rid of'. [242] But this was her view too and she felt deceived by him. In his autobiography Major charitably wrote that Margaret Thatcher's epigones 'poured poison in her ear'. [243] The truth is that she herself, mortified to the core by expulsion from the premiership, helped to turn Tory wounds septic. Contemplating the quasi-Jacobite threat she posed to her successor, Ken Clarke called her the lady over the water. Reflecting on the rancorous in-fighting that plagued Major's government and its eventual defeat by 'New Labour', Chris Patten stated flatly, 'She destroyed the Conservative Party.' [244]

She struck the weightiest blows in her autobiography and in the four-part BBC television series based on the first of its two volumes, *The Downing Street Years*. Even by the standard of rival political memoirs, notably Ted Heath's, her account is a colossal monument to vanity. On rare occasions Lady Thatcher did admit to error, saying, for example, that she should have sacked Lawson. But in the main she produced a heartfelt testament to the superhuman soundness of her judgement and the supreme value of what she had accomplished. The books were competently written by a spectral team of assistants, but from time to time the even tenor of their prose was ruffled by gusts of passion plainly emanating from the acknowledged author. Ungenerous to the 'drys', she slapped down the 'wets' like so many dead fish on a slab. 'When the Norman Fowlers of this world believe that they can afford to rebel,' she characteristically remarked, 'you know that things are bad.'[245] As Ian Gilmour said, her first volume was 'written in anger'.[246] Her second, *The Path to Power*, concluded with a stinging attack on Major's government, which he deeply resented, doing his best to marginalise her politically and shun her personally. But nothing compared with Lady Thatcher's dramatic appearance in the documentary film about her premiership on the small screen. In the words of its producer, 'her eyes flash, she has a look like a laser'.[247] As she defended her record and paid off old scores, living rooms throughout the country were irradiated by her wrath.

She also took more positive steps to celebrate and perpetuate her achievements. In 1991 she established the Margaret Thatcher Foundation, 'to advance the cause of political and economic freedom'.[248] It did valuable educational work, made all her public statements available in electronic form and gave as much access as possible to her private papers, housed at the Churchill Archives Centre in Cambridge, in a new wing that could hardly have been built without her generous support. There was, though, an inevitable conflict between her charitable and propagandist purposes. And this was compounded by the fact that she received large sums of money for acting as a consultant to the tobacco company Philip Morris, despite having supported as prime minister an official campaign to send out 'the message that smoking kills'.[249] No wonder that she resented Tony Blair's indictment of the 'rampant individualism, the atomisation and division or society, the narrow self-interest that characterised the 1980s and helped to fracture our society'. In the event, of course, New Labour did not so much repudiate as embrace the Iron Lady. It prescribed her economic nostrums, imitated her assertive foreign policy and occupied political ground that she had tilted to the right. Like her, Blair was a conservative in radical clothes, and he had no intention of reversing her key policies, privatisation and trade union regulation. She in turn was flattered to hear, from Peter Mandelson, that 'we are all Thatcherites now'. 'In fact,' she remarked sardonically, 'the Road to Damascus has never been more congested.'[250] Far from being honoured as a prophet, however, she was paraded as a fetish, her successors in Downing Street hoping that some of her antique magic would rub off on them.

By the new millennium Lady Thatcher was increasingly erratic. She indulged her taste for whisky. She championed General Pinochet, Chile's former dictator. At a Tory gathering in Plymouth she said that she must have been expected, because she had passed a cinema showing *The Mummy Returns* – failing to realise that it was a horror film. Her computer-like memory began to fail and she suffered a series of minor strokes. In 2002 she stopped public speaking on doctors' advice, occasionally ignored. The following year, Sir Denis – she had secured her husband a baronetcy, which Mark would inherit – died from cancer, leaving her utterly bereft. The Iron Lady faced terminal corrosion. Hesitantly, with flashes of her former spirit, she descended into the twilight world of dementia. This is a tragic fate, but it was especially poignant for one who had commanded others so imperiously to lose command of herself. Despite her pitiable condition, she continued to polarise opinion. The Tory faithful revered her and the press was respectful. Friends remained loyal and Mikhail Gorbachev himself visited her when he came to England. But the old enmities lingered on, expressed in the vandalising of her marble statue in the Guildhall Art Gallery and the sale of T-shirts bearing the motto I STILL HATE MARGARET THATCHER. No fewer than two plays dealt with her death, making it the subject of cruel jokes – she would not be cremated, one said, because the lady's not for burning.

In government circles there was much dispute about how to mark her passing with suitable dignity but without undue cost or controversy. Both Labour and Tory prime ministers decided that there were political advantages to be gained by staging a great patriotic show. What did she think about departing amid official pomp and circumstance? In her prime the radical might have dismissed it as extravagant flummery. In her dotage, the reactionary favoured a ceremony of Churchillian grandeur (while modestly eschewing a lying-in-state and a fly-past) as a fitting honour. This she duly received after her death from a stroke on 8 April 2013. It was a state funeral in all but name, complete with gun-carriage, military pageantry and a service in St Paul's Cathedral graced by the sovereign. Most people evidently approved. But some protested, especially about the bill, estimated at £10 million. And as Lady Thatcher's authorised biographer Charles Moore observed, she was 'reviled in parts of the country that are less important'[251] – in other words, those blighted by her policies. In truth, the national obsequies could hardly have been less fitting; for Margaret Thatcher's most notable achievement was to divide the nation against itself.

Mick Jagger

No one personified the rebellious spirit of the 1960s more stridently than Mick Jagger. As pundits noted at the time, the lead singer of the Rolling Stones was an icon of insurrection. His most famous refrain – 'I Can't Get No Satisfaction' – became an anthem for youth disaffected by the repressive orthodoxies of the day, among them the constraints of grammar. Three years after this global hit, on 17 March 1968, Jagger appeared at a riotous demonstration against the Vietnam war, which took place in London's Grosvenor Square, opposite the American embassy. He enjoyed the experience, remarking that this 'kind of violence gives me a really nice buzz'.[1] And he said afterwards that the protesters should have challenged the mounted police with their own cavalry, '10,000 people on horses'.[2] Soon he was proposing still more drastic courses: abolish private property, change the entire rotten political system, stock the reservoirs with LSD to 'turn the whole country on', support the 'kids [who] are ready to burn down the high-rise blocks and those stinking factories where they are forced to sweat their lives away'. 'The time is right now,' he proclaimed, 'revolution is valid.'[3] He even composed a protest song, 'Street Fighting Man', sending a copy to the Marxist paper *Black Dwarf* with its most Jacobin line emphasised in block capitals: 'I'LL KILL THE KING.' But Jagger's lyrics were incoherent at best and at worst little better than twaddle; it was the music of the Rolling Stones that was really subversive. Their brand of rock 'n' roll was bawdy black blues imported from the United States and amplified into mind-numbing white noise. It was a form of aggression, a tumultuous assault on the proprieties as well as the senses. Modern society could no more resist its seismic power, reckoned the Stones' rhythm guitarist Keith Richards, than Jericho could withstand the blast of Joshua's trumpets. By the end of the decade Mick Jagger was widely identified as the voice on the soundtrack of sedition.

He revolted in style. The antithesis of the melodious Beatles and a world away from moonglow crooners such as Frank Sinatra, he developed a stage persona that was flamboyant and inflammatory. Jagger aroused audiences by his outlandish appearance and his explosive energy, by animal magnetism and sex appeal. With his gaudy clothes and shaggy hair, he was a mix of popinjay and ruffian. And he acted out his songs with gyrations that veered between the callisthenic and the orgiastic. On the boards he would strut, glide, dance, prance, mince, kneel, leap, jerk, shake, wriggle and roll. He seemed to be animated by a potent erotic charge, which some thought 'queer' and others thought 'negroid'. He fluttered his pretty hands and swivelled his skinny hips in a peculiarly sensual manner. Still more lascivious was the way in which he agitated his buttocks. But nothing about him was more provocative than his large, red, tumid lips, which would spread (said the writer Tom Wolfe) into 'the wettest, most labial, concupiscent grin imaginable'.[4] Joan Rivers memorably called them 'child-bearing lips'.[5] Others dubbed Jagger 'King Leer'.[6] Androgynous and narcissistic, he incited both men and women to adore him as much as he seemed to adore himself. To be sure, he was often as hammy as any old trouper exploiting the contrivances of Grand Guignol. He aped the antics of African-American entertainers like James Brown just as he echoed the Mississippi tones of Muddy Waters. But if his routines were imitative, his bad-boy image fabricated and his avowed sympathy for the devil absurd, Jagger evidently possessed a genuine charisma. He had a dissolute, dissident glamour all his own, a unique air of ogling, sneering menace. Anthony Burgess judged that he would be ideal to play the psychopathic protagonist in a cinematic version of *A Clockwork Orange*. The novelist did not admire the vocalist's art, but he said that Jagger 'looked the quintessence of delinquency'.[7] Another author, Truman Capote, said Jagger would be perfect for the film role of a mad killer who cut women's heads off.

Without going that far, he and his fellow Stones went out of their way to affront conventional opinion. After a brief attempt to emulate the wholesome Beatles, they dressed like beatniks and behaved like yahoos. They spat, swore, snarled and sulked. They ostentatiously picked their noses. They were fined for relieving themselves in public. They flouted television decorum, voting down records played on BBC TV's *Juke Box Jury* with uncouth disdain: 'Well, yeah, er, I, er, mean, like, well it's, ha-ha, awful then. Naw, definitely not, innit?'[8] Jagger was said to be 'particularly adroit at playing the guttersnipe'.[9] He chewed gum throughout his numbers and swigged whisky between them. During a performance of 'Satisfaction' in Berlin, he triggered a riot by goose-stepping and giving the Nazi salute. His act became increasingly pornographic, as he stripteased, clutched his genitalia and mimed masturbation. Eventually he bestrode a giant inflatable penis. Jagger's lyrics embodied male chauvinism and race prejudice, occasionally in the same line: 'Black girls just want to get fucked all night.'[10] Often he seemed to celebrate mayhem, misogyny, sadomasochism and drug abuse. Where the Beatles trilled 'Let It Be', the Stones rasped 'Let It Bleed'. Of course much of their truculence was sheer ballyhoo, intended to attract teenagers by repelling their parents. The tactic was gratifyingly successful, and mature critics competed to denounce Jagger's vicious circle as dirty, degenerate and moronic. A favourite charge was that its members were regressing to the Stone Age; they were hirsute Neanderthals with 'primitively imbecile faces'.[11] They even shocked other musicians: George Melly likened the Rolling Stones to chimpanzees and Gene Pitney said that when he met them 'I didn't know whether to shake hands or bark'.[12] However, Jagger insisted that their agitprop against oppressive bourgeois norms was entirely authentic. 'The grown-up world was a very ordered society in the early sixties,' he declared, 'and I was rebelling against it.'[13]

He had much to rebel against. During the first decade of the new Elizabethan Age, Britain was still suffocatingly class-ridden. The country was dominated by an elite, hardly monolithic but christened 'the Establishment'.[14] The monarch herself, venerated like a tribal fetish, headed this privileged order. Its plummy accents were those of 'Auntie' BBC. Its herald was *The Times*, which boasted of being taken by 'top people'. And its essential impulse was restrictive, not to say retentive. Public information was treated as the private property of the ruling caste. The arts were censored. The divorce laws remained archaic. Abortion and homosexual acts were illegal. Criminals were hanged and children were beaten – Jagger's father, a physical training instructor, practised physical correction. Despite a consumer boom fuelled by increasing affluence, little was done to tackle problems such as pollution and urban decay, let alone racial and sexual discrimination. The mood was one of cavalry-twilled complacency, short-back-and-sides conformity. Yet there were signs of ferment, typified by Teddy boys and angry young men, by films such as *Rebel Without a Cause* and songs like 'Rock Around the Clock'. Disaffection blossomed during the early 1960s as the British Empire visibly disintegrated and the Tory government collapsed amid the reek of scandal. Duffel-coated marchers made political protest fashionable. University-educated satirists tweaked the tails of national sacred cows. Progressives embraced libertarianism. Jeaned teenagers defied adult authority. In short, Britain underwent a cultural revolution and Jagger acted out his part in it on a crowded stage.

This was, though, a very English revolution. Moderate, woolly and hesitant, it did not precipitate sudden radical change. Far from arriving at a gallop, the permissive society was hobbled by liberal timidity and bitted by conservative hostility. The new temper of the time found its most characteristic expression in the sprightly irreverence of the Beatles rather than the raucous profanity of the Rolling Stones. Yet paradoxically the Head Stone, as Jagger was sometimes called, could hardly have been more slippery about his own role in the revolt against the old order. Starkly contradicting other assertions, he declared in 1967: 'I'm not rebelling against anything! I never rebelled against my parents.'[15] Denying that he wanted to storm the barricades, Jagger attempted to scale the pinnacles of high society. He toadied to toffs, soliciting tips about etiquette. He cultivated the jet set and joined the Country Gentlemen's Association. Although scorning the British fixation with royalty, Jagger also sucked up to Princess Margaret. Ultimately, despite having condemned the Beatles for receiving their MBEs, he himself accepted a knighthood – a bauble much derided by the other Stones, for whom it symbolised his final sell-out to the Establishment. For all his strictures on capitalism and consumerism, moreover, Jagger was heroically acquisitive. He was more preoccupied by money than anyone that his early girl-friend, Marianne Faithfull, had ever known. And when, later, his wife Jerry Hall received gifts from him, she assumed that they were intended to conceal an infidelity. Jagger regarded music as a get-rich-quick branch of commerce, and he was determined to squeeze cash out of the Stones. A dropout from the London School of Economics, he treated the band as a business in which the most important instrument was his electronic calculator. Not for nothing was he seen as a singing accountant.

Jagger's other ambiguities were legion. Often he played the fiery superstar, assaulting photographers, smashing up hotel rooms and lashing the stage with his studded belt in what audiences saw as a 'carnival of subversion'.[16] Just as often he appeared to be quiet, modest, fastidious and polite, notably in the presence of those he considered his betters – artists, professional cricketers, Fellows of the Royal Society. In many respects he was a Home Counties Tory, cautious, orthodox, old-fashioned. He sympathised with Mrs Thatcher. He was as house-proud as any suburban matron, living 'a prim, prissy, bourgeois life', according to his drug supplier Tony Sanchez, and worrying 'in case someone spilled coffee on his Persian carpets'.[17] In fact, Jagger rationed his intake of dope and drink. Doubtless recalling paternal PE lessons, he disciplined his lean body with all the rigour of a gymnast. Yet, as a devout hedonist, he insisted on nothing but the best and was especially fussy about his food. Similarly, the black impersonator was proud of being white. The professed satanist wore a crucifix around his neck. The serial seducer deplored divorce and fretted about the morals of his children. One minute the career rock 'n' roller admitted that he had 'always wanted to be a pop star';[18] the next he denied ever having had any such ambition,[19] dismissed the Stones' music as adolescent, frivolous and ephemeral, and declared that his only real interests were 'comparative religion and ancient history'.[20] At different times, however, Jagger said that he would prefer to become an actor, music producer, film director or novelist. Improving on the pop singer's clichéd aspiration to be an all-round entertainer, he was particularly attracted by 'the idea of becoming an academic'.[21] Like Peter Cook's comic creation E. L. Wisty lamenting that he'd never had the Latin to become a judge, Jagger told Rudolf Nureyev that he would have wanted to be a ballet dancer himself 'but I never had the opportunity'.[22] To his credit, though, Jagger did confess that he was 'full of shit'.[23]

In other words, he admitted to showing off and shooting a line; but he justified his affectations inventively. Sometimes he attributed them to accident or fantasy or fun, maintaining that he could not seem to tell the same story twice. Sometimes he suggested that the bluff and flash were just put on for the sake of publicity, to keep fans interested and journalists guessing – a tactic that undoubtedly contributed to the astonishing longevity of his career. Sometimes he presented himself as an English dilettante, a man of many parts, a universal figure of the Renaissance. Sometimes he claimed that success had not altered him at all: 'I'm not a chameleon.'[24] More often, though, Jagger explained that he enjoyed changing his personality and did so in self-defence: 'Honestly, I feel I've got to be very . . . uh . . . chameleon-like to preserve my own identity.'[25] Certainly he took on the colour of his surroundings: the yob in the street, the stud at the club, the tycoon in the office, the exhibitionist on stage, the sophisticate in the salon, the gourmet in the restaurant, the paterfamilias at home. Reflecting the varied company he kept, his sexual manner ranged from butch to camp. His accent was equally volatile, slithering from mock cockney to fake Dixie: 'Hi y'all.'[26] At the drop of an aitch the fly boy could metamorphose into a culture vulture, discussing art and books and wine with every sign of connoisseurship. So the questions arise: will the real Mick Jagger stand up? Who was 'the man behind the mascara'?[27] How to lay bare an identity that required such elaborate camouflage – or subterfuge?

The Rolling Stones themselves were puzzled. Keith Richards reckoned that 'you find the pure unadulterated Mick Jagger'[28] when he's playing the harmonica, but added that his friend was a 'bunch of guys' and 'It's up to him which one you meet.'[29] Noting that Jagger was as insincere as he was inconsistent, bassist Bill Wyman branded him as, in many ways, a hypocrite. Jagger's first wife Bianca appeared to agree, remarking that her husband was not famous for honesty. More detached observers attributed his evasiveness less to lack of intellectual integrity than to lack of moral fibre. He would not stand firm. 'He is like a jelly,' wrote one biographer, 'he never really commits himself to anything.'[30] Wary of risk and plagued by insecurity, Jagger qualified almost everything he said. He could not even pin himself down. He was extraordinarily self-absorbed yet, as Marianne Faithfull testified, he had little insight into his own psyche. On the contrary, he often told her that he would rather not know what he was like: '"I am what I am," he used to say.' She thought him shallow, and he seemed to acknowledge that as an adult he was incapable of profound emotion. In fact the evidence suggests that, like many born showmen, Jagger was a triumph of style over substance. On the boards he was a twirling mirror ball reflecting the fantasies of the fans. Off stage he remained all multi-faceted veneer, deeply superficial, sincerely pretentious, genuinely phoney. Refusing to be encapsulated in an autobiography, even for a million pounds, he made himself up as he went along. He was whatever character he happened to be acting at the moment, a concoction of grease-paint, costume and performance. As the music journalist Robert

Greenfield wrote, Jagger was a 'great poseur and role-player, and he knows it'.[31] His life, like his art, owed everything to artifice.

The name Jagger probably derived from the old term for itinerant pedlar, applied especially to a hawker of fish. When the Irish folk musician Ronnie Drew told Mick Jagger that he might be descended from such a travelling salesman, the Rolling Stones' singer 'broke his arse laughin' at the thought'.[32] On further reflection he was perhaps less amused by these fishy antecedents, for he liked to explain that Jagger stemmed from 'jag', meaning to cut or pierce. Thus he was really a knifer, on a par with switchblade characters like Keith Richards and John Lennon, both of whom collected knives. Whatever the truth of this, Jagger found it more difficult to dramatise his immediate origins, which were sublimely prosaic. He did claim, certainly, to be very proletarian on his mother's side as well as bourgeois thanks to his paternal background. But he had to admit that 'we weren't from the gutter at all'.[33] In fact he came from a typical middle-middle-class suburban family, a model of chintz-curtained, bay-windowed, pebble-dashed respectability. His father, Basil Jagger, always known as Joe, was of northern Baptist stock. The son of a headmaster, he had attended university and got a job teaching athletics at East Central School in Dartford, Kent. Mick's mother Eva, née Scutts, had been born in Australia, but her family soon returned to Britain and afterwards she always seemed keen to shed the colonial stigma, particularly the accent. A pretty girl, with protuberant lips and a good voice, she sang in Dartford's Holy Trinity Church choir and became an accomplished ballroom dancer. Both aged twenty-seven, Eva and Joe married in December 1940, shortly after Britain's finest hour. She gave birth to their first child, Michael Philip Jagger, on 26 July 1943 – though Mick's myth, sedulously cultivated, would long put the date a year later.

Mike, as he was called until his late teens, was a war baby who knew nothing of the hardships or perils of the war. Eva was more amused than annoyed when he smeared an entire egg over himself, half the weekly ration. The Jaggers were unscathed by the bombing, which destroyed or damaged 13,000 houses in Dartford, and Mike's first memory was of his mother taking down the blackout curtains. Soon afterwards the family moved from busy Brent Lane to leafy Denver Road, only three miles distant but a distinct rung up the social ladder. Eva, who worked variously as a hairdresser and a cosmetician, was concerned with appearances, and, in the words of a neighbour, 'she seemed eager to have people think that she was, well, refined'.[34] Fortunately for her, amid the rigours of post-war austerity, Joe could afford upward mobility. He had obtained a post with the Central Council of Physical Recreation that would make him a key figure in the promotion of canoeing, basketball and gymnastics throughout the country. At home he practised what he preached, showing three-year-old Mike how to grip a bar bell and teaching him other athletic exercises. Although shy and modest, Joe was a firm taskmaster, slapping or spanking his son for misdemeanours. He was also something of a Puritan, a teetotal non-smoker who said grace before meals. Mike was intimidated by his father but, as a friend noted, anxious to please him. He found it hard to quell his natural exuberance, however, going through phases of shouting, charging about and hitting other children for no reason. He also used his brother Christopher, born in 1947, as a punchbag. At Wentworth County Primary School, where he went in 1951, Mike told his fellow pupils that he had got a chemistry set and was going to blow up the world.

At least one of those pupils, Keith Richards, might have sympathised with this ambition, for he had more than a little dynamite in his composition. He was an instinctive iconoclast, a primitive rebel. Coming from the wrong side of the tracks, he saw a different Dartford from the genteel purlieu of London inhabited by Mike Jagger, and he damned and blasted it comprehensively. The town was a dumping-ground, he later said, for every unwanted Victorian institution – smallpox hospitals, leper colonies, gunpowder factories, lunatic asylums – and not for nothing did it adjoin Gravesend. (Richards' Dartford was a safe Labour constituency, of course, as young Margaret Roberts found in both 1950 and 1951). Keith went on to a technical school, which he regarded as part of the state's apparatus for keeping the 'mob in line'.[35] There his aliena- tion grew fiercer and his mother fretted, 'I just don't understand why Keith isn't normal.'[36] Meanwhile the Jaggers moved to a private road in Wilmington, the smartest district in town. They acquired a Dormobile. They went camping and enjoyed Mediterranean holidays. And Mike, dressed in a gold-piped maroon blazer and cap, attended Dartford Grammar School. Founded in 1576, it was a slavish imitation of traditional public schools, where fags were for roasting rather than smoking. Masters wore gowns and mortar boards. Prefects enjoyed privileges and new boys underwent initiation rites. House spirit, organised games and cadet training were extolled. Caning, which hurt the giver more than the receiver, was the order of the day. For several years Mike visibly flourished under this dispensation. He obeyed the rules, enjoyed sport, worked hard and earned favourable reports – his form master commended him for possessing 'intelligence without brilliance'. In fact Mike seemed intent on laying the educational foundations for a career in business, journalism, politics, banking or accountancy. As Eva said, he had never wanted to be a pilot or an engine driver like other boys. His 'main ambi- tion was to be rich. Money meant a lot to him.' He told his schoolmates that his aim was to be a millionaire.

Adolescence changed his attitudes if not his ultimate goal. Mike was slow to mature, but after reaching puberty in about 1957, he became less amenable to authority. He skimped on his studies, sulked in class and complained that athletics was a bore. He wore his hair longer and his trousers tighter, which got him sent home from school. His first sexual experiences were with boys, but he boasted about his exploits with girls – fantasies that were all the more transparent because he was too spotty and scrawny to attract them. Later he engaged in mild bouts of recalcitrance, opting out of the cadet corps, drinking in pubs and driving a motorbike over the school lawn. He also burlesqued a mannered teacher, who remarked that 'You'd look up and there was Jagger grinning at you like an ape.' Such was Mike's talent for mimicry that he gave passable imitations of hip idioms (everything was 'a gas' or 'a drag') and of pop songs he heard on radio and television. He even parroted Ritchie Valens' rock version of 'La Bamba' in sham Spanish. His mother, who took piano lessons and liked Bing Crosby, thought Mike the least musical member of the family. But after working briefly at a US base outside Dartford, he had become addicted to black American rhythm and blues as performed by artists such as Little Richard and Big Bill Broonzy. Playing them at full volume was also a form of self-assertion. Joe objected to what he called 'jungle music',[37] and when Mike strummed his guitar and sang in this style Eva worried about what the neighbours would say. She told him that he'd wake the dead.

Later the son recalled that 'we never existed as a family'[38] and that his 'father had been bloody awful, he was so disciplinarian'.[39] He further claimed that his headmaster, 'Lofty' Hudson, had been cold, unapproachable and 'an iron-fisted disciplinarian'. These were exaggerations designed to romanticise the young Jagger as a wild and wayward spirit. It is true that Joe was the perennial coach, shouting at him for neglecting his weight training. But although Mike grumbled behind his father's back, he was almost excessively docile to his face. Moreover he enjoyed basketball, with its opportunities for theatrical leaps. He also revelled in the chance to perform as a (self-consciously bored-looking) rock-climber in a television programme entitled *Seeing Sport*, on which Joe acted as consultant. In fact Mike's parents were quite indulgent by the canons of the day. They always liked him, as he acknowledged on occasion, and he responded in kind. Certainly he was no larrikin in the manner of Keith Richards. Mike admitted to living through the Teddy boy era without experiencing it. As one teacher confirmed, he was cautious, conservative and usually well behaved despite conveying the opposite impression. He did well in his examinations, gaining seven passes at O level and two at A level (in English and history – he failed French). Accordingly the headmaster recommended him for a degree course as a lad of some intellectual determination and good general character. In truth, 'Lofty' Hudson was more of a pedant than a martinet – he wrote a history of the school scrupulously excluding anything of the slightest interest. And despite griping about Hudson's regime, his most famous pupil declared when opening the Mick Jagger Centre for Performing Arts at his alma mater in 2000: 'I loved my schooldays.'[40] During the ceremony the octogenarian Joe tearfully confided to his son's chauffeur, 'I'm so very proud.'[41]

Mike began his course at the London School of Economics in September 1960, assisted by a state grant and by cash earned from a summer job as a porter at Bexley Mental Hospital, where he was said to have lost his virginity to a nymphomaniac nurse in a linen closet. His tutor at the LSE, the economic historian Walter Stern, found him a normal, unpolished, middle-of-the-road youth, 'very shy, very polite'.[42] But Jagger was plainly nervous about being at university and he worried especially about his weakness in mathematics, which might thwart his commercial ambitions. Such ambitions were hardly fashionable at the LSE, and Jagger was quick to reflect its radical ethos. He looked bohemian, talked Billingsgate, despised Toryism and espoused communism. He sang with friends – they had earlier formed an amateur band called Little Boy Blue and the Blue Boys – and acted out the lyrics in an ever more brazen manner. Soon he no longer answered to Mike, insisting on the hipper Mick. He also re-established contact with Keith Richards, fortuitously meeting him while going up to London by train and discovering that they shared a passion for Chicago bluesmen, among them Muddy Waters, Chuck Berry, Bo Diddley and Howlin' Wolf. Richards was then at Sidcup Art College, which, like many such institutions at the time, was a nursery for rhythm and blues musicians. Invariably dressed in a purple shirt, denim jacket and drainpipe jeans, he devoted what time he had left from playing the guitar to playing the fool – setting fire to dustbins or feeding pep pills to the cockatoo at a nearby zoo. Jagger was fascinated by this cool desperado and tried to emulate him. When Richards began jamming with the Blue Boys, he told an aunt that 'Mick is the greatest R&B singer this side of the Atlantic and I don't mean maybe.'[43]

In truth Jagger was at first, as George Melly ironically remarked, a blues shouter 'from the Thames Valley cotton fields'. His performances, distinguished only by their sexual dynamism, were 'almost grotesquely derivative'.[44] They were *doubly* derivative: imitations of northern black professionals who drew on the music of their poor relations in the Deep South. To paraphrase Bo Diddley, Jagger's group reproduced his (Diddley's) pulsating rhythms, which owed much to the raw emotion generated by the legendary Delta maestro Robert Johnson, who had learned from the Devil himself. Of course all music is mimetic, echoing and blending different styles. Thus rhythm and blues incorporated elements of soul, jazz, folk and country, and it easily slid into rock 'n' roll. Great pretender though he was, Jagger could hardly conceal the fact that he was a singing ventriloquist, a dancing copycat. Yet he did lay claim to originality. This was because he and his friends alloyed Afro-American R&B – itself a broadside against racial injustice and a tattoo of masculine virility – with their own bolshie, raunchy riffs and jangling, percussive licks. As such their music would transfix newly affluent teenagers bored by a pop scene offering, in the honeyed words of David Jacobs, host of *Juke Box Jury*, 'excellent entertainment for all the family'.[45] What that chiefly meant was candyfloss ballads and bubble-gum tunes rendered by Cliff Richard, Tommy Steele and their ilk. To be sure, Tin Pan Alley was full of other noises, sounds and sweet airs, extending from skiffle to bebop. And dominating the cacophony was the King over the water, Elvis Presley, notoriously accused of stealing the blues from the blacks. A 'godlike hermaphrodite'[46] with a gift for coloured simulation and pelvic oscillation, he largely anticipated Jagger. But Presley descended into grotesque self-parody, said his English epigone, who strove to forge his own kind of authenticity.

Jagger's early efforts were ludicrous yet mesmeric. A student during the week, he rehearsed at weekends and got his first serious chance to sing in public at Alexis Korner's Ealing Jazz Club in the spring of 1962. Korner was another R&B aficionado, and his group, which included Charlie Watts on drums, gave occasional guest spots to Brian Jones on slide guitar. Jones's virtuoso technique, foppish accent and delinquent behaviour intrigued Jagger and Richards. Amazed to find 'their' music being so brilliantly played by a white contemporary, they haunted Korner's Ealing basement, itself about as sordid as Liverpool's Cavern Club, where the Beatles had just begun to make their mark. And aged nineteen, his nerves steadied by draughts of beer but his clothes still sober (blue cardigan, white shirt, striped tie), Jagger took to the tiny stage. Korner thought his singing diabolical. He could not get in key. His vocal range was limited. When performing numbers like Chuck Berry's 'Around and Around' he began what was nastily described as 'niggerising with a fake greasy dialect'. Moreover, his transsexual slinkiness quickly earned him the nickname 'Marilyn Monroe'. From spinning top to writhing bottom, he stunned spectators. 'His mannerisms and his attitude were repulsive in the truest sense of that word,' said one. 'I know people who were simply too *embarrassed* to watch.'[47] But others, both male and female, were captivated by his act. Korner recognised that Jagger had a spellbinding stage presence and offered him paid appearances. Jagger's parents worried that he was neglecting his education and thought that there was no future for him in music. Considering his ability to entertain rather than his technical proficiency, Korner tried to reassure Eva: 'He's the best singer I know.'

Canny to a fault, Jagger kept his career options open. He did not enjoy commuting from Dartford or living on a student grant, telling his tutor that he was fagged out and couldn't afford to buy himself lunch. But when Stern suggested that he should bring sandwiches, Jagger replied: 'I don't eat sandwiches.'[48] He was also bored by most of the subjects he was studying, such as British government and English legal institutions. As he would say in the lingo of a later age, 'It wasn't like it was Oxford and it had been the most wonderful time of my life.'[49] Nevertheless, he did enough to scrape though his first examinations, in June 1962, and he persevered at the LSE well after the Rolling Stones came into being the following month. The formation of the group, its characteristic sound and its name owed almost everything to Brian

Jones. A blond, baby-faced ex-public-schoolboy prone to larceny, brutality and lechery (he had already sired several illegitimate children), Jones craved the sweets of stardom. He hoped to attain them by leading a band that would popularise the transgressive Afro-American music he loved. After holding auditions, he recruited Jagger, Richards, the prognathous-jawed pianist Ian ('Stu') Stewart and others who were soon replaced. Stuck for a moniker, Jones chose 'The Rollin' Stones' (the g was later reinstated) in homage to Muddy Waters, who had used the phrase. Stewart said that it made them sound like Irish acrobats, but in black rock argot the term signifies jiggling testicles, male potency. Nobody knew what to expect at the Stones' first gig, which took place in Oxford Street's Marquee Club on 12 July 1962. Jagger, alone billed by name, hoped that they wouldn't be mistaken for 'a rock 'n' roll outfit'.[50] Blues purists booed them as such. But half the audience cheered and danced, excited by the sensuality of the singer and galvanised by the electric din.

In the ensuing months, as the Stones struggled to define their identity, Jagger sought to determine his destiny. That summer he left home and moved into a Chelsea flat with Richards and Jones. They dwelt in fabled squalor, surrounded by flaking wallpaper, ragged curtains, ramshackle furniture, mouldy food and dozens of unwashed milk bottles. Their habits were equally disgusting. They spat on the walls, threw dirty plates out of the window, made a bonfire of their sheets, and secretly tape-recorded noises emitted by visitors to the bathroom, playing them back with shrieks of mirth. There were also episodes of sadism and vandalism in which, as Jagger remarked, 'we'd go round smashing things up'.[51] All this seemed to mark a revolution in his fastidious bent, but it was more a whimsical experiment in alternative living. So too was the quasi-gay phase he went through for six months. Wearing a blue linen housecoat, flouncing about and gesticulating extravagantly, Jagger behaved, said one witness, like a 'real King's Road queen'.[52] Yet he was simultaneously trying out a laddish persona. At the Marquee Club he was seen pawing drunkenly at a girl in a strapless pink dress. He apparently bedded Jones's current girlfriend. And he sent hackneyed pleas to a black school-girl called Cleo Sylvestre: 'I want somebody to share everything with, someone to respect, not just someone to sleep with. Please make me happy. It's the one thing that's missing in my life right now.'[53] Where did his future lie? To Richards' amusement, Jagger had his palm read and appeared to be impressed by the verdict: 'You've got the star of fame! *It's all there.*'[54] Fame seemed an unlikely prospect during the freezing winter of 1962–3, when the trio sometimes stayed in bed to keep warm. They also scrounged money for the gas meter and for cigarettes, and stole potatoes to stave off hunger. Jones indulged in Chaplinesque fantasies about cutting up their blankets to make sandwiches – hardly Jagger's cup of tea. Stewart dreaded entering the flat because of their bizarre goings-on: 'I used to think they were fuckin' insane at times.'[55]

There was method in their madness, though, as Jagger attended lectures, Richards got his mojo working and Jones jockeyed for engagements. These were thin on the ground, and when the Stones made their first attempt to record a song, Decca told them that their singer was hopeless. There seemed little hope for any of them. Jones apart, they still lacked musical finesse, especially in the rhythm section. Jagger was committed only to Jagger. Richards was widely regarded as a hooligan. And far from being the only pebbles on the beach, the Stones were competing with a proliferation of pop groups that the writer Bernard Levin described as 'the most extraordinary phenomenon in the world of entertainment of the whole decade'.[56] Also extraordinary was the advent of the Beatles, who rose without trace from local heroes to global idols. They were the most celebrated troubadours of an age when, as John Betjeman noted, popular music became the poetry of youth. Stone frenzy could never match Beatlemania, and while the Merseyside quartet was on the scene the Thames delta group would always play second fiddle. However the Stones did start to roll once they acquired a talented bass player, Bill Wyman, who actually possessed an amplifier, and a superb jazz drummer, Charlie Watts, who provided what Jagger called their 'driving beat'.[57] In February 1963, the impresario Giorgio Gomelsky gave them their first real opportunity: regular appearances at the so-called Crawdaddy Club, accommodated at the back of the Station Hotel, Richmond. Gomelsky admired Richards, who was 'always at war', and he liked the way Jagger treated the stage as an 'altar of pleasure'.[58] At first audiences were bemused by the frantic turbulence of the band and by the singer's coquettish capers. But within weeks the exhilaration increased with the decibel level until, Richards said, it exploded in a 'sort of hysterical wail, a weird sound like a hundred orgasms as once'.[59]

Many who packed the Crawdaddy Club as the Beatles' second single 'Please Please Me' topped the charts reckoned that the secret of the Stones' success lay in Jagger's carnal allure. This was the view of George Melly, who disparaged the rest of the group: Jones was admittedly pretty, but Richards was sinister, Watts looked Aztec and Wyman was 'a hole in the air'.[60] Another singer, Phil May, extolled Jagger's ability to 'turn on' both men and women, which required more sophistication than 'just wriggling your ass'.[61] Dick Rowe, the Decca manager who had rejected the Beatles but would accept the Stones, once confessed that although he was a happily married man with a large family, 'I'd love to fuck Mick Jagger.'[62] When the Beatles themselves joined the ululating throng at the Crawdaddy Club in April 1963, John Lennon concluded that Jagger *was* the Stones. Observing his unkempt tresses and unbuttoned gestures, Lennon frankly envied Jagger's 'rebel image'.[63] When they fell out subsequently, however, he changed his tune, saying that he had always thought 'Mick's a joke, with all that fag dancing'.[64] Some early fans were also more amused than impressed by the singer, finding Jones sexier, Richards earthier and Watts straighter. With his golden fleece, his lickerish grin and his hypnotic dexterity, Jones was certainly the initial 'scream-provoker-in-chief'.[65] Richards ruled the stage as an elemental force, an atavistic disturber of the peace, an aboriginal raver whose hair seemed to have been 'cut with a tomahawk'.[66] Watts was resonantly honest. According to a saxophonist who would sometimes accompany them, he and Richards were the 'heart and soul of the band'.[67] So Jagger was a star in the making who shone most brightly as part of a constellation. As the relative failure of his solo efforts would eventually prove, he was at his best in conjunction with the others. It was the group dynamic that thrilled Andrew Loog Oldham, a nineteen-year-old showbiz huckster, who first heard them on 28 April and proposed that he should become their manager. But, as Melly unforgettably observed, Oldham 'looked at Jagger as Sylvester looks at Tweetie Pie'.

Oldham not only signed up the Stones but became a Svengali to Jagger. Another louche ex-public-schoolboy, he modelled himself on the fast-talking, amoral talent agent Johnny Jackson, played by Laurence Harvey in the 1959 film *Expresso Bongo*, and on the vicious American music entrepreneur Phil Spector. Oldham had worked briefly for the fashion designer Mary Quant and had helped to publicise the Beatles. He had also plumbed the depths of the music business while doing jobs for the record producer Joe Meek, who took advice about hits from the ghost of Buddy Holly and eventually committed suicide after murdering his landlady. Meek was tone deaf and, according to the Outlaws' drummer Bobby Graham, 'as queer as a pork chop in a synagogue'; Oldham didn't 'know a crotchet from a hatchet',[68] said the Shadows' drummer Tony Meehan, and everybody assumed that he was homosexual. What mattered, though, was that he had a nose for Jagger's aphrodisiac aura and for the magic atmosphere generated by the Stones. They were producing 'the sort of music and performance that could storm the country'.[69] Furthermore, this 'incredible bullshitter, fantastic hustler', as Richards characterised Oldham, proceeded to use every trick of his ruthless trade to ensure that they did so. Surprisingly, Jagger posed an immediate problem. To get the Stones going Oldham had to team up with a mature but mangy Tin Pan Alley cat called Eric Easton, who wanted to drop Jagger because he couldn't sing. Others in that crooked back street decried the vocalist's giblet lips, and a BBC man said that he sounded 'too black'.[70] Oldham was his guardian demon. He was also his father confessor, kept informed about

Jagger's fiery new inamorata, Chrissie Shrimpton, who hit and cursed him for his sins. Oldham would sit on an Embankment bench listening to the singer's wails 'about the confusion of being in love with oneself, one's girl and one's life'.[71]

Jagger sang falsetto in the first single the Stones cut and he pronounced their whole performance 'shit'.[72] Nevertheless the record, an accelerated version of an old Chuck Berry number called 'Come On', reached No. 20 in what was then called the hit parade. And its appearance under the Decca label, thanks to Oldham's bare-faced chutzpah, signalled a breakthrough. On the strength of it Jagger left the LSE, retaining the option to return. His parents deplored the decision, but, as Eva said, he thought the fruits of an ordinary career would arrive too late for him to enjoy them and seized the chance to make a lot of money fast. Jagger himself fretted about the risk and expressed reluctance to become a rock 'n' roll star – it was 'just too tacky'.[73] But he easily overcame such qualms once fame and fortune beckoned, condoning Oldham's distasteful schemes to promote the band. Thus he winked at the harsh dismissal of Ian Stewart from the line-up, though the pianist remained their road manager. 'Stu' looked too normal, thought Oldham, who initially tried to recreate the Stones in the svelte image of the Beatles. For their first television appearance, on *Thank Your Lucky Stars*, he dressed them in matching houndstooth-check jackets with velvet collars. Despite the uniforms, which Jagger reviled, the programme's presenter Pete Murray treated them like lepers. And viewers protested about their tousled locks. Oldham soon realised that bad publicity was good publicity and that the Stones could best be marketed as anti-Beatles. Thus he encouraged them to play like fiends and to act like louts. He aggravated the resultant bedlam, bribing girls to squeal and inciting boys to riot. He also prompted Jagger to discard any remaining inhibitions. At Decca Jagger and Richards behaved like 'complete animals', one witness recalled, putting their feet on Dick Rowe's desk and 'saying "sod this" and "eff that"'.[74] When the actor Anthony Steel asked Jagger in a King's Road restaurant whether he was male or female, the singer unzipped his trousers and 'slammed his cock on the table'.[75]

In September 1963 Jagger and Richards moved to a house in Kilburn with Oldham, who was obviously intent on protecting his investment. It was an unstable ménage, since Jagger had frequent squabbles with Chrissie Shrimpton. Despite his acne she found him attractive and especially admired the fleck of brown in one of his blue eyes. But she hated his arrogance and occasionally saluted him, to his fury, with '*Heil* Jagger!'[76] She also caught him naked in bed with Oldham, and although this sleeping arrangement was apparently chaste, she concluded that Jagger was bisexual. Without doubt he was hyperactive heterosexually. He continued his relationship with Cleo Sylvestre. And as the Stones began a ceaseless programme of performances, he became the willing victim of what Richards called 'feral body-snatching girls'.[77] Indeed, Jagger, Jones and Wyman solicited their attentions and competed with each other about how many they scored, promiscuous to the point of satyriasis. Richards expressed surprise that his friend could divorce copulation from emotion and he attributed it to a basic contempt for the opposite sex. 'Mick's attitude towards women is that they are *cattle*,' he said. 'They are *goods*.'[78] Jagger did affirm that they were all groupies, and he frequently treated them as such. Of course this was not unusual in the world of pop music, which endorsed John Lennon's ineffable maxim that 'Women should be obscene, not heard.'[79] Yet Marianne Faithfull was moved to describe Jagger as a repulsive male chauvinist, and the feminist Caroline Coon called him 'a fucking macho pig'.[80] He claimed to like women but it is clear that, in patriarchal fashion, he really liked them under his thumb. And he desired them enough to pursue them compulsively, achieving a remarkable record of high infidelity.

Jagger said that everything the Stones did as they catapulted to success, especially during their first three British tours (autumn 1963 and early winter 1964), was spontaneous. They prided themselves on their sincerity and made no concessions to commercialism. Far from calculating his own effects, Jagger performed as the spirit moved him. 'Nobody has had to suggest things to us,' he declared. 'We just act ourselves.'[81] None of this was true. From the first the group was a money-making machine, appearing everywhere it could and even providing the soundtrack on two television commercials for Kellogg's Rice Krispies. Jagger himself studied to please. He scrutinised the techniques of other performers – the whooping curvets of Little Richard, the funky stomping of Tina Turner – and tried to replicate them. His eurhythmics were far from being an impromptu response to the music, said the singer George Gallacher, who once saw him rehearsing James Brown's movements in front of a full-length mirror – he looked 'like a stick insect in some weird mating dance'.[82] Egged on by Oldham, the Stones adapted their sound to suit popular taste. Acknowledging the cult status of 'pure' rhythm and blues, they invigorated it with a ferocious rock 'n' roll beat. The antisocial reverberations and the anarchic spectacle, accentuated by Jagger's transvestite rig, were in some sense an expression of Oldham's fissile personality. In manic moods he was not so much an agent as an *agent provocateur*. Wearing greasepaint and employing a hoodlum as a minder, he enveloped the Stones in an ambience of lewdness and menace. Demanding that they turn out their own material, he allegedly locked Jagger and Richards in a kitchen until they had written a song, thus inaugurating their productive partnership. Oldham got *Melody Maker* to publish the notorious headline, 'Would You Let Your Daughter Go With A Rolling Stone?'.[83] He also put advertisements in the musical press for 'Mick Jagger lips. Order now. Be with the in-crowd. Full details from your local lip dealer.'[84]

Jagger upstaged Jones literally and metaphorically as the Stones rose to national fame. With curling lips and twirling hips, with a shudder of the torso and a shimmy of the feet, he stimulated pubescent girls – teeny-boppers – into paroxysms of ecstasy. They howled and jived and stamped. Sometimes they pelted him with underwear. Often they lost control completely – old stagers would quip that there was not a dry seat in the house. Scenes of mayhem occurred that Richards brightly likened to the Western Front:

'people gasping, tits hanging out, chicks choking, nurses, ambulances. We couldn't hear ourselves.'[85] Audiences were equally deafened, and for fun the Stones would occasionally bash out 'Popeye the Sailor Man'. Jagger relished the adulation and took easily to stardom. He enjoyed hobnobbing with notables such as David Bailey and the Marquess of Bath. And he emerged as the spokesman of the Stones, frequently amiable and candid with reporters but just as frequently sullen and rude. He also became boorish towards his chief rival as the band's heart-throb. In alliance with Richards, he took to needling Jones, disdaining his pretensions to lead the band, mocking his peacock taste in clothes. Oldham encouraged the Stones to strike sparks off one another. But Jones, who was asthmatic and neurotic, became increasingly demoralised by the animosity of the songwriting duo. Moreover, he was marginalised as Jagger and Richards began to improve on their first efforts. These were schmaltzy ballads containing such mighty lines as:

> Last night I needed you so bad
> I was alone and feeling sad.

But although songs like 'As Tears Go By' did well in the charts, even their authors agreed with Oldham that they were 'pretty shitty'.[86]

In the same vein Stu would usher his 'three-chord wonders' out of their dressing-room with the words: 'Come on my little shower of shit – you're on!'[87] But Jagger believed that the Stones would only last for a couple of years, and he was impatient to emulate the Beatles, who had just conquered the New World – while seventy-three million people watched them on *The Ed Sullivan Show*, it was said, 'there wasn't a hubcap stolen anywhere in America'.[88] After all, the Stones seemed to have earned the right to take the blues back to the States. They had broadcast often, played live almost every evening for a year and issued their first album, which knocked *With the Beatles* off the top spot. Entitled simply *The Rolling Stones*, it was made at Regent Sound (in Denmark Street), where the acoustics were regulated by a mosaic of egg boxes. Here was a suitably crude venue for an obscene ditty, recorded for fun, in which Jagger hymned Oldham's supposed taste for cunnilingus. But the studio's primitive equipment reproduced the edgy tones of the group in unmixed form, particularly effective in the key, and off-key, Jagger–Richards pop ballad 'Tell Me'. This did well as a single across the Atlantic and when the Stones landed at the newly named John F. Kennedy airport, in June 1964, they were greeted by a posse of yelling girls specially recruited for the occasion. But despite the publicity Oldham drummed up, they achieved only sporadic success on their first tour of the United States. They were quite alien to a country that remained psychologically rooted in the conservative Eisenhower era, those eight long years of 'golfing and goofing' and 'the bland leading the bland'.[89]

Crew-cut Americans expressed horror at the hirsute, furtive, freakish, simian Stones, who were, Jagger said, almost driven potty by hair questions. Hosting one of their television appearances, the crooner Dean Martin, who failed to appreciate that he was the past and they were the future, said that the Stones merely had low foreheads and high eyebrows, a taunt that flummoxed Jagger. Amid the turmoil of the incipient civil rights movement, his performances offended opinion by crossing the colour line; he also crossed the gender line in what seemed a deliberate affront to contemporary correctness. Dandyish in silk shirt and white trousers, Jagger induced gasps by swaggering through the foyer of his Chicago hotel with a nubile black woman. And he made no attempt to imitate the waggish courtesy of the Beatles, who were acclaimed as the best-mannered musical group that ever perforated an eardrum. Indeed, Jagger led the Stones through what the Australian rock 'n' roll pundit Lillian Roxon termed 'the full slummy English lout barrow-boy gutter-rat routine'.[90] Suspected of subversion and lacking an American hit, they often played to half-empty auditoriums, the one at Hershey in Pennsylvania smelling strongly of chocolate. They were eclipsed by tumbling acts, performing horses and trained monkeys. Even groupies were in short supply, though the journalist Al Aronowitz did see Jagger on his bed in the New York Sheraton surrounded by a 'flock of elegantly styled chicks fluttering as if they all wanted to rub his body. That's what one of them was doing.'[91] At all events, the band caught a lot of venereal disease, thanks to what Oldham called 'indiscriminate fucking'.[92] For Richards the high-light of the tour was meeting Muddy Waters and Chuck Berry and recording, as they did, at the Chess Studio on Chicago's Michigan Avenue. Jagger himself was cool about this experience, though he boiled with rage about their lukewarm reception in the States. Refusing to take any blame himself for their premature arrival, he bawled at Easton: 'Fuck you, Eric, for doing this to us! Never, ever AGAIN. Got that?'[93]

Nothing like this did happen again: Jagger sometimes provoked hostility, occasionally physical assault, but never indifference. And the Stones, touring incessantly at home and abroad, were greeted with increasing delirium – belying the pessimistic title of their first No. 1 single, issued in July 1964, 'It's All Over Now'. Often their opening chords were a signal for chaos. In Blackpool dozens of people were injured, the group's instruments were smashed to pieces and the Stones had to flee for their lives. In Stockton Jagger picked up a shoe thrown at him and sang to it, prompting a barrage of footwear – soon, said Wyman, they had more shoes than Dolcis. Serious disturbances occurred in Belfast. The Hague's opera house was sacked. Fans besieged Brussels airport and wrecked the Olympia Theatre in Paris, where police put the Stones in an armoured van full of sub-machine guns. Jagger seemed to revel in the pandemonium that he helped to excite, notably by turning his back on audiences and shaking his trim behind. There were some 'nice riots' in Germany, he said, where 'real bodily violence breaks out'.[94] During the Stones' second American tour, in October 1964, they still caused outrage – after protests about their unwashed appearance on Ed Sullivan's show, he called them scum and vowed never to have them again. It was a promise he would not keep, since they now also sparked frenetic enthusiasm

Mick Jagger

in the States. Jagger moved wantonly to the beat and he trumped
James Brown by imitating a 'kind of paraplegic funky chicken'.[95]
This phrase was coined by Oldham, who remained chic in hexag-
onal glasses, silk Cossack blouses, long leather coats and stretch
limousines, but was increasingly deranged by psychedelic drugs.
Jagger too began dabbling in drugs, first smoking marijuana and
prompting wisecracks about the rolling joints. But he never became
a junkie like Richards, being more addicted to groupies and
celebrities, who massaged his vanity in their different ways. Jagger's
best trips were ego trips and he mainlined on fame.

Mick Jagger became a potent symbol of the sexual revolution
of the 1960s, that post-Pill and pre-AIDS decade that began with
the *Lady Chatterley* trial and ended with the legal publication of
Fanny Hill. Actually, according to the band's calculations, he was
less priapic than Brian Jones and Bill Wyman, sleeping with some
thirty different women between 1963 and 1965 whereas their
tally was, respectively, 130 and 278.[96] But as the Stones band-
wagon, which traversed the globe, became a rolling saturnalia,
he certainly enjoyed the ride. In America he picked up groupies
in the street, acknowledging that it was a sordid business. In
Australia he and the others sent out for females in the crowd
around their hotel as if ordering room service. In Singapore they
encountered dollies as disposable as doilies. On the boards Jagger
aroused such passion that, in the words of one devotee, Pamela
Des Barres, he impelled 'girls in the audience to poke and prod
at their private parts'. Afterwards he would sometimes assuage
their lust. Des Barres recalled how 'he inched up my thigh, leaving
a sticky trail like a snail had been crawling into my panties' and
then 'we made love for hours'.[97]

Jagger did not attract all females and he disappointed some.
Jenny Fabian, the author of *Groupie*, found him distinctly unap-
pealing: 'He is a great strutting little cock, isn't he, all plumed,
definitely bisexual in appearance.' Another groupie memorably
reported that the lover did not live up to the legend: 'He was
only so-so. He tried to come on like Mick Jagger, but he's no
Mick Jagger.'[98] Perhaps there was substance to the feminist joke

213

that many women who had not slept with him regretted it, but that many who had slept with him regretted it even more. Some of his bed partners may have felt let down by what Richards recently called Jagger's 'tiny todger'.⁹⁹ But there was conflicting testimony over the size of his manhood. Certainly he made the most of what he'd got, wearing jumpsuits on stage, the *New York Times* later reported, so tight as to push his genitalia 'up and out – a sexual display as aggressively protuberant as a fifties teen-age girl in a pointy bra'.¹⁰⁰ And in general he seems to have given ample satisfaction. An expert witness, the Labour MP Tom Driberg, made Jagger blush by gazing hungrily at his groin and exclaiming: 'Oh my, Mick, *what* a big basket you have!'¹⁰¹

During the summer of 1965, Jagger lamented his own lack of satisfaction in the rock song that captured the mood of alienated youth all round the planet. Ironically this heavily promoted, endlessly broadcast hit, penned by a renowned libertine, was a litany of discontent about commercialism, media manipulation and sexual frustration. However the words of 'Satisfaction' hardly signified – Jagger slurred them in any case, to ensure that radio stations did not ban the song on grounds of indecency. Like his other writing, a stream of semi-consciousness (soon polluted by dope), the lyric was a verbal hotchpotch. It did not lapse into gibberish – Little Richard's 'awopaloobop alopbambboom' made Jagger sound like Cole Porter.¹⁰² But Jagger's fractured sentences were so vacuous that teenagers could inject their own meaning, as they did with Bob Dylan's surreal whimsy – 'don't follow leaders, watch parking meters'. 'Satisfaction' seemed to convey the angst of the era. Despite scansion worthy of William McGonagall, it was in tune with the zeitgeist. And the song was ultimately effective because of the macho intensity of Jagger's rendition and the primal energy of the playing, notably Richards's fuzz guitar riff. The success of 'Satisfaction', coming on top of the Stones' earlier No. 1 disc 'The Last Time', laid the foundation for their future claim to be the greatest rock 'n' roll band in the world. But it added to Jagger's current dissatisfaction. Instead of whirling from gig to gig and scribbling in foul dressing rooms, he craved the company of ritzy blue-bloods. Instead of being reduced to tears by an irate Chrissie Shrimpton, who was appalled when Jagger suggested that their Portuguese maid should come up the back stairs, he expressly yearned to date classy birds like Julie Christie. Instead of begging Easton for handouts, he longed for real opulence and kept asking if he had become a millionaire yet.

So Jagger, best equipped of the Stones to understand finance, endorsed the sacking of Easton and the appointment of an American manager called Allen Klein, only to find that he had replaced a leech with a vampire. Jagger said that Oldham sold Klein to them as a gangster, and they were impressed when this tough-talking, hard-drinking, gun-toting New Yorker made them rich by squeezing large gobs of cash out of the record companies. But their short-term gains were dwarfed by long-term losses. Klein was rapacious on his own behalf and, after buying out Oldham in 1966, he tied the Stones up in contractual knots and held on to many of the band's royalties and copyrights. Jagger himself became chairman of their production company – he enjoyed going to the office with a briefcase and, according to an assistant, 'exercised a *droit de seigneur* with all female staff'.[103] Reflecting on the millions of dollars Klein cost them, however, Jagger acknowledged that in business he had often been 'terribly wrong'.[104]

Still, he had much on his mind in the mid-sixties. The Stones worked unremittingly, rehearsing, touring, broadcasting, publicising themselves and recording some of their most celebrated numbers. Among them were 'Get Off My Cloud', 'Stupid Girl', 'Paint It, Black' (the imperative comma, perhaps inserted by Oldham, ensured that this song did well in apartheid South Africa) and '19th Nervous Breakdown', of which Jagger said: 'We're not Bob Dylan, y'know. The song's not supposed to mean anything.'[105] The strain of all this activity produced constant ructions, quarrels with the press, brushes with the law, attacks on rival bands – without irony, Jagger condemned copyists seeking 'a quick fortune'.[106] The Stones fragmented further as a result of drugs, booze and sex. Jones's exquisite new paramour Anita Pallenberg, who took a sinister interest in Nazism, witchcraft and narcotics, had a deeply disruptive impact on the group. Its members were ever more unruly: after filming in drag to promote 'Have You Seen Your Mother, Baby, Standing in the Shadow?', Jones, lifted his skirt and masturbated on camera, a sequence that Jagger would replay to entertain dinner guests. He regarded Pallenberg as poison, while she thought him lippy and crude. As it happened, Jagger was busy consorting with just the kind of people whose refinement would, he hoped, rub off on him. He favoured especially artistic Old Etonians such as Desmond Guinness, Robert Fraser and Christopher Gibbs. Dining with Gibbs, Jagger said: 'I'm here to learn how to be a gentleman.'[107] Evidently he aimed to complete this strangely obsolescent makeover with the help of a lady.

She was Marianne Faithfull, the voluptuous daughter of an Austro-Hungarian aristocrat. Marianne seemed to have been genetically programmed by Eros: one forebear was Baron von Sacher-Masoch, who wrote *Venus in Furs* and gave his name to masochism, while another was a sexologist who invented a so-called Frigidity Machine for unlocking libidinal energy. It was superfluous to her needs, since a convent education did not stop her from becoming, as she confessed, 'very promiscuous'.[108] Belying her name and her angelic appearance, she had flings with both Jones and Richards prior to settling for Jagger. His advances had ranged from the uncouth (spilling wine on her dress) to the unsubtle – writing a song for her, a seduction technique he often used. Having first discounted him as a crass schoolboy, she subsequently fancied him as a decadent romantic. So in December 1966, nineteen-year-old Marianne Faithfull left her husband and infant son (consigned to her mother) for Jagger, who cut the suicidal Chrissie Shrimpton off with a penny. He delighted in the social cachet that this ravishing new mistress brought him and hankered to say on his passport that his occupation was 'English Gentleman'. But on Jagger's odyssey from villa to chateau he treated Faithfull more as a fashion accessory than as an object of desire. She complained that after the beginning of their relationship 'Mick was never very interested in having sex'.[109] Since there was nothing wrong with his libidinal energy, he was presumably expending it on other horizontal liaisons or on vertical orgies of self-love in concert. According to Faithfull, he liked to watch her engaging in lesbian activities, and for her part, 'I didn't mind Mick sleeping with men.' She recorded him as saying in Richards' hearing, 'God, I'd like to lick him all over and then . . . suck his cock.'

Faithfull fostered Jagger's interest in literature as well as gentility, while he assisted her singing and acting career. They were both obsessed by clothes – he liked wearing hers – and no couple was more sartorially à la mode. Gossip columnists spied them in swish nightspots. In fact they became a cliché, trend-setters in swinging London. Yet simultaneously she tried to elevate him from the mire of materialism. Faithfull believed that astrology enabled her to see deeply into the nature of things and she discerned, for example, that 'there was a mystic link between druidic monuments and flying saucers'.[110] Jagger had little time for such insights, let alone for nutritional charts telling Faithfull when to meditate or for her lucubrations on the Group Mind. Eventually he burned all her magic books. He also disdained idealistic manifestations of the hippy counterculture such as flower power, crafting cynical aphorisms that turned out to be the merest commonplaces. For instance, he dismissed the Beatles' Indian guru, the Maharishi Mahesh Yogi, as a 'bloody old con man' and derided 'all that peace, love and pay-the-bill crap'.[111] Yet Jagger was less of a sceptic than he liked to pretend. He proposed to have a 'groovy time' in India with Robert Fraser since the Maharishi had 'really showed us some nice things'.[112] Jagger used the *I Ching Book of Changes* (a Chinese system of divination) to make even humdrum decisions. He sometimes claimed to be a very spiritual person, and though he didn't endorse the church, he thought Jesus 'fantastic'.[113] Jagger and Faithfull attended a Technicolor Dream Be-In at Alexandra Palace, billed as an 'all-night psychedelic freakout', which he also pronounced fantastic. His metaphysical impulses were doubtless confused by cannabis and they became even more erratic when he followed Marijuana Faithfull, as *Private Eye* dubbed her, in trying to open the doors of perception with hallucinogenic drugs. These Aldous Huxley had described as 'toxic short cuts to self-transcendence'.[114] Initially at least, Jagger found them life-enhancing. With LSD, he said, 'One's brain works not on four cylinders but on four thousand.'[115] Faithfull recorded that during one acid trip they took together he did an eerie dance in front of her. His hands moved in 'stroboscopic flutters' and his body vibrated in 'shimmering phosphorescent particles'. He had 'become Shiva'.[116]

Early in February 1967, Jagger issued a libel writ against the *News of the World* for erroneously attributing to him Brian Jones's more catholic ingestion of pharmaceuticals. Even in its pre-Murdoch days this scandal sheet enjoyed a symbiotic relationship with the police, regularly exchanging money for information. It also had the same propensity to eavesdrop on telephone calls, since the paper tipped off Scotland Yard that Jagger was going to Redlands, Richards' newly acquired Elizabethan farmhouse in Sussex, for a party involving illegal substances. There Jagger and his friends duly sampled 'white lightning' supplied by a mysterious dealer called David Schneiderman, known as the Acid King, who may have been in cahoots with the *News of the World* and afterwards vanished without trace. So, on the evening of Sunday 12 February 1967, nineteen officers of the West Sussex constabulary, armed with a search warrant, raided Redlands. They found hashish, heroin pills (belonging to Fraser) and four amphetamine tablets in the pocket of Jagger's green velvet jacket. They found Marianne Faithfull dressed (after a bath) only in an orange fur rug, which she sometimes let slip. They found chocolate – often used to give drug takers a sugar rush. And it was said that they also found Jagger eating a Mars bar from Faithfull's vagina. This was a canard, widely disseminated but obviously forged in the fevered imaginations of gendarmes and journalists. The reality proved more prosaic. Along with Richards and Fraser, Jagger was charged with possession of drugs – having apparently tried and failed to bribe his way out of trouble. He was mortified by the publicity, fearful of further surveillance and distressed by the legal proceedings, sometimes weeping uncontrollably. He was also genuinely shocked by the corruption of the guardians of law and order. Fleeing to Marrakesh, he told Cecil Beaton that he wanted to leave England because it was a 'police state'.[117]

Like other photographers and homosexuals, Beaton was fascinated by Jagger. As well as taking pictures of the singer, he penned a striking portrait. It was a collage of contradictions. With his hairless concave body, his chicken-breast-white skin, his delicate arms and legs, his albino-fringed eyes and his fantastically rounded lips, Jagger was 'beautiful and ugly, feminine and masculine, a "sport", a rare phenomenon'.[118] He possessed the arrogance of Nijinsky and an inborn elegance, smoking with pointed finger held high. Moreover he was a natural model, 'sexy, yet completely sexless. He could nearly be a eunuch.' But after a hard night Jagger's face was transformed into 'a white, podgy, shapeless mess', the eyes piggy, the nose squidgy, the hair sandy.[119] His manners varied with his moods and he was as inarticulate as his friends, said Beaton, none of whom ever finished a line of conversation. Of course they did finish lines of drugs, becoming increasingly disorientated. Jones was in an especially crazed condition – he became hysterical when the apes on Gibraltar ran away screeching as he tried to play them his music – and he drove Pallenberg into the arms of Richards, who became the father of her three children. But Jagger too was in an unsteady state. Feeling persecuted, he sought refuge in anonymity and registered at hotels under false names. He beat up Faithfull when she unexpectedly flew to join him during a hectic European tour. He went berserk when Robert Fraser made a half-hearted pass at her, 'swelled up like a bullfrog' and split his tight silk jacket.[120] He also tried to inflate his status by posing as a medium for the apocalyptic emotions of the younger generation: 'when I'm on stage, I sense that the teenagers are trying to communicate to me, like by telepathy, a message of some urgency . . . about the world and the way we live . . . This is a protest against the system. I see a lot of trouble coming in the dawn.'[121] Jagger may have hoped that such an oracular pronouncement would help his case in court.

If so, he was grievously disappointed. At the trial, which took place in Chichester on 27 June 1967, a hostile magistrate directed the jury to find Jagger guilty. He became rigid with terror at the prospect of a term behind bars, a truly petrified Stone. He spent two nights in Lewes jail, where Faithfull found him whimpering, 'What am I going to do? What am I going to do?' She suggested that he should write a song, but he replied: 'I can't think of anything but being in this fucking hole and wanting to get out.'[122] Finally Jagger was sentenced to three months' imprisonment, Fraser to six months and Richards to a year. Handcuffed to Fraser, Jagger was taken to Brixton and locked up. The whole experience left him shaky and tearful. He was 'thoroughly cowed, white with fear', said Ian Stewart, 'a nervous wreck'.[123] But the next day Jagger and Richards were released (without Fraser) pending an appeal. Fans and supporters had protested about the severity of their punishment but most people, even among the young, thought they had got what they deserved. However, as if to refute the charge that Jagger was the victim of an Establishment vendetta, *The Times* took up his cause. Its editor, a maverick Tory called William Rees-Mogg, argued that his sentence was unjust because it reflected a prejudice against the influence, the anarchic performances and the suspected decadence of the Rolling Stones. This article has always been interpreted as a sterling defence of the singer. But that is not quite the message of its title, WHO BREAKS A BUTTERFLY ON A WHEEL?.[124] The quotation (actually a slight misquotation) comes from Alexander Pope's venomous attack on the epicene Lord Hervey, and the subsequent lines were hardly flattering to Jagger:

> Yet let me flap this bug with gilded wings,
> This painted child of dirt that stinks and stings.[125]

Nevertheless, the appeal court gave him a probationary discharge. 'I hated the bust,' he said afterwards. 'That's why I turned bourgeois.'[126] Richards, who was also freed, responded that Jagger had never been anything but bourgeois.

After this costly trauma Jagger did become more discreet, but he went on experimenting with hallucinogens and much else besides. LSD seemed to have been the inspiration behind the Beatles' dazzling masterwork *Sergeant Pepper's Lonely Hearts Club Band*, and he hoped that the Stones would echo its success with a psychedelic extravaganza of their own. The result was *Their Satanic Majesties Request*, a piece of diabolical kitsch full of electronic gimmickry and phantasmagoric imagery. The album's cover centred on Jagger wearing a pointed wizard's hat decorated with a crescent moon – he himself chose the motif, which signalled his final break with, or rather messy divorce from, Andrew Oldham. Jagger was later scathing about the record, saying that it was the product of too much acid. This did have a corrosive effect on the band. But chemicals stimulated Jagger's continuing flirtation with the occult, as did Pallenberg's dalliance with the black arts – she kept garlic in her handbag to ward off vampires. High on LSD, he engaged in a kind of flying sorcery. For example, he composed weird music for the avant-garde film *Lucifer Rising*,[127] a mishmash of narcotics and necromancy made by that disciple of Aleister Crowley and self-appointed magus Kenneth Anger. Jagger declined to play the title role, however, and in truth his satanism was little more than fuddled naughtiness. It was the converse of his fuddled righteousness: 'I'm just . . . being very religious . . . just getting into all that . . . My soul just keeps telling me what's right for me to do at the present time and I just follow it.'[128] Jagger could easily have gone the way of Richards and Jones, who got hooked and famously became old men in their twenties. Instead he used drugs recreationally and in moderation, raging when stoned Stones wrecked their combined endeavours. Even so, he found it hard to perform and 'reckoned he'd lost his ego through acid'.[129]

Actually his ego seemed much in evidence during the tempestuous year of 1968, when he paraded it in many guises. With Tom Driberg he seriously discussed going into politics, asking which party someone with his anarchistic feelings should join. Jagger appeared on television as a spokesman for youth, once scoring off Mary Whitehouse, flail of the permissive society, whom he invited to 'Call me Mick, dear.'[130] He watched football, cricket and ballet. He read Jung and Yeats. He drove by Bentley to march against the Vietnam war. He was variously reported as 'hiding, running away' during the Grosvenor Square riot and 'throwing rocks and having a good time' – before making a lot of money from 'Street Fighting Man'.[131] He set up as a country gentleman, purchasing the Stargroves estate in Hampshire where he entertained well-born hippies such as Sir Mark Palmer, who found him very neurotic and surrounded by toadies, 'a bit like the royal family'.[132] As a man about town Jagger acquired a smart house in Cheyne Walk and furnished it sumptuously. He was willing to lavish cash on himself and he even let Faithfull persuade him to buy a £6,000 chandelier; but he kept her on a tight financial leash and she felt like a concubine in a seraglio, embraced by opiates and luxury, awaiting the arrival of the sultan. Although Jagger resented anything in the way of instruction from a woman, he did listen to her advice over his role as the reclusive rock star in Donald Cammell's cult movie *Performance*. Faithfull said that he was too straight to play himself and should try to imitate poor, paranoid, coked-up, freaked-out Jones, mixed with a bit of Richards' 'tough, self-destructive, beautiful lawlessness'.[133] As his other, best forgotten, movies showed, Jagger lacked talent as an actor. But in *Performance* he threw himself into the part so vigorously that the sex scenes with Pallenberg became all too genuine. Such was the nightmarish atmosphere conjured up by the shooting that Jagger was not alone in being confused. But then he was never comfortable in his own skin, never certain of his true identity. Richards, who began taking heroin to numb the pain of jealousy over Pallenberg, said that it was 'a tremendous hassle to keep Mick in reality because he's so easily influenced'.[134]

Yet Jagger was realistic enough to see that Jones was becoming a hopeless liability. Jean-Luc Godard's *nouvelle vague* film *Sympathy for the Devil*, which juxtaposed a Stones rehearsal with images of black power and white revolt, revealed Jagger's sensible direction and Jones's total immersion in dope. Jones made a small but versatile contribution to the group's seventh studio album *Beggar's Banquet*, an acclaimed return to its Delta roots featuring songs like 'Jumpin' Jack Flash' (a spring-heeled jig of liberation) and 'Stray Cat Blues' (a lip-smacking appreciation of underage groupies). By now, though, he was barely capable of playing, in thrall to morphine and enmeshed in the toils of the law – where the drug squad was concerned, Jagger scarcely exaggerated when he sang 'every cop is a criminal'.[135] Jagger variously lambasted and assisted Jones, once even trying to save him from an apparent suicide bid in the Redlands moat. It turned out to be only a few feet deep and Jagger was furious, pulling Jones under the water by his hair. 'You want to drown, you bastard?' he said. 'Well, I'm going to bloody well drown you, then. Look at these velvet trousers – cost me fifty quid! – you've ruined them.'[136] Jagger had troubles of his own towards the end of 1968. Faithfull was sinking into heroin addiction and she lost their baby in a miscarriage. The Stones were defeated in a long battle with Decca over the design of the record sleeve for *Beggar's Banquet*, on which they wanted to depict a lavatory wall daubed with graffiti. Meanwhile they were being robbed blind by Allen Klein, whom Jagger called 'Fatso' and aimed to 'dump' with the help of his new financial adviser, a suitably elevated merchant banker named Prince Rupert Loewenstein, soon known as 'Rupie the Groupie'.[137] Finally a rival rock band, the Who, outplayed the Rolling Stones so shatteringly when recording for their Christmas television spectacular, the *Rock and Roll Circus*, that Jagger refused to let it be shown. He thus suppressed his own performance as ringmaster, replete with top hat, red tailcoat, boots and whip, as well as stifling Brian Jones's last hurrah.

Baudelaire had regarded opium as a *'machine à penser'*[138] and it seems that drugs can temporarily stimulate creativity, however damaging they are in the long run. Apparently they gave Jagger a quick fix, for he was at his most prolific just as the Stones were starting to get smashed. Having extolled the power of LSD, Jagger wrote so fast that his thought could hardly keep pace with his pen. The result was a clutch of songs, some engendered on holiday with Richards, others included in the landmark album *Let It Bleed*, which became central to the band's repertoire. Their themes – sex, drugs, violence – chimed with the anxieties of the age. And although anything but lucid, the songs were highly commercial. They were tabloid sensationalism rendered as sonic boom. Thus 'Brown Sugar', which Jagger initially wanted to call 'Black Pussy', was a prurient celebration of the sexual sweets of slavery. 'Honky Tonk Women' was a melange of whoremongering and mind-blowing. 'Sister Morphine' extolled cousin cocaine and 'Monkey Man' sounded like a bad acid trip. 'Gimme Shelter' announced that rape and murder were just a shot away. 'Midnight Rambler' evoked the Boston Strangler and contained the line 'I'll stick my knife down your throat'. Some thought that Jagger had himself disposed of a competitor when Jones was ousted from the band in June 1969 – one witness said that 'Mick was being the Godfather'.[139] But Jones had become so unhinged that his expulsion was inevitable, the Stones replacing him with Mick Taylor. And no one was more shocked than Jagger when, the following month, Jones accidentally drowned in his swimming pool. He had not died, Jagger insisted, but gone to another life. 'I have really lost something,' he said. 'I just say my prayers for him. I hope he becomes blessed.'[140]

This was the message that Jagger tried to convey at the free concert the Stones staged in Hyde Park on 5 July. Originally intended as a means of selling Taylor to the fans, it was seamlessly transformed into a commemoration of Jones. Jagger told the press that the dead Stone would have wanted the show to go on, and he himself proposed to appear in a snakeskin suit on a platform embellished with palm trees and parakeets. These proved imprac-tical, and because of the heat Jagger wore instead a frilly tunic with an ornamental choker and white bell-bottoms. He also, as one witness put it, made himself up like a tart – which did not worry the 250,000 spectators, many of whom sported beads, kaftans, headbands and joss sticks. 'Aaawrite,' intoned Jagger as he grabbed the microphone, 'now will you just cool it just for a minute.' He then read from *Adonais*, Shelley's elegy to Keats, two stanzas suggested by Faithfull that he hoped would express everyone's feelings about the prematurely departed guitarist:

> Peace, peace! He is not dead, he doth not sleep,
> He hath awaken'd from the dream of life.

Jagger delivered the lines woodenly, but when he finished stagehands released hundreds of white butterflies, as if to represent the liberation of Jones's spirit. This piece of theatre fell flat, since many of the creatures fluttered from their stifling boxes only to expire on members of the audience. Good judges thought Jagger's whole performance more than usually meretricious. His recitation of Shelley's poem, concluded the writer Philip Norman, 'seemed less a memorial to his dead companion than one further medium for his own primping narcissism'.[141] And his coarse frolics left nothing to the imagination. In his defence, it should be said, Jagger had hay fever and the band, breaking in its nervous new recruit, played abominably. Yet the crowd applauded, hypnotised by the myth and assured by Jagger that they had all had a good time. As one newspaper remarked, 'Love 'em or loathe 'em, the Stones are still the Pied Pipers of Britain's youth.'[142]

The following day Jagger and Faithfull flew to Australia, where they were to star in Tony Richardson's film *Ned Kelly*. Their relationship was by now on the rocks, not least because both persisted in having other affairs. Stigmatised at the trial as 'a drug-taking nymphomaniac',[143] Faithfull even slept with Tony Sanchez in return for heroin; while Jagger was heavily involved with the black singer Marsha Hunt, whom he called 'Miss Fuzzy'. In Sydney, where he was greeted with placards saying 'POOFTER', Faithfull took a near-fatal overdose of sleeping pills. Jagger told her that he was 'utterly devastated to realise that you felt you were in such agony you had to kill yourself'.[144] He was equally upset by Richardson's film, in which his own performance was about as clanking as the outlaw's suit of armour. To compensate for this debacle, itself compounded by a gun accident to his hand and Digger outrage at his suggestion that all men (including Ned Kelly) were latent homosexuals, Jagger hired Albert and David Maysles, exponents of *cinéma-vérité*, to record the Stones' next venture. This was a tour of the United States, their first for three years. In New York Jagger gave a pretentious answer to the corny question about whether he was satisfied: 'Financially dissatisfied, sexually satisfied, philosophically trying.'[145] Rubbish though he later labelled this reply, it did contain grains of truth. Jagger had recently discovered the word 'messianic', and he was struggling to realise the confused aspirations of the time – though unwilling to commit himself and unsure whether to give the peace sign or the clenched-fist salute. The tour poster, which featured a naked woman, might have been an advertisement of Jagger's off-stage activities. Finally he was determined to make America pay since, thanks largely to Allen Klein, the Stones were broke. Critics complained about their high ticket prices, accusing them of monstrous cupidity. But Jagger insisted that the band was playing for fun not money. He professed a complete lack of interest in business: 'I don't want to become a weirdo, pseudo-capitalist.'[146]

There seemed little danger of this as Jagger fronted a band that, according to the writer Albert Goldman, had a 'public image of sado-homosexual-junkie-diabolic-sarcastic-nigger-evil unprecedented in the annals of popular culture'.[147] Jagger was more garish than ever, appearing on *The Ed Sullivan Show* in an orange and black satin shirt with voluminous sleeves and a choker hung with gold medallions. He performed with undiminished zest, snarling and howling 'in the finest man-woman blues tradition', reported the *New York Times*, 'and flaunting his hips at the audience like a stoned flamenco dancer'.[148] His titillations were more flagrant and, however puerile, they provoked squeals from swooning fans: 'I think I busted a button on my trousers,' he smirked, 'you don't want my trousers to fall down, now do ya?' Indeed the rapture he triggered, as the Stones criss-crossed America in a haze of hash and hooch, fed suspicions that Jagger was a musical mob-orator, a kind of rock Führer presiding over concerts that were the teeny-bopper version of the Nuremberg rallies. In fact, of course, Hitler had starred in a brutal theatre of power, whereas Jagger was a pantomime demagogue. His were the histrionics of an all-singing principal boy, an all-dancing demon king. He whipped up emotion as part of the entertainment, conjuring with sex, drugs, violence and devilry because they were good box office. But at a time of ferment over Vietnam, civil rights and youthful protest, and in the wake of murders such as those of Martin Luther King and Sharon Tate, Jagger was playing a dangerous game. It came to life, as Faithfull said, when he tried to assuage resentment about the Stones' avarice by organising a free concert, to eclipse the Woodstock music festival, at the end of their American tour. There were disputes about the cost, since, as the ex-student of economics sagaciously observed, 'It's free, but it still has to be paid for.' Jagger aimed to sell the film rights profitably, and a cheap last-minute venue was found fifty miles east of San Francisco, at Altamont Speedway.

There, on Saturday 6 December 1969, Jagger and the other Stones landed by helicopter in the midst of a vast beatnik bivouac filled with 300,000 fans and awash with drink and dope. The singer was dressed in high-heeled knee-length burgundy suede boots, honey-coloured velvet trousers, thick studded belt, a frilly, wing-sleeved orange and black silk shirt, a brown suede jerkin piped in red and a leather cape with a feathery collar. As he arrived, a young druggie darted forward and hit him in the face, shouting: 'I hate you! I hate you!' While supporting bands played, fights broke out elsewhere. Many were provoked by Hell's Angels, motorbike gangsters who were paid in beer to provide security but ran amok on bad acid and rotgut liquor. In the cool of the evening, after a long wait, the Stones mounted the low improvised stage to a roar of applause. 'All right! Whooooh!' Jagger responded. 'Oww babe! Aw yeah! Aww, so good to see ya *all*! Whoo!'[149] The group opened with 'Jumpin' Jack Flash' and spectators swirled and surged. They were held back by a phalanx of tattooed Angels, who struck out indiscriminately with pool cues, knuckledusters and cleated boots. 'Oooh, babies – there are so many of you,' cried Jagger, 'just be cool down the front there now, don't push around.'[150] The clashes continued, and Jagger artlessly remarked that something funny always happened when they struck up 'Sympathy for the Devil'. His appeals for calm became increasingly tremulous. 'I mean like people, who's fighting and what for?' he babbled, looking pale and panicky but going on with the show. He urged everyone to stay cool and sit down, adding that 'when we get to really like the end and we all want to go absolutely crazy and like jump on each other then we'll stand up again, d'you know what I mean?' The end came early for Meredith Hunter, a black man in a green suit who was just behind the footlights as Jagger sang of

> The squirmin' dog who's just had her day
> Under my thumb.

During another skirmish with the Hell's Angels, Hunter drew a gun and was stabbed to death.

Jagger was not sure what had happened, but with increasing desperation he pleaded for peace and love. 'All I can ask you, San Francisco, is like the whole thing – this could be the most beautiful evening we've had this winter. We really – y'know, why, why, – don't fuck it up, man, come on – let's get it together – everyone – come *on* now.' Calling for medical help, he urged the fans to relax, get into the groove and 'fucking well *show* that we're all one'.[151] But benign unity could scarcely be imposed by the paeans to torture, rape, murder, racial hatred and drug abuse that were audible in subsequent numbers. Moreover, the savage pugnacity of the group's playing and the 'feral intensity'[152] of Jagger's singing were calculated to excite Dionysiac frenzy. Further affrays took place. A large naked woman who tried to mount the stage was badly beaten by Hell's Angels, much to Jagger's disgust: 'Hey – heyheyheyheyheyheyhey*hey*! One cat can control that chick, y'know what oi mean.' But rather than issuing reprimands and exhortations, he tried to appease the audience. 'Are y'havin' a good ti-i-me?' he shouted over the melee. 'OOH-yeah!' As the Stones worked up to their finale, 'Street Fighting Man', he told the throng 'you've been beau-ti-ful' and 'we gonna kiss you goodbye'.[153] Then the band members fled for the helicopter, escaping not only from the rampant fans but from the Hell's Angels, whom Richards described as homicidal maniacs. 'Shit, that was close,' said Jagger. 'But it's going to make a fucking terrific film.'[154]

The Maysles brothers' rock doc *Gimme Shelter*, which reaches its climax as Jagger himself appears on camera gazing in horror at footage of Meredith Hunter's killing, possesses all the hideous fascination of a snuff movie. However the film, controlled by its stars, has more in common with cinema than verity. As the critic Pauline Kael wrote in a controversial review, it was fashioned to 'whitewash' the Stones.[155] It established no link between their barbed music and the carnage, incriminating only the Hell's Angels. It omitted mention of the Stones' greed, opportunism and ineptitude, all of which had helped to precipitate the calamity. And by focusing on their sorrowful response to clips of the murder, it gave them expiation without blame and atonement without penalty. Actually, in the aftermath of Altamont, Jagger seems to have felt some genuine remorse. He told Pamela Des Barres that it was his fault and for a while he became less incendiary, avoiding songs such as 'Sympathy for the Devil'. However, he would soon imply that Altamont was an act of God: 'If Jesus had been there he would have been crucified.'[156] He dismissed as modish mercenaries those writers who said that the event symbolised the death of the 1960s, 'Woodstock beatitude' being overtaken by 'Californian *Götterdämmerung*'.[157] Such opinions were commonplace indeed, and they sounded trite as Vietnam so bloodily sapped the idealism of the decade. Still, Altamont did add to contemporary disillusionment, and Jagger's own reflection on it was hardly perspicacious: 'Sometimes I think that the only two people that didn't have a good time were me and the guy that got killed.'[158] But he had scant leisure to dwell on the many injured fans, quickly jetting off to deposit the Stones' takings, perhaps a million dollars, in a

Swiss bank. As a person Jagger was 'an egotistical creep', concluded the concert promoter Bill Graham, adding disgustedly, 'But you know what is the greatest tragedy to me? That cunt is a great entertainer.'[159]

More problems beset Jagger as the 1970s dawned. Having been humiliatingly cuckolded by the painter Mario Schifano, whom he addressed as 'dago', Jagger got Faithfull back only to lose her again to the poppy. He himself was convicted of cannabis possession. The Stones, facing huge bills from the Inland Revenue if they stayed in England, finally sacked Klein. Richards' drug habit made recording difficult, and the band's autumn tour of Europe was chaotic. Jagger was among those who snorted lines of cocaine laid out behind the amplifiers, and no turn was left unstoned. Meanwhile, according to Tony Sanchez, he emulated the depraved pop star in *Performance*, establishing a *ménage à trois* and pitting the rival women 'against each other until they were at screaming point'.[160] In November Marsha Hunt gave birth to his first child, Karis, though he refused to acknowledge or support her until obliged to do so by paternity orders. Jagger quarrelled bitterly with Marsha, telling her that she was mad to think he had ever loved her. But by now he was besotted with a female version of himself.

She was Bianca Pérez-Mora Macias, to whom Donald Cammell had introduced him in Paris saying that they were made for each other. Cammell regarded this Nicaraguan of obscure origins and slender means as 'an old style courtesan',[161] and she herself would state that one previous lover, Michael Caine, had treated her as 'his geisha'.[162] However, with her lithe body, deep voice and pouting crimson lips, Bianca did bear an uncanny resemblance to Jagger, her 'golden animal languor' forming a counterpart, in the view of one witness, to his 'careless vitality'.[163] Jagger's fascination with this exotic lookalike was such that, it was said, he now 'entered the most solipsistic stage of his career'.[164] He became more and more preoccupied with himself and his mirror image, a reflection as admiring as it was alluring. Richards accordingly detested Bianca, who threw fits, put on airs and once remarked that she might have had more character if only she had been less beautiful. Pallenberg, who likened her conversation to elevator music, asserted that Bianca was really a man and threatened to put a voodoo curse on her. Certainly Bianca was a disruptive presence. She encouraged Jagger to hold aloof from the other Stones and to ingratiate himself further with the international smart set. So, as Marianne Faithfull observed, he increasingly organised his social calendar around events like debutantes' balls, petromillionaires' brunches and formal dinners with titled folk, which he had formerly delighted to scorn. Under Bianca's influence, he basked in the flattery of the famous and acted the spoilt brat. In March 1971, after a final British tour before becoming tax exiles in France, the Stones held a farewell party at Skindles Hotel in Maidenhead; but when the management presumed to end it at four o'clock in the morning, Jagger was so cross that he flung a chair through a plate-glass window.

Jagger's virility was given novel, if superfluous, advertisement on the sleeve of the Stones' potent album *Sticky Fingers*, which was devised by Andy Warhol and featured a jeaned crotch that literally unzipped to reveal bulging underpants. Equally salacious was the band's new brand, a large tongue protruding from a deep throat. This ubiquitous trademark was created by a young designer called John Pasche, who got the idea from Jagger's tumescent mouth. *Sticky Fingers*, the first album to appear under the Rolling Stones' own label, was supposed to denote the end of their exploitation by crooked managers and to usher in a fresh period of musical endeavour. But Jagger immediately sabotaged work on their next album, *Exile on Main Street*, which was being recorded in Richards' rented villa Nellcôte, formerly the Gestapo headquarters at Villefranche on the Riviera, by making hasty but elaborate arrangements to marry the pregnant Bianca. Like other superstars, he demanded that the event be kept secret but somehow managed to get it maximum publicity.

Jagger had submitted to Roman Catholic instruction, but on their wedding day, having ordered 'a little c-o-k-e to get him through',[165] he imposed a prenuptial agreement to secure his wealth in case of divorce. Bianca was livid, deeming their marriage dead before it began and calling him, with fierce tautological emphasis, 'a penny-pinching Scrooge'.[166] A scrum of paparazzi disrupted the civil ceremony, which took place in the town hall at St-Tropez, where a scowling, cream-suited Jagger lashed out and almost halted the proceedings. The subsequent chapel service was more decorous, with music taken, at Bianca's request, from the film *Love Story*. The reception so pullulated with celebrities (though none of the Stones was invited except Richards) that Jagger could not find a quiet moment to see his parents. Noting the oodles of caviar and champagne, as well as the yacht trip to honeymoon in an Italian palazzo, critics accused him of selling out to the beau monde and *la dolce vita*. For all his supporting the Black Panthers, marching for Angela Davis and announcing that one American revolution was not enough, Jagger had evidently become more chic than radical. The street-fighting man had changed into the playboy of the Western world. Still, as Michael Caine predicted, Jagger would have fights galore with Bianca, for she herself underwent a metamorphosis – from *grande horizontale* to prima donna. The birth of their daughter, who was christened Jade Sheena Jezebel, in October 1971 did produce an interval of peace, since Jagger, though a philandering husband, was a doting father. But soon Jade's parents were behaving as though they really wanted to hurt each other. Jagger later declared that he had only got married for something to do.

The Rolling Stones gathered much moss, a clinging growth of agents, lawyers, accountants, bodyguards, chauffeurs, musicians, technicians, drug peddlers, freeloaders, pimps, bimbos, lackeys and flunkeys of all sorts. Bianca loathed Jagger's entourage, which she described as a 'Nazi state',[167] and he himself admitted that hangers-on delayed progress on the new album. Its production, in the humid, warren-like basement of Nellcôte, which Richards compared to 'Hitler's bunker',[168] was further impeded by deficient acoustics and abundant narcotics. The recording sessions were constantly interrupted: Richards fell asleep at the guitar, Jagger visited Bianca in Paris and Nellcôte became a shambles. Sporadic jamming did yield some exhilarating tracks, notably 'Tumbling Dice'. Richards claimed that their songs stemmed from hard graft as well as from an ethereal inspiration that was 'Blake-like, a revelation, an epiphany'.[169] Yet the guitarist acknowledged that he and Jagger also relied on serendipity, once even assembling a lyric from headlines randomly torn out of newspapers. Drawing from diverse sources, among them reggae and gospel, they also put together a musical collage. As Jagger said, 'You're kind of throwing this mish-mash in.'[170] The mish-mash was refined by a slick Los Angeles studio, but in essence it remained rough and crude. Although at the time many people panned *Exile on Main Street*, the rawness of the material was eventually seen as the mark of its authenticity and the source of its continuing appeal. Having made France too hot to hold them, the Stones planned to promote the album on another lucrative circuit of America. Just as Margaret Thatcher declared that she must govern, Jagger said that he 'must perform'. With inimitable logic he explained his need to the chronicler of the 1972 tour, Robert Greenfield: 'Well . . . oi mean . . . it's more or less what oi do, inn't it? So I've got to do it. Oi mean, either I do it or . . . I don't do it. If I don't do it . . . what am I going to do? Do ya know what oi mean?'

During a bacchanal including fifty concerts in thirty cities, Jagger was 'scared shitless'[171] that he was going to be shot. He instituted fierce security measures, surrounding himself with bouncers and having spectators frisked for weapons. It was ironic, as one journalist wrote, that such precautions were required for a group that had embodied 'the desire of many young people to rip society open, to destroy the shibboleths and throw the older generation on the scrap heap'. It was still more ironic that Jagger and Richards, who were arrested after a fracas with a photographer, had to be released at the behest of the mayor of Boston to prevent their fans from going on the rampage. Since Altamont the Stones had become more cautious, though Jagger still mouthed obscenities and mimed brutalities, slinking round the stage like a latter-day Messalina or a 'reincarnation of Jack the Ripper'.[172] Faint crow's feet were now etched on his face, but his dervish energy was unabated and with it his capacity to induce an incalculable catharsis. While working up audiences he witnessed extraordinary displays of passion: one fan bit his lip until it bled, another crushed a cigarette in the palm of his hand, while yet another begged to be whipped. Groupies became so sexually aroused that they would get off with anything, said Truman Capote, 'boys, women, dogs, fire hydrants'.[173]

Jagger acknowledged that he became a monster on the road, and this tour afforded him occasions for debauchery that might have piqued the imagination of Rabelais. Highlights included a three-day orgy of sex, dope and havoc at Hugh Hefner's Chicago mansion. Richards, who nearly burned the place down, damned it as 'basically a whorehouse'.[174] But Jagger liked the company of glossy Playmates and smack-happy bunny girls. He told one, 'Don't worry, dear, I'll fuck you later.'[175] And when another expressed a wish to bite his ass, he flipped open his bathrobe and said, 'Have at it, luv.'[176] The Stones' Lockheed Electra turboprop, emblazoned with the lapping tongue logo, became a flying bordello. Especially hooked on fornication was the tour doctor, who from his bulging pharmacopoeia prescribed drugs for the rest of the party while dosing himself with nymphets. On the plane to New York Jagger enjoyed watching a gang-bang staged for a film of the tour entitled *Cocksucker Blues*, which he subsequently suppressed. The concluding concert took place in Madison Square Garden, where, as the *New York Times* reported, special effects were 'geared to elicit a frantic blood-pounding response'. An immense green serpent adorned the stage floor, a large overhead mirror reflected lights on to the arena and Jagger danced with Corybantic abandon, ultimately blowing kisses and throwing rose petals to the audience. After this 'brilliantly raunchy, magnificently exciting' performance, he marked his twenty-ninth birthday with a huge party full of celebrities. It reached a witty climax when a naked woman jumped out of a cake and rotated tassels on her nipples.

Jagger applauded her enthusiastically, delighted by what was described as the tour's 'Felliniesque finale'.[177] Despite complaining that for his sins he was enmeshed in a spider's web of socialites, he was also thrilled by the band's lengthening train of well-known followers. Among them was Truman Capote, whose comments on the Stones were idiosyncratic but incisive. He thought them 'complete idiots' and reckoned that Jagger was 'about as sexy as a pissing toad'.[178] His lyrics made no sense and he could not dance or sing. Yet through sheer dynamism, through a rare gift for throwing himself totally into a role, Jagger was 'an extraordinary performer'. Once out of the limelight, the singer reverted to being rational and emotionally mature. But on or off the boards he thought mainly about the takings, said Capote, for he was 'a businessman *par excellence*'.[179] Jagger, of course, denied that he wanted riches and presented himself as an artist. However he frankly preferred America, where no one cared how much he earned, to Britain, where money 'has got to be rather a dirty word'.[180] And he valued the status that wealth conferred when added to fame. He relished the power to attract and repel. He became more capricious, beguiling people one minute, cutting them dead the next. Journalists particularly were subjected to this treatment, now dazzled by his smile, now instructed to 'await my presence in the next office'.[181] Trophy friends were treated to his charm and, an inveterate name-dropper, he courted the likes of Nureyev, Jackie Onassis, Princess Lee Radziwill, Andy Warhol and Gore Vidal. As Jagger soared into the social stratosphere, though, Richards plunged into what Thomas de Quincey had called the 'abyss of divine enjoyment'.[182] Their divergent trajectories pulled the Stones apart. Jagger deplored Richards' junkie state, while Richards despised his friend's addiction to 'that jet-set shit'.[183]

The band went on rolling into the mid-1970s, but mainly from past momentum, and even Jagger was gloomy about its future. There were hints that each tour would be the last (which boosted attendances) and he vowed to retire at the age of thirty-three, though always putting off the evil day – 'I'd rather be dead than sing "Satisfaction" when I'm 45.'[184] Albums such as *Goat's Head*

Soup and *It's Only Rock 'n' Roll* were below par. In more senses than one, Wyman played away from home. Mick Taylor left the group and Jagger treated his replacement, Ronnie Wood, as a buffoon, keeping him on a salary for over fifteen years. Advocating social revolution while struggling to develop a global corporation, Jagger supervised everything and became hysterical about the details. He once telephoned a tour manager at six in the morning to say that Watts's eyeshadow was the wrong colour. He worried about the emergence of fresh styles and young rivals: glam rock as personified by David Bowie, who projected a sexuality that was more glaringly ambivalent than Jagger's, and punk rock, epitomised by the Sex Pistols, safety-pinned nihilists who dismissed the Stones as 'boring old farts'.[185] Punks such as Johnny Rotten and Joe Strummer derided rock stars who were guilty of 'turning rebellion into money'.[186] Jagger angrily accused *them* of selling out and publicised his occasional contributions to good causes, such as earthquake relief in Nicaragua. He ranged about in a restless search for novelty – new rhythms, new ventures, new places, new women. Diverting attention from his wrinkles, he had a diamond embedded in an upper front tooth.

Jagger also experimented with new shocks. He sang 'Starfucker', which contained this immortal couplet:

> Your tricks with fruit was kind of cute,
> I bet you keep your pussy clean.

He himself tied up the half-naked woman who was pictured thanking the Rolling Stones for her bruises in a repulsive flier for their album *Black and Blue*. And for the American tour of 1975 he played dirty games with a white rubber phallus, which, when pumped up fully, was some twenty feet long. This erection was part of Jagger's drive to make Stones concerts more of a spectacle. He also splurged on his own costumes, designed by Giorgio Saint Angelo: white Lycra jumpsuits slashed to the loins, lavender stretch tops embroidered with rhinestones, satin jackets with beige shirts, red cummerbunds and green pants. Jagger performed on a ten-ton touring stage shaped like a lotus flower, the scene of a dramatic sound and light show featuring both a trapeze and a Chinese dragon that disgorged confetti, all powered by twenty-two tons of electrical equipment. In lieu of musical innovation he provided circus, theatre, rock vaudeville. Some observers were disenchanted, charging that his act had 'stylised itself up its own ass'[187] and that the Stones were 'burnt-out imitations'[188] of their former selves. Many others found the singer a compelling presence and hailed the band as the best of its kind in the world. To retain that accolade and to keep the Stones on the road, Jagger made shamefaced compromises. He bowdlerised 'Starfucker', changing its name to 'Star Star'. He withdrew the masochistic *Black and Blue* image. And he heeded protests over the colossal obscenity that the Stones proposed to unleash on America. Leading the outcry was Rupert Murdoch's gutter press, but, as Richards himself sagely remarked, the inflatable cock was 'a millstone round our neck'.[189] Jagger ensured that it remained largely flaccid.

The singer could now hardly tolerate anything less than riotous adulation, and he was variously distressed, depressed and enraged by criticism. 'Are you feeling good?' he asked audiences. 'ARE YOU FEELING GOOD?' 'Not at all,' responded the novelist Martin Amis, leaving Earl's Court prematurely even though his earplugs muffled the 'strangled monotone holler' in which Jagger delivered 'frenzied approximations' of familiar songs.[190] The monstrous amplifiers made him sound like a railway tannoy announcer while the strobe lights just made him look old. After another such concert the cartoonist Stan Franklin remarked, 'Well, it will never take the place of music, will it?'[191] Charles Shaar Murray accused Jagger of dancing like 'a faggot chimpanzee' and travestying blackness with exclamations such as 'All *right*!' and '*Yeah*!' and 'Sssssssss-*guh*!'[192] Jagger threatened to set his heavies on Murray. He boycotted and vituperated other critics. He fired his press agent. He stormed out of the BBC when the disc jockey John Peel denied him 'awestruck worship'.[193] At a Toronto club in 1977 he doused journalists with water. By then, though, he was under grave stress, because Richards had been charged with heroin trafficking and faced the likelihood of a long prison sentence. It took the Canadian authorities several years to conclude that he had smuggled in such large quantities of dope for his personal use. So the Stones were stymied for the nonce. Where his friend was concerned, Jagger veered between commiseration and exasperation. But while urging sobriety on Richards, he himself sometimes got drunk. Nevertheless Jagger wanted to prove that the band remained relevant and that it could out-punk the punks. Even wearing a torn T-shirt in the style of Johnny Rotten, he was quite clear about his own status, telling an American reporter: 'I'm, along with the Queen, you know, one of the best things England's got. Me and the Queen.'[194]

While Jagger was struggling to hold the Stones together, his marriage to Bianca finally fell apart. The split was painful, particularly as people said that he was becoming ever more her twin. 'I'm glad I'm as beautiful as my fucking wife,' he once retorted. 'But she looks like me.'[195] The pair indulged in mutual recriminations about multiple adulteries. They fought over the divorce settlement – she got custody of Jade and perhaps a million pounds. Bianca scolded him for being a skinflint and he slated her as a gold-digger. Jagger found solace in the arms of a Southern belle called Jerry Hall, overcoming her initial reluctance to enter his bedroom with the stock reproach: 'Oh, girl, you're so uptight.'[196] Hall was tall, blonde, gorgeous, amiable and effervescent. No one, though, could have accused her of being a highbrow. Like all models, wrote Andy Warhol, she talked 'baby talk'. In fact, said Keith Richards, talking to her was like talking to a window. Nevertheless Jagger sustained a long relationship with her, perhaps because she had sexual as well as financial resources of her own. Hall explained her hold on him to Warhol, who thoughtfully informed Bianca: 'she gives Mick a blow job before she lets him out of the house'.[197] Hall adored her new lover and wanted to settle down. 'I'm a Cancer,' she said. 'I have a huge nesting instinct.'[198] Jagger did make various domestic dispositions, selling Stargroves, buying a chateau in the Loire valley, an apartment in Paris, a ranch in Texas and a brownstone house in New York, and building a Japanese-style villa on the exclusive island of Mustique. However, he liked to keep on the move, insisting that 'Domesticity is death.'[199] Jagger was both physically and psychologically mercurial. As Jerry Hall found, he adopted 'all these different personas': sometimes the 'nice gentlemanly guy' at home, often on tour the 'incredible egomaniac'.[200]

He needed all the egomania he could muster during the impromptu American tour of 1978, when the Stones sometimes played so badly that audiences bombarded them with opprobrium and garbage. Gulping brandy and sniffing cocaine, Jagger himself missed cues, forgot words and sang flat. He admitted later that the group was unfit to appear, and observers wondered whether these ageing 'geezers were still capable of generating the old road show madness'.[201] The speculation was all the more poignant since the band had just produced its most kinetic record since *Exile*. This was *Some Girls*, Jagger's answer to Johnny Rotten. With it, raved one fan, the Stones emerged from 'the shadows to kick the shit out of their punk detractors by recording a monumental masterwork of rock music'.[202] Jagger was condemned for his witless remark about the habits of black girls, but, although claiming that it was a parody of prejudice, he defiantly announced that the next album would be the better for containing even more sexism and racism. Actually the next album, *Emotional Rescue*, was much less contentious. But it did reignite a smouldering conflict between Jagger and Richards, which, despite periodic reconciliations, ultimately ravaged their friendship.

Their differences were various. Jagger followed musical fashion and hankered to try genres that might prove commercial, while Richards was adamant that the Stones were a rock 'n' roll band. Jagger had enjoyed complete control of the business when Richards was incapacitated by heroin, and he resented it when his friend recovered enough to challenge his dominance. 'Oh, shut up, Keith,' he often exclaimed. 'Don't be stupid.'[203] Richards thought that Jagger had fallen in love with power. The singer had become unbearable, he said, puffed up with sycophancy and prone to treat other members of the group as minions. They retaliated by calling him 'Her Majesty' and 'that bitch Brenda' – a name appropriated from the romantic novelist Brenda Jagger. Richards and Jagger almost came to blows when the latter refused to go on the road in 1980, and matters got worse during subsequent American and European tours. Jagger demanded fancy props to support his act, and once, when he flounced out in a huff, Richards told journalists that this was 'a fair example of the kind of cunt I've had to deal with for the last 25 years'.[204] Perhaps the root cause of Jagger's animus was that he hated being regarded as a calculating machine and craved recognition as a man of passion like Richards. Yet the prudent, scheming, suspicious Jagger must have known that, however much he tried to reinvent himself, he was a bean-counter at heart; whereas Richards was an avatar of Orpheus who, when torn to pieces by the maenads, continued to pluck his lyre. Personal discord obviated musical harmony. It is true that the Stones sometimes played with breathtaking vigour in their latter days. But even their best efforts, such as the 1981 album *Tattoo You*, were revivals of the past. Together the Rolling Stones went through the motions. Individually they went their own way, preceded by Jagger.

The singer had sound motives for pursuing a solo career. The Stones were so demoralised by drink and drugs that, he reckoned, they were unfit to cross the Champs-Elysées, much less go on the road. He was particularly offended by Ronnie Wood, whose vagaries sometimes made Richards look like a member of the Band of Hope. Jagger himself was increasingly abstemious. Like a matador, he dieted, exercised and honed his slim body for its gruelling ordeals in the arena. He employed a masseur and a personal trainer. He even took singing and dancing lessons, much to the disgust of Richards, who thought that musicians should do what came naturally. But Jagger had a middle-class faith in the virtues of self-improvement and felt that he could do better unencumbered by a troupe of mazed bohemians. No doubt he also aimed to be famous in his own right, as Bill Wyman said, adding that he had lost touch with whoever Mick was now and thought that Mick had too. Anyway Jagger refused to tour with the Stones between 1982 and 1989. He contributed little to the two substandard albums they issued during those years – one critic said that his vocals sounded as if they had been phoned through as an afterthought. Moreover Jagger turned an abdication into what looked like a betrayal. In 1983 he did a lucrative deal to make solo discs for CBS Records, the company that signed a multimillion dollar contract with the Stones themselves. Richards accused Jagger of piggybacking on their contract and called him a 'back-stabbing cunt'.[205] Charlie Watts was less polite. When Jagger drunkenly summoned 'my little drummer', Watts gave him a right hook to the jaw and pronounced, 'You're my fucking singer.'[206] Richards threatened to slit his childhood friend's throat if he toured without the Stones and sang their songs. Jagger did just that, scurrying round the world and dismissing the Rolling Stones as 'a bunch of tired old men'. Entering his forties, he felt compelled to distinguish himself from them. As Richards later explained, Jagger was consumed by the need to seem hip and boyish. Instead of growing up, he pined to be Peter Pan. 'Mick has been searching for the Fountain of Youth.'[207]

Jagger put on a remarkable display of juvenile gusto at the Live Aid charity concert in 1985, when, at the climax of his act, he ripped off Tina Turner's dress; whereas, playing separately, Richards and Wood sounded sclerotic. Jagger's libido also remained in lusty form, a fact he advertised by siring a total of four children on Hall, boasting to her about his amorous escapades with the likes of 'eighteen-year-old debutantes'[208] and asserting publicly that recreational adultery was essential to secure their relationship. What this meant, of course, was that he should tomcat freely while she looked after the babies. When Hall flouted the traditional double standard for an affair of her own, Jagger became almost insanely jealous. In 1990 he married her. The Hindu ceremony, which took place in Bali, was of dubious legality and wedlock did nothing to harness his raging sex drive – about which Richards, now a family man, thought he should consult a doctor. Almost as impressive was the brio Jagger invested in his solo albums, *She's the Boss* and *Primitive Cool*. They were not without merit, though made amid complaints from the hired musicians about his stinginess. But they did badly enough by the Stones' standards to count as commercial fiascos. Indeed the second album, which contained a coded attack on Richards entitled 'Shoot Off Your Mouth' and an implausible renunciation of Casanova conduct for a love too good to 'Throwaway', was described as 'one of 1987's most embarrassing stiffs'.[209]

As a result advance ticket sales for Jagger's planned American tour were so poor that it had to be cancelled. Thoroughly chastened, the singer concluded that he could only achieve twenty-two-carat distinction in alliance with the Stones. In 1989 he met Richards on Barbados, where, after first shouting and then laughing, they were reconciled. Thus ended what Richards had characteristically called World War III, though détente did not preclude further hostilities.

The band, which resumed its fitful routine of producing albums and touring to promote them, had all the novelty of age. Moreover to Jagger's chagrin, the sight of old codgers playing the music of raw youth prompted much mockery. Where Jimi Hendrix had embodied galactic rock, the Stones supposedly typified 'geriatric rock'.[210] They performed crock 'n' roll in an antiques roadshow or rocking-chair roll in the greyest show on earth. They were universally known as the Strolling Bones. Jagger's face was said to have more lines than Richards had snorted. The singer riposted tetchily that such jokes would not be made about black performers such as Louis Armstrong. 'Besides,' he bragged, invoking the size of his lingerie collection, 'the chicks still dig me.'[211] It was a fair point. Even as a wrinkly he retained an awesome ability to woo and wow fans right round the globe. Jagger re-established his rapport with them during the Stones' 1989 tour of America, where he 'jittered with energy'.[212] Returning five years later, now a grandfather, he still appeared 'eternally youthful'.[213] Critics expressed amazement at his stamina and declared that time had done nothing to diminish his magic. At Wembley in 1995 Salman Rushdie marvelled at 'the sheer quality and freshness of Mick's singing' as well as his 'athleticism and grace of movement'.[214]

While the other Stones played their instruments, he wrote, Mick played the audience, coaxing, caressing and controlling this vast hydra. Such ripe charisma invited hyperbole. One puritanical academic, Allan Bloom, was so sickened by the corrupting effects of the vocalist's gutter glitz that he denounced him as a menace to Western civilisation. In a best-selling book Bloom stated that Jagger played the same role in the lives of contemporary young Americans as 'Napoleon played in the lives of ordinary young Frenchmen throughout the nineteenth century'.[215]

Actually Jagger had cause for concern about the evanescence of stardom, and he took elaborate steps to prolong the Stones' Indian summer. The lyrics in their first new albums, *Steel Wheels* and *Voodoo Lounge*, were conventional to the point of banality, and Jagger himself acknowledged that rock songs involved much 'recycling of subject matter'. Furthermore the music, as he was later almost to concede, sounded like echoes from the past. So did his regurgitation of vintage hits like 'Street Fighting Man' though, unlike more recent numbers, they invariably struck a chord. Unwilling to rely on the appeal of nostalgia, Jagger arranged that the band's live shows should develop still further into a choreographed Mardi Gras. 'People coming to a stadium,' he said, 'expect to see pizzazz as much as hear music.' Jagger performed against backdrops that grew ever more fabulous: a glamorised urban jungle of ramps, pipes, girders, trusses, boilers, gantries and decrepit oil refineries, resembling the set of *Bladerunner*; or a futuristic panorama like something out of Fritz Lang's *Metropolis*, with lasers, pyrotechnics, animations on a Jumbotron video screen, sixty-foot inflatable dolls and a phallic column spitting fire, part cobra, part brontosaurus. To discerning eyes, however, such razzle-dazzle scarcely disguised the fact that the Stones had nothing new of substance to contribute. Indeed, it confirmed the critical view that they were 'wasted emblems of decadent hedonism'.[216] Preening himself in front of this lurid scenery, Jagger looked a picture of the *fin de siècle* sybarite.

The production of these gigantic tableaux was costly as well as logistically demanding, and Jagger invariably focused his attention on the bottom line. He drove hard bargains with record companies, once yelling at the boss of CBS: 'You fat fucking record executives! What do you know?'[217] He promoted the Stones by other means, not just through artistic photo shoots and well-directed films but via Imax and the internet. He also exploited many merchandising and sponsorship opportunities to augment their income – some £500 million during the 1990s, more than twice the sum earned by any other group. (By 2010 his personal fortune, supplemented by more tours, offshore tax management and investment in outside enterprises, was put at about £200 million.) As always, Jagger was far more coy about his commercial priorities than his sexual proclivities, repeating that he was interested in business 'from the creative point of view'.[218] But he did not deceive acquaintances such as the cartoonist Barry Fantoni, who found his posturing personality repellent and said that Jagger was 'absolutely obsessed by wealth'.[219] And the singer sometimes dropped his guard on the subject. In 1989 he admitted that he was just touring for the money. He insisted that not to get as much as possible was 'fuckin' stoopid'.[220] And he once confessed that 'there's something spiteful in me which makes me hold on to what I've got'.[221] Making savings, paying slowly and tipping badly, he might have modified the Beatles' mantra to 'All You Need is Lucre'. An Australian entrepreneur reportedly thought it worth offering twenty million dollars for Jagger's ashes, which he proposed to put into egg-timers.

Rolling in riches, the Stones were increasingly remote from their fan base, and Jagger, the erstwhile effigy of rock rebellion, now deliberately cultivated his image as a man of wealth and taste. After his marriage to Hall he bought a Georgian mansion overlooking the Thames at Richmond to accommodate his growing family. He embellished his properties with the help of fashionable interior decorators and garden designers. He purchased expensive works of art, spending hours on the telephone to auction houses and even acquiring a couple of watercolours painted by Prince Charles. He built Hall a heart-shaped swimming pool in Texas. He put his private jet at the disposal of patrician guests and entertained liberally in his French chateau, presiding over charades and other amusing games, among them a contest to see who could go furthest with a coin clenched between the buttocks. Jagger also aspired to high-mindedness. He paid serious, if inter-mittent, attention to his parental duties, even making enquiries about his children's religious education. Distant from his youthful radicalism, though occasionally hitting out at alien dictatorships, Jagger took refuge in a hazy idealism. He evinced an eclectic interest in other-worldly matters, now having his auras cleansed by a South American shaman, now wearing a Kabbalah bracelet to ward off the evil eye. Above all he essayed to tread the Eightfold Path. Hall said that he was 'totally into this Buddhist thing'.[222] He sought enlightenment in the Orient, often travelling to Thailand and Laos, where, as recently as 2010, he visited temples to chant and 'meditate with monks'.[223] However Jagger made sure that the rigours of his spiritual quest were alleviated by fleshly nirvana. Usually accompanying him was his latest *maîtresse en titre*. This was an office he liked to fill with tall models, ranging from Carla Bruni in the 1990s to, more currently, L'Wren Scott, who (at six foot five) made him look almost as much of a homunculus as the motor-racing mogul Bernie Ecclestone.

Rather than lose Jagger, Hall wrote to him saying, 'I won't be mad if you fuck other girls.'[224] He should be free, she thought, to fulfil his ambition 'to go down in history as one of the world's great lovers'. However, Hall soon became agitated, humiliated and depressed by his ruttishness. According to his chauffeur, Jagger would sometimes go from one woman to another in a single night, cajoling potential lovers by telephone: 'Come on baby, you know you want me.'[225] Latterly he took to making propositions by text message and received as many rejections as acceptances. Even so he reserved suites in luxury hotels for days at a time to accom-modate his women and, as one journalist wrote, 'His bedpost is not so much notched as whittled to a fine point.'[226] Jagger's affairs caused angry break-ups and tearful make-ups with Hall. Occasionally she locked him out of the house. She cried on Richards' shoulder, 'Oh, what a bastard that guy is.'[227] The last straw was Jagger's impregnation of a Brazilian underwear model called Luciana Morad. He tried to deny it, hoping to avoid maintenance and to mollify Hall. But when a DNA test proved the truth she sued for divorce, denouncing Jagger publicly as a 'lying, cheating, no-good slimeball'.[228] Jagger countered her claim for a reported £30 million by asserting that their marriage was invalid. But this would have made his children with her (Elizabeth, James, Georgia and Gabriel) bastards – just like his son Lucas, born to Morad. So in 1999 an amicable settlement was reached for a much smaller, though undisclosed, sum. In his paternal role, emphasised in a vanity television film called *Being Mick* that he produced in 2002, Jagger kept a base in Richmond. Otherwise he went his own way, a raddled roué pursuing girls young enough to be his grandchildren and demonstrating once again the aphrodisiac power of variety. Perhaps senile impotence will be as much of a relief to him as it was to George Melly, who likened the experience to being unchained from a maniac.

The Stones had been disintegrating for years, and by the end of the second millennium only three members of the original band remained: Jagger, Richards and Watts. Ian Stewart had died in 1985, and when Bill Wyman quit in 1993, tired of rehashing the same golden oldies, no permanent replacement was appointed. Jagger's relations with Richards fluctuated wildly. They could still collaborate, sometimes doing so at a distance, but their differences ran deep. Jagger liked musical as well as theatrical experimentation. He was keen to employ computers and synthesisers, for example, hoping that an investment in novelty would produce a dividend of hits. Richards just wanted to go on playing the blues and he loathed being turned into a sideshow, though he looked increasingly suitable for one – his face seemed to have been invaded by termites and his hair, encompassed by a headband, resembled a triffid escaping from a plant pot. Richards's favourite T-shirt bore the legend *Obergruppenführer*, and he became furious when Jagger continued trying to dictate the policy of the group. Occasionally they had incandescent rows, and Jagger walked out of the last recording sessions for their 1997 album *Bridges to*

Babylon. Richards not only disparaged Jagger's guitar playing but seemed delighted when his solo albums did badly. The third, *Undercover Spirit*, though favourably received, did not produce a significant single, and the fourth, *Goddess in the Doorway*, barely entered the charts. Richards nicknamed it *Dogshit in the Doorway*.

When Jagger accepted a knighthood in 2002, Richards went, as he put it, 'fucking berserk'. He regarded receipt of this 'fucking paltry honour' as a betrayal of everything the rebel Stones stood for and a surrender to the 'establishment that did their very best to throw us in jail'.[229] Richards thought Sir Mick had destroyed Jagger's credibility and he ridiculed the singer's plea that the prime minister had insisted that he should take the gong. Of course Tony Blair was personally concerned, having as a long-haired undergraduate aspired to be a pop star himself – in the Oxford rock band Ugly Rumours he had been known for giving his performances 'a bit of serious Mick Jagger'.[230] Blair must also have calculated that a sexagenarian plutocrat who graced the covers of magazines like *Saga* and *Fortune* was now less likely to be regarded as a vile tearaway than as a national treasure. Still, Jagger could easily have resisted his blandishments. Richards' own reaction was ribald when Blair told him that 'you've always been one of my heroes'[231] – he said it was frightening that someone with such bad judgement should be running the country. But Richards' own judgement was hardly impeccable: he urged Blair to 'stick to his guns'[232] over the Iraq war, which Jagger, who excoriated American neoconservatives, opposed. More specifically, Richards naively assumed that Jagger shared his own contempt for the gewgaws of rank, whereas Watts rightly observed that the singer had always coveted them. Jagger only regretted that his mother Eva, who had died in 2000, could not accompany the ninety-two-year-old Joe to Buckingham Palace, where Prince Charles conferred the chivalric accolade on 'Sir Michael'.

Jagger's dissident stance had never been firm. Veering between the equivocal and the ersatz, it was one of many attitudes he affected, a masquerade of mutiny. The singer was a symptom of the sixties, a stagey reflection of the radical temper of the age, more a creature than a creator of fashion. Such subversion as he did foment was essentially a product of the Stones' music, amplified until (he once complained) his ears bled. It seemed to bear out Plato's view that rhythm and melody accompanied by dance were the barbarous idiom of the soul in its primal state of passion. To the clangour Jagger contributed spicy lyrics and sizzling performances, enhanced by a sexual allure second only to that of Marilyn Monroe – to judge, at any rate, from the sales figures of Andy Warhol's images of the stars. A cynosure of lust, which he did his level best to satisfy, Jagger was also a prodigy of greed. More than anyone, he had transformed the Stones into a corporate leviathan. Bound together in a cash nexus relationship and able or willing to do no other, they continued working together despite every quarrel and every setback. World tours in 2002–3 and in 2005–6, this one to plug their last album *A Bigger Bang*, made them record-breaking sums of money. As usual Jagger was dolled up to the nines, having chosen his costumes for their sparkle, as the *New Yorker* sardonically remarked, 'with no more fuss than marks the change of government in a small country'.[233] Like the others, he displayed phenomenal dynamism on the boards, as appears in Martin Scorsese's documentary *Shine a Light* (2008). During the burst of activity with which the Stones celebrated and exploited their fiftieth anniversary, he still had fans rolling in the aisles. Yet no euphoria could dispel a sense that Jagger, his hearing impaired, his body gaunt and his face deeply grooved with age, was participating in the march of the dinosaurs. He was the incarnation of Jurassic rock. What Jagger had once played as erotic melodrama was coming to be repeated as tragic farce.

Notes and References

Introduction

1 All my current protagonists went to university (though Mick Jagger dropped out before taking his degree), as compared to only one in four Eminent Edwardians (Arthur Balfour).

Rupert Murdoch

1 Taylor, 151.
2 Kiernan, 51.
3 Shawcross, 81.
4 *New York Post*, 28 April, 7 May and 24 May 1982.
5 Kiernan, 197.
6 Watkins, 162.
7 *Village Voice*, 29 November 1976.
8 Welles, 52.
9 Morgan, 75.
10 Curtis, III, 177.
11 F. Waldrop, *McCormick of Chicago* (Westport, Conn., 1966), 152.
12 R. Thomson, *After I Was Sixty* (1973), 87.
13 Welles.
14 Belfield, Hird and Kelly (1991), 23.
15 R. D. Blumenfeld, *The Press in My Time* (1937), 49.
16 T. Driberg, *Beaverbrook* (1956), 213. The phrase was, of course, invented by Baldwin's cousin, Rudyard Kipling.
17 Russ.
18 *New York Times*, 13 July 1982.
19 Shawcross, 3. See also H. Brenton and D. Hare, *Pravda* (1985), 9,

where the villain Lambert Le Roux, obviously based on Murdoch, is described as 'that Satan'.

20 *Columbia Journalism Review*, January/February, 1980.
21 Pearl, 160–1.
22 M. Cannon, *That Damned Democrat* (Melbourne, 1981), 52. The law, supposedly designed to protect the living from the consequences of the sins of their forebears, was a dead letter.
23 S. K. Padover (ed.), *Democracy by Thomas Jefferson* (1943), 150.
24 Zwar, 120.
25 *New York Post*, 22 April 1982.
26 Kiernan, 120
27 Curtis, I, 592, and III, 359.
28 *Ekklesia*, 10 December 2007.
29 Curtis, III, 285.
30 Griffen-Foley, 280.
31 *Guardian*, 21 February 2009.
32 E. Berliner, 'Rupert Murdoch and the Black Art of Journalism' (internet).
33 Zwar, 1, 10, 12, 13, 15, 1 and 10.
34 Ibid., 27.
35 S. Roskill, *Hankey: Man of Secrets*, I (1970), 220.
36 Zwar, 34.
37 L. A. Carlyon, *Gallipoli* (2002), 498.
38 Zwar, 36.
39 Shawcross, 36.
40 W. Hughes, *The Splendid Adventure* (1929), 41.
41 Brendon, 238–9.
42 Younger, 123.
43 Zwar, 64 and 89.
44 N. Richardson, 'Sir Keith Murdoch's relationship with Prime Minister Joseph Lyons' (National Archives of Australia, 2006), 7.
45 Zwar, 100.
46 Kiernan, 17 and 28.
47 Welles, 54.
48 Crainer, 6.
49 Heren, 263.
50 J. Grant and G. Serle, *The Melbourne Scene 1803–1956* (Melbourne, 1957), 267.
51 Inglis, 94.

52 Barry, 89.
53 Shawcross, 106.
54 Kiernan, 67.
55 Leapman, 30.
56 Somerfield, 161.
57 Kiernan, 82.
58 Menadue, 104.
59 Murdoch, 148.
60 D. Cryle, '"A Wild Idea": Rupert Murdoch, Maxwell Newton and the Foundation of *The Australian* Newspaper', in *Media International Australia* 123 (May 2007), 56.
61 Menadue, 90.
62 *The Australian*, 6 January 1968.
63 Page, 116.
64 Menadue, 107.
65 Tuccille, 62.
66 B. Cohen, *The Almost Complete Gough* (Crows Nest, NSW, 2001), 131 and 49.
67 Ibid., 109 and 112.
68 Chadwick, xix.
69 J. Walter, *The Leader* (St Lucia, Queensland, 1980), 89 and 43.
70 J. Button, *As It Happened* (Melbourne, 1998), 160.
71 Porter, 171.
72 Page, 156.
73 Menadue, 101.
74 Bower, 94.
75 Horrie, 160.
76 Thompson and Delano, 22.
77 Munster, 117.
78 Page, 123.
79 Thompson and Delano, 145.
80 Leapman, 49.
81 Munster, 126.
82 M. Hussey, *Chance Governs All* (2001), 98.
83 D. Frost, *An Autobiography* (1993), 500.
84 P. Howard, *The British Monarchy in the Twentieth Century* (1977), 90.
85 Wolff, 134.
86 Kiernan, 120.
87 *More*, February 1977.

88 S. Jenkins, *The Market for Glory* (1986), 119.
89 Chippindale and Horrie, 49.
90 Taylor, 249.
91 Ibid, 314.
92 Stewart, 128.
93 Coleridge, 389.
94 Belfield et al. (1991), 70.
95 Dunn.
96 *Time*, 17 January 1977.
97 Morgan, 24.
98 *Sunday Times Magazine*, 21 April 1974.
99 P. Brendon, 'Bulldog Editor', in *Columbia Journalism Review* (January–February 1984), 54.
100 Neil, 175.
101 Chippindale and Horrie, 458 and 396.
102 Curtis, III, 43.
103 Neil, 32.
104 Welles.
105 Page, 126.
106 Evans, 2 and 401.
107 P. Brendon, *Eminent Edwardians* (1979), 31.
108 Evans, 179.
109 Stewart, 34.
110 Evans, 169.
111 Shawcross, 223.
112 Evans, 215.
113 Giles, 203.
114 Young, 385.
115 Giles, 203.
116 D. Torbett, 'Who's Afraid of Rupert Murdoch?', *Frontline* WGBH.
117 Stewart, 171.
118 Shawcross, 261.
119 Evans, 404.
120 Neil, 42.
121 Sisman, 470.
122 Littleton, 49.
123 Melven, 149, 11 and 117.
124 Leapman, 199.
125 Chenoweth, 61.

126 Melven, 79.
127 Stewart, 218.
128 Neil, 147.
129 Melven, 170.
130 Littleton, 88.
131 Curtis, I, 359.
132 Hamilton, 184.
133 Curtis, I, 567 and 619.
134 Neil, 169.
135 Curtis, I, 366.
136 Young, 386.
137 Neil, 182.
138 Curtis, II, 254.
139 Munster, 158.
140 Kiernan, 259 and 206.
141 *Wall Street Journal*, 5 June 2007.
142 *Time*, 17 January 1977.
143 *Vanity Fair*, December 2004.
144 Welles.
145 *New York Times*, 13 July 1982.
146 Crainer, 86.
147 *New York Post*, 20 April 1982.
148 Welles.
149 *New York Post*, 15 April 1983.
150 *Forbes*, 15 May 2008.
151 *Village Voice*, 19 May 1982.
152 Munster, 180.
153 Kiernan, 215.
154 Welles, 51.
155 Shawcross, 321.
156 Tuccille, 134.
157 Belfield et al. (1991), 224.
158 Munster, 188.
159 Ibid., 123.
160 Chadwick, 16.
161 Belfield et al. (1991), 266.
162 Belfield et al. (1994), 15 and 329.
163 Menadue, 281.
164 Auletta.

165 Chenoweth, 152.

166 *Guardian*, 11 August 2011.

167 Kitty, 100. Despite its partisanship, or perhaps because of it, Americans trusted Fox News more than other television news networks. But those who watched it, mostly white and elderly, were the most misinformed of all news consumers according to recent polls. Even Murdoch's son-in-law, Matthew Freud, was ashamed and sickened by its 'horrendous and sustained disregard of journalistic standards' (*Guardian*, 28 January 2010).

168 Larry Johnson in *Outfoxed*, TV programme.

169 Chadwick, 107.

170 Dover, 18, 29, 144.

171 *New York Times*, 7 March 1998.

172 Rohm, 31.

173 Dover, 126, 92, 178 and 238.

174 Wolff, 96.

175 Chenoweth, 309.

176 Wolff, 59.

177 Ellis.

178 Campbell, 74.

179 Ibid., 363.

180 *Guardian*, 1 July 2006.

181 Morgan, 315.

182 *British Journalism Review* 13, No. 4, 2002. The former Culture Secretary Chris Smith told a fellow MP that 'Tony felt he had to give something to Murdoch'. (C. Mullin, *A View from the Foothills* [2010 edn.], 332).

183 *Independent*, 18 April 2005.

184 *Guardian*, 26 April 2010.

185 Campbell, 603.

186 Wolff, 243 and 271.

187 *Guardian*, 21 July 2011.

188 *International Herald Tribune*, 19 July 2011.

189 *Guardian*, 21 July 2011.

190 *Private Eye*, 4 February 2011.

191 It seems that the voicemail messages were deleted automatically and not, as the *Guardian* initially reported, because of the hacking. See *Guardian*, 13 and 14 December 2011.

192 *Guardian*, 21 July 2011.

193 *Newsweek*, 17 July 2011.
194 Guardian Datablog, transcript, 20 July 2011.
195 *Guardian*, 21 July 2011.
196 Watson and Hickman, 311.
197 B. Hagerty, 'I don't do it for the money', in *British Journalism Review* X, No. 4.

Prince Charles

1 York, 11 and 95.
2 Dimbleby, 249.
3 Benson, 101.
4 S. Curtis (ed.), *The Journals of Woodrow Wyatt*, III (2000), 423.
5 A. N. Wilson, *Our Times* (2008), 323.
6 Jones, 399.
7 *Daily Telegraph*, 14 November 2007.
8 Lorimer, 163.
9 Bradford (1996), 458.
10 C. Hibbert, *George IV*, II (1973), 16 and 185.
11 Magnus, 146.
12 Godfrey, 266.
13 J. Bryan III and C. J. V. Murphy, *The Windsor Story* (1979), 58.
14 D. Thompson, *Queen Victoria: Gender and Power* (1990), 116.
15 M. Carter, *Anthony Blunt: His Lives* (2001), 376.
16 A. Hare, *In My Solitary Life* (1953), ed. M. Barnes, 270.
17 Clark, 235.
18 Dempster and Evans, 80.
19 P. Vansittart (ed.), *Happy and Glorious* (1988), 171.
20 Brandreth, 124.
21 Bedell Smith, 105.
22 *Sunday Times*, 16 November 2008.
23 Bagehot, 119.
24 *Sunday Times*, 16 November 2008.
25 Magnus, 211.
26 *Guardian*, 22 February 2006.
27 Dimbleby, 140.
28 Benson, 213.
29 *Sunday Times*, 16 November 2008.
30 Lorimer, 146.
31 Brendon, 115.

32 Bradford (1996), 488.
33 Lacey (1977), 121.
34 Roberts, 9.
35 Bradford (1989), 399.
36 Crawford, 44.
37 T. C. Worsley, *Flannelled Fool* (1967), 186 and 191.
38 Alexandra of Yugoslavia, 60.
39 R. Rhodes James (ed.), *Chips: The Diaries of Sir Henry Channon* (1967), 287.
40 Heald, 69.
41 Eade, 155.
42 D. Kynaston, *Austerity Britain 1945–51* (2007), 244.
43 Turner, 106.
44 Kelley, 153 and 497.
45 Heald, 92.
46 Dimbleby, 21.
47 Kelley, 148.
48 Pimlott, 97.
49 Heald, 103.
50 Morrah, 52 and 59.
51 I. Hamilton, *When I Was a Boy* (1939), 89.
52 Shawcross, 631.
53 Bradford (1996), 326.
54 Morrah, 80.
55 Boyd, 14.
56 Dimbleby, 62.
57 Shawcross, 807.
58 Benson, 96.
59 *Daily Telegraph*, 4 March 2005.
60 Benson, 103.
61 Rogers, 70.
62 Morrah, 132 and 133.
63 York, 11.
64 *Economist*, 19 July 1986.
65 Benson, 113.
66 Ibid., 23 and 19.
67 *The Times*, 23 February 1970.
68 M. Butler, *August and Rab* (1987), 110.
69 *The Times*, 20 June 1969.

70 Pearson, 194.

71 Brandreth, 155.

72 *The Times*, 2 July 1969.

73 York, 25.

74 Hillier, 369.

75 L. Mitchell, *Maurice Bowra: A Life* (Oxford, 2009), 195.

76 E. Wyn James, 'Painting the World Green: Dafydd Iwan and the Welsh Protest Ballad', *Folk Music Journal* 8:5 (2005), 594 ff.

77 Strong, 89.

78 Keay, 98.

79 York, 68.

80 Keay, 182.

81 Dimbleby, 136.

82 Strong, 257.

83 Benson, 133.

84 York, 35, 31, 64 and 50.

85 Dimbleby, 169 and 164.

86 York, 54.

87 *The Times*, 2 July 1969.

88 Dempster and Evans, 79.

89 Graham, 29.

90 Brandreth, 208.

91 Dimbleby, 260 and 229.

92 Rogers, 72.

93 Turner, 129.

94 York, 122.

95 *The Times*, 5 January 1977.

96 National Archives of Australia: Media Release, 15 February 2008, 'Molly Meldrum and his royal faux pas'.

97 Hillier, 389.

98 *Daily Telegraph*, 22 February 2006.

99 *Independent*, 13 December 1992.

100 B. Donoughue, *Downing Street Diary* (2008), 443.

101 K. O. Morgan, *Callaghan: A Life* (1997), 512.

102 Strober, 444.

103 Barry, 79.

104 Kelley, 148.

105 Brandreth, 214.

106 Barry, 78

107 Holden, 207.

108 *Daily Mail*, 30 January 2007.

109 *Daily Mail*, 10 March 2003.

110 Jones, 398–9, 397, 363, 358, 393, 396 and 75.

111 Roberts, 90.

112 Evans, 79.

113 York, 76.

114 Vickers, 166.

115 Hoey, 145.

116 Quoted in P. Brendon, *The Decline and Fall of the British Empire* (2007), 405.

117 York, 76.

118 *People*, 31 October 1988.

119 Brown, 166.

120 York, 97.

121 Barry, 202.

122 Godfrey, 121.

123 Brown, 124.

124 Lacey (2002), 315.

125 Ibid., 145.

126 *The Times*, 25 February 1981.

127 Carpenter, 221.

128 *The Times*, 30 July 1981.

129 A. Morton, *The Royal Yacht Britannia* (1984), 29.

130 Burrell, 65.

131 Brown, 152.

132 Morton, 35 and 43.

133 Lady Colin Campbell (1993), 142 and 138.

134 Lady Colin Campbell (1992), 268.

135 Morton, 43 and 39.

136 *Scotsman*, 22 September 2001.

137 Lady Colin Campbell (1992), 316.

138 Berry, 78.

139 Jephson, 37.

140 Lady Colin Campbell (1993), 144.

141 Berry, 47 and 45.

142 Lady Colin Campbell (1993), 142.

143 *News of the World*, 15 January 1995.

144 N. Henderson, *Mandarin* (1994), 397.

145 Brown, 178.

146 Morton, 63.

147 Prince Charles and Clover (1993 edn.), 28, 13, 25 and 10.

148 Dimbleby, 432.

149 *Economist*, 19 July 1986.

150 Bradford (1996), 457.

151 Dimbleby, 493 and 366.

152 Holden, 17.

153 *Independent*, 8 April 2009.

154 www.princeofwales.gov.uk/speechesandarticles.

155 *Guardian*, 25 October 2009.

156 *Observer*, 10 May 2009.

157 Charles set out ten principles of good architecture in his book *A Vision of Britain*. In a paper entitled 'A Critique of the Prince of Wales' prescription for architecture', Professor Marcial Echenique demonstrates that Wren's masterpiece meets virtually none of the Prince's 'simplistic prescriptions' and that there is no easy 'recipe for producing good architecture'.

158 *Guardian*, 1 August 2011.

159 *Guardian*, 31 March 2009.

160 www.princeofwales.gov.uk/speechesandarticles.

161 *The Times*, 4 November 2009.

162 *Guardian*, 19 October 2009.

163 *Sunday Telegraph*, 15 March 2009.

164 *Scotsman*, 11 March 2009. When Ernst criticised a report on alternative medicine commissioned by Charles, the Prince's private secretary complained to Exeter University about an alleged breach of confidence. Ernst endured 'a gruelling 13 months of inquiry' before he was cleared. Commenting on this in the *Guardian* (31 October 2008), Lord Taverne said that if Charles wanted to speak out, he should renounce his claim to the throne; if 'he wants to succeed as a constitutional monarch, he must shut up'.

165 J. Campbell, *Margaret Thatcher II The Iron Lady*(2003), 467.

166 *New York Times*, 12 April 1988.

167 Dimbleby, 386.

168 *Economist*, 8 July 1989.

169 J. Barnes, *Letters from London 1990–1995* (1995), 154.

170 Dimbleby, 392.

171 Berry, 147.

172 A. Horne, *A Bundle from Britain* (1993), 86.
173 Shawcross, 891.
174 Burrell, 156.
175 Berry, 159.
176 Brown, 243.
177 Morton, 150.
178 *Economist*, 29 August 1992.
179 Jephson, 248.
180 *Sun*, 24 August 1992.
181 Burrell, 164.
182 Brown, 285.
183 Lacey (2002), 329.
184 *Economist*, 16 January 1993.
185 Brandreth, 258 and 263.
186 *Sun*, 19 January 1993.
187 Wharfe, 197.
188 Brandreth, 275.
189 Tomlinson, 276.
190 S. Simmons, *Diana: The Secret Years* (1998), 23 and 46.
191 Burgess, 128.
192 Brown, 336.
193 *Guardian*, 12 June 2000.
194 Lacey (2002), 352 and 385.
195 *The Times*, 23 February 2006.
196 Campbell and Stott, 426.
197 *Guardian*, 2 July 2011. Campbell further recorded that Blair was 'very pissed off' about Charles, inveighed against his 'straightforward anti-science position' and said that he was deliberately 'screwing' New Labour. But in an oleaginous comment on Campbell's revelations, Blair said that he had found discussions and correspondence with Charles 'immensely helpful'. The Prince's contributions were not only constitutionally proper but 'informative and insightful' (*Guardian* 5 July 2011).
198 Campbell and Stott, 324.
199 Bradford (1996), 519.
200 Berry, 26. Despite the global financial crisis, Charles's official household increased from 94 in 2005 to 125 in 2010 (*Sunday Times*, 27 June 2010).
201 Burrell, 111.

202 Burgess, 217.
203 K. Middlemas, *The Life and Times of Edward VII* (1972), 26.
204 *Guardian*, 12 November 2002.
205 *Daily Mirror*, 12 November 2002.
206 *Guardian*, 4 December 2002.
207 *Independent*, 6 May 2004.
208 *Evening Standard*, 11 November 2002.
209 *Evening Standard*, 23 June 2010.
210 *Daily Mail*, 16 November 2010.
211 *Daily Telegraph*, 19 December 2009.
212 *The Prince and the Composer*, BBC 4, 6 June 2011.
213 *Daily Telegraph*, 19 December 2009.

Margaret Thatcher

1 *The Times*, 20 July 1984.
2 Pugliese, 383.
3 *Independent*, 13 April 2003.
4 Hoskyns, 403.
5 Powell, 142.
6 Curtis, II, 275.
7 MTF, Speeches, BBC TV interview, 10 June 1987.
8 *New Statesman*, 26 February 2009.
9 Speech of 11 October 1906, quoted by V. Brendon, *The Edwardian Age* (1996), 42.
10 MTF, Speeches, *Woman's Own* interview, 23 September 1987.
11 Cole, 267.
12 MTF, Archive, Sherman MSS, T. E. Utley to David Wolfson, 6 December 1978.
13 MTF, Speeches, 3 March 1989.
14 CAC, THCH, 5/1/3/11.
15 *Independent*, 13 April 2003.
16 Campbell (2000), 123.
17 Vinen, 70.
18 Harrison, 229.
19 Campbell (2000), 45.
20 Garnett, 94.
21 Crick, 298.
22 MTF, Speeches, 8 February 1984.
23 Davenport-Hines, 6.

24 Prior, 106.
25 *Guardian*, 17 April 1979.
26 D. Parker, *The Official History of Privatization*, I (2009), 76.
27 Young (2009), 152.
28 *Daily Mirror*, 5 February 1975.
29 MTF, Speeches, 19 January 1976.
30 MTF, Speeches, 10 October 1980.
31 Vinen, 58.
32 Hoskyns, 125.
33 Parris, 204.
34 Campbell (2003), 21.
35 M. Thatcher (1995), 5.
36 R. Southey, *Life of Wesley*, II (1925 edn.), 306.
37 M. Thatcher (1995), 6.
38 Weiss, 30. This dissertation, in the CAC, maintains that the dictum that
   only work entitled people to eat and the parable of the talents were
   central to Mrs Thatcher's religious beliefs. It also observes that she
   cites Christ's injunction to 'render unto Caesar that which is Caesar's,
   and unto God that which is God's' in all three of her 'sermons'.
39 Quoted by R. Hyam, *Understanding the British Empire*
   (Cambridge, 2010), xvii.
40 *Daily Mail*, 5 May 1979.
41 Gardiner, 25.
42 Campbell (2000), 49.
43 Harrison, 231.
44 MTF, Speeches, 25 June 1945.
45 Howe, 201.
46 Campbell (2000), 67.
47 Murray, 42.
48 M. Thatcher (1995), 74.
49 MTF, Speeches, 28 January 1950.
50 C. Thatcher (1996), 65.
51 *Sunday Graphic*, 17 February 1952.
52 *Scotsman*, 7 December 2005.
53 C. Thatcher (1996), 86.
54 MTF, Archive, 18 August 1958.
55 Walters, 104.
56 *Sunday Pictorial*, 23 April 1961.
57 MTF, Archive, 7 January 1960.

58 M. Thatcher (1995), 125 and 115.

59 Campbell (1993), 214.

60 *The Times*, 6 May 1966.

61 P. Brendon, *Eminent Edwardians* (1979), 134. The phrase was Ethel Smyth's.

62 M. Thatcher (1995), 166.

63 *The Times*, 6 October 2009.

64 M. Thatcher (1995), 188 and 182.

65 Abse, 27.

66 MTF, Speeches, 18 November 1971.

67 M. Thatcher (1995), 190.

68 MTF, Archive, Report to US State Department, 22 May 1973.

69 Heffer, 453. The term 'rivers of blood' was of course coined by the press.

70 This clerihew won a *New Statesman* competition at the time. I quote from memory.

71 MTF, Speeches, 30 December 1988.

72 Gardiner, 143.

73 MTF, Archive, 'Margaret Thatcher & the Centre for Policy Studies'. The sinister Alfred Sherman contributed to this speech but the eugenicist phrases were apparently written by Joseph himself.

74 MTF, Archive, 'Lord Hailsham's coded diary', 29 March 1977.

75 Clarke.

76 Healey, 488. Cooper was a freakish comedian given to wearing a fez.

77 Ziegler, 482.

78 Campbell (1993), 675.

79 Baker, 44.

80 Ranelagh, ix.

81 Castle, 561, 562 and 557.

82 MTF, Archive, Margaret Thatcher to Alcon Copisarow, 11 August 1977.

83 Parris, 160.

84 MTF, Archive, Hailsham Diary, 29 March 1977.

85 Millar, 319.

86 Prior, 108.

87 M. Thatcher (1995), 430.

88 Lawson, 14.

89 Sherman, 89.

90 Campbell (2000), 343.

91 Parris, 187 and 203.
92 MTF, Archive, Hailsham Diary, 29 March 1977.
93 Healey, 488.
94 Ranelagh, 71.
95 Campbell (1993), xviii.
96 Parris, 191 and 211.
97 K. Harris, 73 and 80.
98 CAC, THCR 2/6/1/147, Industry, May 1978–April 1979.
99 CAC, THCR 2/6/1/13D, draft article for the *News of the World*.
100 Hoskyns, 86 and 92.
101 Millar, 262.
102 M. Thatcher (1993), 19 and 10.
103 S. Bradford, *Elizabeth* (1996), 380.
104 Young (2009), 190
105 Lamont, 321.
106 MTF, Archive, Carter Library, Brzezinski to Carter, 12 May 1979.
107 Young (2009), 150.
108 Hoskyns, 105.
109 Campbell (2003), 42.
110 Hoskyns, 236
111 Pugliese, 383.
112 Blake, 339.
113 R. Harris, 92.
114 CAC, THCR 5/1/3/16.
115 Young (1991), 203.
116 Heath, 574.
117 Healey, 490.
118 Gilmour, 25.
119 MTF, Speeches, 1 May 1981. For Margaret Thatcher's views on individual morality, see CAC, THCR 5/1/4/4.
120 M. Thatcher (1993), 147.
121 Berlinski, 127.
122 Campbell (2003), 114 and 173.
123 MTF, Archive, Sir Nicholas Henderson's diary, 23 December 1979.
124 Young (2009), 547.
125 Campbell (2003), 60.
126 Carrington, 346.
127 C. Thatcher (1996), 152. Margaret Thatcher herself liked to say that CHOGM stood for 'Compulsory Hand-outs for Greedy Mendicants'

(P. Brendon and P. Whitehead, *The Windsors* [1994], 208).

128 C. Thatcher (1996), 147. To some extent life imitated spoof and Denis Thatcher played up to the image of himself projected in *Private Eye*'s 'Dear Bill' letters. In reality he was, according to their co-author Richard Ingrams, 'a hardfaced businessman' (H. Thompson, *Richard Ingrams: Lord of the Gnomes* [1995 edn.], 288).

129 Quoted in P. Brendon, *The Decline and Fall of the British Empire* (2007), 596.

130 Baker, 58.

131 M. Thatcher (1993), 26.

132 C. Thatcher (1996), 201.

133 Freedman, 163.

134 Nott, 257.

135 Leach, 221.

136 Benn, 206.

137 L. Freedman, *The Official History of the Falklands Campaign* II (2005), 171.

138 MTF, Archive, Jim Rentschler's Falklands diary, 8 and 12 April 1982.

139 *Sunday Times*, 8 March 1992.

140 MTF, Archive, Jim Rentschler's Falklands diary, 3 June and 12 April 1982.

141 Benn, 227.

142 R. Fox, *Eyewitness Falklands* (1982), 8.

143 BBC *Nationwide*, 24 May 1983.

144 MTF, Archive, Falklands, 30 April 1982.

145 M. Thatcher (1993), 184.

146 C. Sandford, *Mick Jagger: Rebel Knight* (2003), 271.

147 MTF, Speeches, 3 July 1982.

148 Gilmour, 6.

149 F. Walsh, *A History of Hong Kong* (1993), 507 and 508.

150 Cottrell, 94.

151 *Daily Telegraph*, 23 February 2006.

152 M. Thatcher (1993), 493 and 492.

153 Morgan, 390 and 432.

154 Millar, 293. The echo of Mr Gradgrind was plainly unconscious, suggesting Mrs Thatcher's failure to grasp that the Victorian values that she now began to espouse were by no means wholly

admirable.
155 C. Thatcher (1983), 136.
156 C. Thatcher (1996), 243.
157 Ridley, 45.
158 Young (2009), 236
159 Andrew, 676.
160 Lawson, 314.
161 Howe, 347.
162 Wright, 56.
163 CAC, THCR 2/6/1/204, Margaret Thatcher to James Callaghan, 14 July 1978.
164 MTF, Speeches, 12 October 1984.
165 Milne, 252.
166 Sisman, 521.
167 Horne, 626.
168 C. Thatcher (1996), 220.
169 MTF, Speeches, 12 October 1984.
170 T. P. Coogan, *The IRA* (2000), 579.
171 Crick, 187 and 280.
172 Watkins, 54.
173 Jenkins, 189.
174 Heseltine, 332.
175 R. Harris, 132 and 140.
176 Heseltine, 310.
177 Benn, 437.
178 MTF, Speeches, 23 January 1986.
179 Clark, 135.
180 CAC, KNNK, 1/1/4, letters between Mrs Thatcher and Kinnock, 13 and 14 February 1985.
181 MTF, Speeches, 23 January 1986.
182 Lawson, 679.
183 MTF, Speeches, 17 October 1987. The following year she retreated from these words.
184 Curtis, I, 224.
185 Pimlott, 513.
186 CAC, British Diplomatic Oral History Project, Sir Bryan Cartledge, 56.
187 Fowler, 307.
188 Private information.

189 Sisman, 521.
190 CAC, KNNK 2/1/86, unfinished hand-written text.
191 Halloran and Hollingsworth, 137.
192 MTF, Speeches, 11 May 1987.
193 Marsden-Smedley, 243.
194 Baker, 256.
195 Mount, 347.
196 Baker, 257.
197 R. Harris, 122.
198 Curtis, I, 531.
199 Berlinski, 26. The same remark was attributed to General Montgomery.
200 Young (2009), 267.
201 MTF, Speeches, 10 March 1988.
202 Mrs Thatcher was simultaneously lecturing Ronald Reagan on the desirability of imposing 'tax increases as one of the means of reducing the [American] budget deficit'. MTF, Archive, Thatcher to Reagan, 22 October 1987.
203 Garnett, 245. The phrase was Robin Cook's.
204 M. Thatcher (1993) 709–12.
205 Gibson, 332.
206 J. Barnes, *Letters from London* (1995), 62.
207 Ridley, 139.
208 *Independent*, 11 September 2009.
209 MTF, Speeches, 28 October 1989. Brian Walden made this comment in a television interview.
210 Private information.
211 S. Bell, *Bell's Eye* (1999), 74.
212 Clark, 136.
213 Currie, 174.
214 Young (2009), 299.
215 M. Thatcher (1993), 783.
216 Cole, 290.
217 A. Neil, *Full Disclosure* (1996), 237.
218 Lawson, 957 and 895.
219 Baker, 329.
220 MTF, Speeches, 30 October 1990.
221 *Independent*, 26 November 2000. The journalist was Alan Watkins.
222 MTF, Speeches, 12 November 1990.

223 *The Times*, 14 November 1990.
224 M. Thatcher (1993), 840.
225 Campbell (2003), 723.
226 Watkins, 179.
227 M. Thatcher (1993), 846.
228 Baker, 407.
229 Heseltine, 370.
230 Clark, 368. Hansard's version is: 'You can wipe the floor with these people.'
231 Hurd, 404.
232 C. Thatcher (1996), 274 and 278.
233 Major, 215.
234 Millar, 368.
235 Sergeant, 202.
236 Ziegler, 575.
237 M. Thatcher (1995), 466 and 465.
238 Major, 200.
239 Curtis, II, 498.
240 Hogg and Hill, 131.
241 *Newsweek*, 27 April 1992.
242 Curtis, III, 605.
243 Major, 215.
244 *Sunday Herald*, 13 February 2005.
245 M. Thatcher (1993), 440.
246 I. Gilmour, 'The Thatcher Memoirs', *Twentieth Century British History* V, 2 (1994), 257.
247 A. Seldon, 'Making *The Downing Street Years*: An Interview with Denys Blakeway', *Contemporary British History* 8,1 (1994), 102.
248 MTF website.
249 Halloran and Hollingsworth, 263.
250 MTF, Speeches, 22 November 1996.
251 *Guardian*, 18 April 2013.

Mick Jagger

1 Doggett, 261.
2 *Independent*, 9 March 2008.
3 Sanchez, 82.
4 Wolfe, 160.
5 Anderson, 248.

6 *New York Times*, 7 August 1994.
7 Oldham (2002), 169.
8 Paytress, 62.
9 Anderson, 75.
10 *The New Republic*, 27 January 1979.
11 Laurie, 84.
12 Dalton, 35.
13 Davis, 94.
14 N. Annan, *Our Age: Portrait of a Generation* (1990), 402.
15 Sandbrook, 516.
16 Green, 41.
17 Davis, 227.
18 Charone, 32.
19 Sandford (2003), 238.
20 Miles, 79.
21 Paytress, 262. He subsequently dismissed this remark as 'crap'.
22 Anderson, 274.
23 Miles, 52.
24 Salewicz, 76.
25 Kent, 144.
26 Norman (1993), 289.
27 *High Times* 58 (June 1980), 36.
28 Holland and Loewenstein, 67.
29 Richards, 458. Richards was echoing Nick Kent's well-known verdict.
30 Aldridge, 119.
31 Greenfield, 94.
32 D. O. Muirithe, 'Serial Jagger', *The Oldie*, October 2010, 29.
33 Miles, 18.
34 Anderson, 15.
35 Richards, 50.
36 Charone, 15.
37 Sandford (2003), 15, 26 and 29.
38 *The Times*, 11 December 1968.
39 Anderson, 24.
40 Paytress, 430.
41 Badgery, 65.
42 Sandford, 33.
43 Richards, 78.
44 Melly, 88.

45 Chambers, 37.
46 Padel, 326.
47 Marks, 92 and 80.
48 Sandford, 43 and 39.
49 *Rolling Stone*, 7 November 1995.
50 Wyman, 104.
51 Charone, 46.
52 Hotchner, 81.
53 Paytress, 21.
54 Wyman, 109.
55 Booth (1985), 65.
56 Levin, 318.
57 *The Rolling Stones Book* No. 8 (10 January 1965), 23.
58 Dalton, 26.
59 Bockris, 48.
60 Melly, 88.
61 Hotchner, 115.
62 Oldham (2002), 127.
63 Davies, 44 and 311.
64 Hotchner, 370.
65 Dalton, 38.
66 Booth (1991), 181.
67 Richards, 154.
68 Oldham (2000), 192, 142 and 232.
69 *Rolling Stones Book* No. 8 (10 January 1965), 27.
70 Phelge, 128.
71 Oldham (2000), 196 and 247.
72 Davis, 58.
73 Paytress, 19.
74 Sandford (2003), 59.
75 Haslam, 142.
76 Anderson, 77.
77 Richards, 131.
78 Charone, 78.
79 Goldman, 312.
80 Savage, 472.
81 Bonanno, 20.
82 Oldham (2002), 273.
83 Schofield, 60.

84 Wyman, 290.
85 Davis, 83.
86 Sandford (2003), 63.
87 Davis, 77.
88 Lewis, 86.
89 P. Brendon, *Ike: The Life and Times of Dwight D. Eisenhower* (1987), 5.
90 Wyman, 233.
91 Oldham (2002), 214.
92 Hotchner, 135.
93 Anderson, 90.
94 Booth (1985), 245.
95 Oldham (2002), 150.
96 By comparison, Eric Clapton claimed to have 'laid a thousand' groupies, though how long it took him is not clear (Sandford [1994], 105).
97 Des Barres, 40 and 170.
98 Hotchner, 177 and 169.
99 Richards, 256.
100 *New York Times*, 16 July 1972.
101 Wheen, 356. Marianne Faithfull said that Richards was not quite right 'but nearly' (*Daily Mirror*, 4 April 2011), whereas Jerry Hall declared that he was 'well endowed', a verdict supported by other enthusiasts. He seems, in fact, to have been averagely equipped.
102 Philip Larkin could not imagine Jagger singing anything distinguished by feats of 'rhyme and reference' commonplace in Porter's 'highly literate' time (*Required Writing: Miscellaneous Pieces 1955–1982* [1983], 227).
103 *Daily Telegraph*, 14 January 2010. The claim was made by Chris O'Dell.
104 Charone, 75.
105 Whitcomb, 227.
106 *Rolling Stones Book* No. 25 (June 1966), 21.
107 Schofield, 83.
108 Faithfull, 38.
109 Hotchner, 203.
110 Faithfull, 169, 95 and 65.
111 Sanchez, 84.
112 Vyner, 197.

113 *The Times*, 16 July 1969.
114 G. Woodcock, *Dawn and the Darkest Hour* (1972), 275.
115 Buckle, 382.
116 Faithfull, 93.
117 Buckle, 381.
118 Vickers, 511.
119 Buckle, 383 and 382.
120 Faithfull, 140.
121 Schofield, 121.
122 Faithfull, 114.
123 Hotchner, 275.
124 *The Times*, 1 July 1967.
125 A. Pope, *Epistle to Dr Arbuthnot* (1735).
126 Charone, 101.
127 The music was used in Anger's film *Invocation of My Demon Brother*.
128 Paytress, 148.
129 Green, 181.
130 Rawlings and Badman, 181.
131 Green, 245.
132 Hotchner, 293.
133 Bockris, 124.
134 Charone, 112.
135 'Sympathy for the Devil'.
136 Davis, 245.
137 *Independent*, 23 August 1992.
138 Quoted by A. Hayter, *Opium and the Romantic Imagination* (1971 edn.), 160.
139 Hotchner, 312. This was John Dunbar's view.
140 Paytress, 166.
141 Norman (1981), 379.
142 Havers, 160.
143 Hodkinson, 88.
144 Faithfull, 190.
145 *New York Times*, 28 November 1969.
146 Paytress, 177.
147 *Sunday Telegraph*, 29 August 2005.
148 *New York Times*, 28 November 1969.
149 Booth (1985), 221, 351 and 357.

150 *Gimme Shelter.*
151 Booth (1985), 359 and 367.
152 Kael, 209.
153 Booth (1985), 368 and 371.
154 Anderson, 11.
155 Kael, 208.
156 Booth (1985), 373.
157 Marks, 123.
158 Miles, 38.
159 Schofield, 177 and 187.
160 Sanchez, 191 and 200. Both Sanchez and Hotchner (353) comment on Jagger's cocaine consumption.
161 Schofield, 198.
162 *People Magazine*, 2 May 1977.
163 Haslam, 257.
164 Dalton, 128.
165 Sanchez, 222.
166 *Evening Standard*, 15 November 2001.
167 Sandford (2003), 200.
168 'Exile of the Stones', BBC Radio 2, 20 May 2010.
169 Richards, 143.
170 'Stones in Exile', BBC 1, 23 May 2010.
171 Sandford (2003), 203 and 205.
172 *New York Times*, 16 July 1972.
173 Inge, 265.
174 Richards, 328.
175 Greenfield, 154.
176 Watts, 272.
177 *New York Times*, 25, 27 and 28 July 1972.
178 Greenfield, 192–3.
179 Inge, 256 and 259. Capote's view was confirmed by Jagger himself, who told Ian Whitcomb that the only way to survive in the pop world was to 'be a businessman', adding that 'I let 'em have bumps and grinds on-stage and off-stage I run the corporation' (Whitcomb, 195).
180 Miles, 127.
181 Paytress, 226.
182 T. de Quincey, *Confessions of an English Opium Eater*, ed. A. Hayter (1971), 71.

183 Bockris, 170.
184 *New York Times*, 15 May 1975.
185 Dalton, 127.
186 *The Times*, 24 December 2002.
187 Murray, 159.
188 *New York Times*, 2 June 1975.
189 Bockris, 203.
190 Amis, 96–7.
191 Private information: Graeme Davies.
192 Murray, 158.
193 Peel and Ravenscroft, 333.
194 Flippo, 143.
195 Paytress, 276.
196 Hall, 88.
197 Hackett, 393 and 263.
198 Hall, 108.
199 Miles, 117.
200 Hall, 85 and 98.
201 Flippo, 150.
202 Gene M. Broxson, 'The Rolling Stones 1978 US Tour' (internet).
203 Richards, 432.
204 Bockris, 289.
205 Kent, 152.
206 Bockris, 298.
207 *New York Times*, 4 June 1989.
208 Hall, 172.
209 Dannen, 240.
210 *Economist*, 9 September 1989.
211 *Orlando Sentinel*, 7 December 1997.
212 *New York Times*, 2 September 1989 and 4 September 1994.
213 *New York Times*, 4 September 1994.
214 Rushdie, 97.
215 Bloom, 79.
216 MacDonald, 59.
217 Dannen, 240. Jagger was apparently out-yelled and, as often happened when people stood up to him, he backed down.
218 *New York Times*, 27 August 1989, 4 May 1994 and 21 February 1993.
219 Hodkinson, 75.

220 Dalton, 177.
221 Palmer, 254.
222 Hall, 125.
223 *Sun*, 17 September 2010.
224 Sandford (2003), 343.
225 Badgery, 21 and 24.
226 *Independent*, 10 July 1999.
227 Richards, 294.
228 *Daily Telegraph*, 27 August 2010.
229 *Guardian*, 5 December 2003.
230 J. Critchley and M. Halcrow, *Collapse of Stout Party* (1997), 29.
231 Richards, 542.
232 *Guardian*, 18 October 2010.
233 *New Yorker*, 9 September 2002.

Select Bibliography

Books were published in London unless otherwise stated.

Rupert Murdoch
Auletta, K., 'The Pirate', in *New Yorker*, 13 November 1995
Barry, P., *The Rise and Rise of Kerry Packer* (Sydney, 1993)
Belfield, R., Hird, C. and Kelly, S., *Murdoch: The Decline of an Empire* (1991)
Belfield, R., Hird, C. and Kelly, S., *Murdoch: The Great Escape* (1994)
Bower, T., *Maxwell: The Outsider* (1988)
Brendon, P., *The Life and Death of the Press Barons* (1982)
Campbell, A., *The Blair Years* (2007)
Chadwick, P., *Media Mates* (Melbourne, 1989)
Chenoweth, N., *Virtual Murdoch* (2001)
Chippindale, P. and Horrie, C., *Stick It Up your Punter!* (1999)
Coleridge, N., *Paper Tigers* (New York, 1994)
Crainer, S., *Business the Rupert Murdoch Way* (Padstow, 1998)
Curtis, S. (ed.), *The Journals of Woodrow Wyatt*, 3 vols (1998, 1999, 2000)
Dover, B., *Rupert's Adventures in China* (Edinburgh, 2008)
Dunn, M., 'How to Survive Rupert Murdoch', in *British Journalism Review*, 18 (November 2007)
Ellis, E., 'Wendi Deng Murdoch', in *Monthly*, 5 June 2007
Evans, H., *Good Times, Bad Times* (1983)
Giles, F., *Sundry Times* (1986)
Griffen-Foley, B., *The House of Packer* (St Leonards, NSW, 1999)
Hamilton, D., *Editor-in-Chief* (1989)

Heren, L., *Memories of Times Past* (1988)

Horrie, C., *Tabloid Nation* (2003)

Inglis, K. S., *The Stuart Case* (Melbourne, 1961)

Kiernan, T., *Citizen Murdoch* (New York, 1986)

Kitty, A., *Outfoxed: Rupert Murdoch's War on Journalism* (New York, 2005)

Leapman, M., *Barefaced Cheek* (1983)

Littleton, S. M., *The Wapping Dispute* (Aldershot, 1992)

Melven, L., *The End of the Street* (1986)

Menadue, J., *Things you Learn Along the Way* (Melbourne, 1999)

Morgan, P., *The Insider* (2005)

Munster, G., *Rupert Murdoch: A Paper Prince* (Harmondsworth, 1985)

Murdoch, S., *Maxwell Newton* (Fremantle, 1993)

Neil, A., *Full Disclosure* (1996)

Page, B., *The Murdoch Archipelago* (2003)

Pearl, C., *Wild Men of Sydney* (1966)

Porter, H., *Lies, Damned Lies and Some Exclusives* (1984)

Rohm, W. G., *The Murdoch Mission* (New York, 2002)

Russ, B., 'Murdoch's Mean Machine', in *Columbia Journalism Review* (May-June 1998)

Shawcross, W., *Murdoch* (1992)

Sisman, A., *Hugh Trevor-Roper* (2010)

Somerfield, S., *Banner Headlines* (1979)

Stewart, G., *The History of The Times: VII 1981–2002 The Murdoch Years* (2005)

Taylor, S. J., *Shock! Horror!: The Tabloids in Action* (1991)

Thompson, P. and Delano, A., *Maxwell: A Portrait of Power* (1988)

Tuccille, J., *Murdoch: A Biography* (1990)

Watkins, A., *A Short Walk Down Fleet Street* (2000)

Watson, T. and Hickman, M., *Dial M for Murdoch: News Corporation and the Corruption of Britain* (2012)

Welles, C., 'The Americanization of Rupert Murdoch', in *Esquire* (22 May 1979)

Wolff, M., *The Man Who Owns the News* (2008)

Young, H., 'Rupert Murdoch and *The Sunday Times*: A Lamp Goes Out', in *Political Quarterly* 55 (October–December 1984)

Younger, R. M., *Keith Murdoch: Founder of a Media Empire* (Sydney, 2003)

Zwar, D., *In Search of Keith Murdoch* (Melbourne, 1980)

Select Bibliography

Prince Charles

Alexandra, Queen of Yugoslavia, *Prince Philip: A Family Portrait* (1959)

Bagehot, W., *The English Constitution*, ed. R. H. S. Crossman (1964)

Barry, S. P., *Royal Secrets* (New York, 1985)

Bedell Smith, S., *Diana* (1999)

Benson, R., *Charles: The Untold Story* (1993)

Berry, W., *The Housekeeper's Diary* (New York, 1995)

Boyd, W., *School Ties* (1985)

Bradford, S., *Elizabeth* (1996)

Bradford, S., *George VI* (1989)

Brandreth, G., *Charles and Camilla* (2006 edn.)

Brendon, P., *Our Own Dear Queen* (1986)

Brendon, P. and Whitehead, P., *The Windsors: A Dynasty Revealed* (2000)

Brown, T., *The Diana Chronicles* (2007)

Burgess, C., *Behind Palace Doors* (2006)

Burrell, P., *A Royal Duty* (2003)

Campbell, A. and Stott, R. (eds.), *The Blair Years: Extracts from the Alastair Campbell Diaries* (2007)

Campbell, Lady Colin, *Diana in Private* (1992)

Campbell, Lady Colin, *The Royal Marriages* (1993)

Carpenter, H., *Robert Runcie* (1996)

Charles, Prince, *A Vision of Britain* (1989)

Charles, Prince and Clover, C., *Highgrove: Portrait of an Estate* (2002 edn.)

Clark, A., *Diaries* (1993)

Crawford, M., *The Little Princesses* (1950)

Dempster, N. and Evans, P., *Behind Palace Doors* (1993)

Dimbleby, J., *The Prince of Wales* (1994)

Eade, P., *Young Prince Philip: His Turbulent Early Life* (2011)

Evans, W., *My Mountbatten Years* (1989)

Godfrey, R. (ed.), *Letters from a Prince* (1998)

Graham, C., *Camilla –The King's Mistress* (1995 edn.)

Heald, T., *The Duke: A Portrait of Prince Philip* (1991)

Hillier, B., *Betjeman: The Bonus of Laughter* (2004)

Hoey, B., *Mountbatten: The Private Story* (1994)

Holden A., *Charles* (1988)

Jephson, P. D., *Shadows of a Princess* (2000)

Jones, J. D. F., *Storyteller: The Many Lives of Laurens van der Post* (2001)

Keay, D., *Royal Pursuit: The Media and the Monarchy in Conflict and Compromise* (New York, 1984)

Kelley, K., *The Royals* (1977)

Lacey, R., *Majesty* (1977)

Lacey, R., *Royal: Her Majesty Queen Elizabeth II* (2002)

Lorimer, D., *Radical Prince* (Edinburgh, 2003)

Magnus, P., *King Edward the Seventh* (Harmondsworth, 1967 edn.)

Morrah D., *To be a King* (1968)

Morton, A., *Diana: Her True Story – In Her Own Words* (1997)

Pearson, J., *The Ultimate Family* (1986)

Pimlott, B., *The Queen: Elizabeth II and the Monarchy* (2001)

Roberts, A., *Eminent Churchillians* (1994)

Rogers, B., *An Audience with an Elephant* (2001)

Shawcross, W., *Queen Elizabeth The Queen Mother* (2009)

Strober, D. H. and G. S., *The Monarchy: An Oral History of Elizabeth II* (2002)

Strong, R., *The Roy Strong Diaries 1967–1987* (1997)

Tomlinson, D., *Divine Right: The Inglorious Survival of British Royalty* (1994)

Turner, G., *Elizabeth* (2002)

Vickers, H., *Elizabeth The Queen Mother* (2005)

Wharfe, K. with Jobson, R., *Diana: Closely Guarded Secret* (2002)

York, R. (ed.), *Charles in His Own Words* (1981)

Margaret Thatcher

Abbreviations
CAC Churchill Archives Centre
MTF Margaret Thatcher Foundation

Abse, L., *Margaret, daughter of Beatrice* (1989)

Andrew, C., *The Defence of the Realm: The Authorized History of MI5* (2009)

Annan, N., *Our Age: Portrait of a Generation* (1990)

Baker, K., *The Turbulent Years: My Life in Politics* (1993)

Benn, T., *Diaries 1980–90*, ed. R. Winstone (1992)

Berlinski, C., *'There is No Alternative'* (New York, 2008)

Blake, R., *The Conservative Party from Peel to Major* (1997)

Select Bibliography

Campbell, J., *Edward Heath* (1993).

Campbell, J., *Margaret Thatcher I: The Grocer's Daughter* (2000)

Campbell, J., *Margaret Thatcher II: The Iron Lady* (2003)

Carrington, Lord, *Reflect on Things Past* (1988)

Castle, B., *The Castle Diaries 1964–1976* (1990)

Clark, A., *Diaries* (1993)

Clarke, P., 'The Antagoniser's Agoniser', in *London Review of Books* (19 July 2001)

Cole, J., *As It Seemed to Me* (1995)

Cottrell, R., *The End of Hong Kong: The Secret Diplomacy of Imperial Retreat* (1993)

Crick, M., *Michael Heseltine* (1997)

Currie, E., *Diaries 1987–1992* (2002)

Curtis, S., *The Journals of Woodrow Wyatt*, 3 vols. (1998–2000)

Davenport-Hines, R., *The Macmillans* (1992)

Fowler, N., *Ministers Decide* (1991)

Freedman, L., *The Official History of the Falklands Campaign*, I (2005)

Gardiner, G., *Margaret Thatcher* (1975)

Garnett, M., *From Anger to Apathy: The British Experience since 1975* (2008)

Gibson, J., 'The Presentation of the Poll Tax', in *Political Quarterly* 60 (July 1989)

Gilmour, I., *Dancing with Dogma* (1992)

Halloran, P. and Hollingsworth, M., *Thatcher's Gold* (1995)

Harris, K., *Thatcher* (1988)

Harris, R., *Good and Faithful Servant* (1990)

Harrison, B., 'Mrs Thatcher and the Intellectuals', in *Twentieth Century British History*, 5:2 (1994)

Healey, D., *The Time of My Life* (1989)

Heath, E., *The Course of My Life* (1998)

Heffer, S., *Like the Roman* (1998)

Heseltine, M., *Life in the Jungle* (2000)

Hogg, S. and Hill, J., *Too Close to Call* (1995)

Horne, A., *Macmillan 1957–1986* (1989)

Hoskyns, J., *Just in Time: Inside the Thatcher Revolution* (2000)

Howe, G., *Conflict of Loyalty* (1994)

Hurd, D., *Memoirs* (2003)

Jenkins, P., *Mrs Thatcher's Revolution* (1987)

Lamont, N., *In Office* (1999)

Lawson, N., *The View from No. 11: Memoirs of a Tory Radical* (1992)

Leach, H., *Endure No Makeshifts* (1993)

Major, J., *The Autobiography* (1999)

Marsden–Smedley, P. (ed.), *Britain in the Eighties* (1989)

Millar, R., *A View from the Wings* (1993).

Milne, S., *The Enemy Within: MI5, Maxwell and the Scargill Affair* (1994)

Morgan, K. O., *Michael Foot* (2007)

Mount, F., *Cold Cream* (2008)

Murray, P., *Margaret Thatcher* (1980)

Nott, J., *Here Today, Gone Tomorrow* (2002)

Parris, M., *Chance Witness* (2002)

Pimlott, B., *The Queen: Elizabeth II and the Monarchy* (2001)

Powell, A., *Journals 1982–1986* (1995)

Prior, J., *A Balance of Power* (1986)

Pugliese, S. (ed.), *The Political Legacy of Margaret Thatcher* (2003)

Ranelagh, J., *Thatcher's People* (1991)

Ridley, N., *'My Style of Government': The Thatcher Years* (1991)

Sergeant, J., *Maggie: Her Fatal Legacy* (2005)

Sherman, A., *Paradoxes of Power* (Exeter, 2005)

Sisman, A., *Hugh Trevor-Roper* (2010)

Thatcher, C., *Below the Parapet: The Biography of Denis Thatcher* (1996)

Thatcher, C., *Diary of an Election* (1983)

Thatcher, M., *The Downing Street Years* (1993)

Thatcher, M., *The Path to Power* (1995)

Vinen, R., *Thatcher's Britain: The Politics and Social Upheaval of the 1980s* (2009)

Walters, D., *Not Always with the Pack* (1989)

Watkins, A., *A Conservative Coup* (1991)

Weiss, A. E., 'The Religious Mind of Mrs Thatcher' (Churchill Archives Centre, 2008)

Wright, P., *Spycatcher* (Toronto, 1987)

Young, H., *One of Us* (1991 edn.)

Young, H., *The Hugo Young Papers*, ed. I. Trewin (2009)

Ziegler, P., *Edward Heath* (2010)

Select Bibliography

The Margaret Thatcher Foundation website affords a wealth of speeches, letters and other documents. This resource is supplemented by original documents in the Thatcher collection at the Churchill Archives Centre in Cambridge, which contains papers such as those of Lord Hailsham and Neil Kinnock, as well as other unpublished material such as that in the British Diplomatic Oral History Project.

Mick Jagger

Aldridge, J., *Satisfaction* (1984)

Amis, M., *Visiting Mrs Nabokov and Other Excursions* (1993)

Anderson, C., *Jagger Unauthorised* (1993)

Badgery, K., *Baby You Can Drive My Car* (2002)

Bloom, A., *The Closing of the American Mind* (1987)

Bockris, V., *Keith Richards: The Unauthorised Biography* (2006)

Bonanno, M., *The Rolling Stones Chronicle* (1990)

Booth, S., *Rhythm Oil* (1991)

Booth, S., *The True Adventures of the Rolling Stones* (1985)

Buckle, R. (ed.), *Self-Portrait with Friends: The Selected Diaries of Cecil Beaton 1926–1974* (1979)

Chambers, I., *Urban Rhythms: Pop Music and Popular Culture* (Basingstoke, 1985)

Charone, B., *Keith Richards* (1979)

Dalton, D., *The Rolling Stones: The First Twenty Years* (1981)

Dannen, F., *Hit Men: Power Brokers and Fast Money Inside the Music Business* (1990)

Davies, H., *The Beatles* (1985 edn.)

Davis, S., *Old Gods Almost Dead: The 40-year Odyssey of the Rolling Stones* (2006 edn.)

Des Barres, P., *I'm with the Band* (1987)

Doggett, P., *There's a Riot Going On* (2007)

Faithfull, M. with Dalton, D., *Faithfull* (1994)

Flippo, C., *It's Only Rock 'n' Roll* (New York, 1985)

Goldman, A., *The Lives of John Lennon* (1985).

Green, J., *Days in the Life: Voices from the English Underground 1961–1971* (1988)

Greenfield, R., *Stones Touring Party: A Journey Through America with the Rolling Stones* (1974)

Hackett, P. (ed.), *The Andy Warhol Diaries* (1989)

Hall, J. with Hemphill, C., *Tall Tales* (1985)

Haslam, N., *Redeeming Features* (2009)

Havers, R., *The Stones in the Park* (2009)

Hodkinson, M., *Marianne Faithfull* (1991)

Holland, J. and Loewenstein, D., *The Rolling Stones: A Life on the Road* (1998)

Hotchner, A. E., *Blown Away: The Rolling Stones and the Death of the Sixties* (1990)

Inge, M. T. (ed.), *Truman Capote: Conversations* (1987)

Kael, P., *Deeper into Movies* (1975)

Kent, N., *The Dark Stuff* (1994)

Laurie, P., *The Teenage Revolution* (1965)

Levin, B., *The Pendulum Years: Britain and the Sixties* (1970)

Lewis, L. A., *The Adoring Audience: Fan Culture and Popular Media* (1992)

MacDonald, I., *The People's Music* (2003)

Marks, J., *Mick Jagger* (1973)

Melly, G., *Revolt into Style* (1972 edn.)

Miles, *Mick Jagger in His Own Words* (1982)

Murray, C. S., *Shots from the Hip* (1991 edn.)

Norman, P., *Shout* (1981)

Norman, P., *The Stones* (1993 edn.)

Oldham, A. L., *2Stoned* (2002)

Oldham, A. L., *Stoned* (2000)

Padel, R., *I'm a Man: Sex, Gods and Rock 'n' Roll* (2000)

Palmer, T., *All You Need is Love* (1976)

Paytress, M., *The Rolling Stones off the Record* (2003)

Peel, J. and Ravenscroft, S., *Margrave of the Marshes* (2006 edn.)

Phelge, J., *Nankering with the Rolling Stones* (Chicago, 1998)

Rawlings, T. and Badman, K., *Good Times Bad Times: The Definitive Diary of the Rolling Stones* (1997)

Richards, K. with Fox, J., *Life* (2010)

Rushdie, S., *Step Across this Line* (2002)

Salewicz, C., *Mick and Keith* (2002)

Sanchez, T., *Up and Down with the Rolling Stones* (New York, 1979)

Sandbrook, D., *White Heat: A History of Britain in the Swinging Sixties* (2006)

Sandford, C., *Mick Jagger: Rebel Knight* (2003)

Sandford, C., *Clapton* (1994)

Select Bibliography

Savage, J., *The England's Dreaming Tapes* (2009)

Schofield, C., *Jagger* (1983)

Vickers, H., *Cecil Beaton* (1985)

Vyner, H., *Groovy Bob: The Life and Times of Robert Fraser* (1999)

Watts, S., *Mr Playboy: Hugh Hefner and the American Dream* (2009)

Wheen, F., *Tom Driberg: His Life and Indiscretions* (1990)

Whitcomb, I., *Rock Odyssey: A Chronicle of the Sixties* (1983)

Wolfe, T., *The Kandy-Kolored Tangerine-Flake Streamline Baby* (1981 edn.)

Wyman, B. with Coleman, R., *Bill Wyman: Stone Alone* (1990)

Two bibliographical works provide a comprehensive guide to early writing about the Rolling Stones. The first contains useful summaries of the content.

Dimmick, M. L., *The Rolling Stones: An Annotated Bibliography* (Pittsburgh, 1979)

MacPhail, J. H. W. (ed.), *Yesterday's Papers: The Rolling Stones in Print 1963–1984* (Ann Arbor, MI, 1986)

Index